HEROES OF GREECE AND TROY

HEROES OF GREECE AND TROY

Retold from the Ancient Authors by

Roger Lancelyn Green

WITH DRAWINGS BY

HEATHER COPLEY AND

CHRISTOPHER CHAMBERLAIN

THE BODLEY HEAD

LONDON SYDNEY TORONTO

DEDICATED TO THE MEMORY OF

Emily and Gordon Bottomley

'Once we fared with the Argo, sailing
The ancient seas for the Fleece of Gold,
The distant gleam and the song prevailing
Over the dragon guards of old;

And we have wandered the Islands ringing
With the Aegean thunder still,
Plucked the unfaded blossoms springing
Yet for us on the Muses' hill.'

AFTER EURIPIDES: *Hypsipyle*

This edition © Roger Lancelyn Green 1960
Illustrations © The Bodley Head 1960
ISBN 0 370 01273 9
Printed in Great Britain for
The Bodley Head Ltd
9 Bow Street, London, WC2E 7AL
by Unwin Brothers Limited, Old Woking
Set in Monotype Ehrhardt
First published in 1958 by Penguin Books Ltd
in two volumes entitled *Tales of the Greek
Heroes* and *The Tale of Troy*
First published in this revised edition 1960
Reissued with an index 1973
Reprinted 1975

CONTENTS

Author's Note, 9

1. The Coming of the Immortals, 13

2. Hermes and Apollo, 23

3. The Story of Prometheus, 31

4. How Zeus and Hermes Went Visiting, 41

5. Typhon the Terrible, 51

6. The Adventures of Dionysus, 61

7. Perseus the Gorgon-Slayer, 71

8. The Birth of Heracles, 81

9. The Choice of Heracles, 89

10. The Beginning of the Labours, 97

11. The Story of Admetus, 107

12. The Wanderings of Heracles, 117

13. The Golden Apples, and the Hound of Hell, 127

14. The Adventures of Theseus, 137

15. The Quest of the Golden Fleece, 147

16. The Return of the Argonauts, 157

17. Meleager and Atalanta, 165

18. The First Fall of Troy, 173

19. The Battle of the Giants, 179

20. Helen of Sparta, 189

21. The Marriage of Peleus and Thetis, 199

[continued overleaf

CONTENTS

22. The Judgement of Paris, 207

23. The Gathering of the Heroes, 215

24. The Siege of Troy, 225

25. The Horses of Rhesus, 235

26. The Death of Hector, 243

27. Neoptolemus and Philoctetes, 253

28. The Theft of the Luck of Troy, 263

29. The Wooden Horse, 273

30. The Fall of Troy, 281

31. Agamemnon and His Children, 291

32. The Adventures of Menelaus, 299

33. The Wanderings of Odysseus, 309

34. Odysseus in Ithaca, 321

35. The Last of the Heroes, 331

Index, 340

MAPS

1. *Heracles and the Voyage of the Argonauts*, 336

2. *The Trojan Wars and the Wanderings of Odysseus*, 338

AUTHOR'S NOTE

The stories of the ancient Greek myths and legends have been told and re-told more frequently than any others by poets, dramatists and scholars; but among re-tellings for younger readers only *The Heroes* by Charles Kingsley, made just over a hundred years ago, has become a real classic. Several others are remembered: Charles Lamb's *Adventures of Ulysses*, Nathaniel Hawthorne's *Tanglewood Tales* and, best of all, Andrew Lang's *Tales of Troy and Greece*: but none of these can compare with Kingsley's version of the stories of Perseus, Theseus and the Argonauts.

My own version is fuller than any of these, and does I believe, approach the old tales in a new way. My predecessors have taken isolated stories and re-told them at some length—but they have, as a rule, remained isolated. My attempt has been to tell the Tale of the Greek Heroes, the history of the Heroic Age, as that single whole which the Greeks believed it to be.

On the other hand this is not a mere outline of Greek myths but a series of some of the world's best and most famous stories. Therefore the most noteworthy have chapters to themselves—sometimes with a minor tale as an inset. I do not think that any of the better known myths have been omitted, except for the misfortunes of Oedipus and the subsequent expeditions of the Seven against Thebes and their sons the Epigoni – all of which, like the darker corners in the tale of 'Pelops' line', are best kept until they can be met in their most satisfactory form in the works of the Greek dramatists.

There are, of course, many small omissions, such as several metamorphosis legends like those of Narcissus and Hyacinthus, Syrinx and Echo: these are really items in a Classical Dictionary, though many re-tellers who use Ovid as their main source spin them out into separate tales.

As for my sources, a detailed list of these would be pointless in a book of this kind, ranging as they do throughout Greek literature during the two thousand years which separate Homer from Eustathius. While Apollodorus has been my guide, assisted by Hesiod, I have wherever possible used an epic, whether by Homer or Apollonius Rhodius, Quintus Smyrnaeus or Nonnos, Colluthus or Tryphiodorus, Virgil, Statius or Valerius Flaccus; a dramatist; a lyric poet – Pindar, Theocritus or Ovid as best might serve; a mere mythographer like Parthenius or Hyginus, or an historian like Herodotus or Plutarch for a chance passage.

Sometimes the dialogue is modelled on an original, sometimes it is my own: but it would be as merely pedantic to indicate which line is taken from a play or fragment of Euripides as it would to distinguish in the story of the Argonauts where I have followed Pindar, where Apollonius Rhodius, where Valerius Flaccus and where the 'Orphic' *Argonautica*.

I may, however, add that to the best of my ability I have used my multitudinous sources honestly: I have selected, but I hope that I have never falsified my originals; I have assumed dialogue but added no single incident, so far as I am aware, nor made any alteration in a legend, though I have sometimes omitted where desirable.

I must confess three small exceptions to this statement. Firstly, as a connected sequence made chronology hold rather more importance than the Greeks attached to it, I suppressed the name of the 'witch-wife' who tried to poison Theseus when he first came to Athens: if she were Medea, as some authorities suggest, Theseus could not have been an Argonaut! Secondly, I have suggested that Helen became separated from Menelaus on the return from Troy, and so was able to be in Egypt before him and allow the introduction of the adventures added by Stesichorus and dramatised by Euripides in his *Helena* without having recourse to the 'eidolon' myth. My third confession is that I have followed Kingsley in allowing an old servant, the only man who ever fitted the Bed of Procrustes exactly, to warn Theseus: Kingsley may have had an authority for this, but I have not been able to trace it.

Apart from a reference to the story of Troilus, I have otherwise full classical authority for everything in this book: indeed, though I have sometimes used Ovid, Virgil, Statius, Valerius Flaccus and Lucan for details, I can say that I have ancient *Greek* authority for everything except the wanderings of Aeneas and the story of Cacus.

To avoid the risk of influence, I have taken care not to consult any of the modern re-tellings – though Kingsley and Lang could not altogether be forgotten. I sternly repressed the temptation to use *The World's Desire*, the romantic sequel to the *Odyssey* which Lang and Rider Haggard wrote in 1890, to replace the unsatisfactory summaries of the last adventures and death of Odysseus which are all that have come down to us: but I may here advise readers to substitute that delightful book for my last chapter!

At this date it is hardly necessary to make any remark about the use of the correct Greek names for the gods and heroes of Ancient Greece. In deference to the general literary tradition I have used the Latinised spellings – Phœbus Apollo for Phoibos Apollon, Circe for Kirke, Pirithoüs for Peirithoös, and so on. I have called the son of

Telamon Ajax, the Latin form, merely to distinguish him from Aias the son of Oileus; and it has seemed better to retain such slight variations as Hector, Priam and Hecuba. But against Ulysses and Hercules I have set my face firmly: they are as different from Odysseus and Heracles as Jupiter and Juno are from Zeus and Hera: the Roman names belong to the artificial epic and the calculated convention of Virgil and Ovid; the Greek names fling wide the magic casements on the instant – led by them we step right back into the Heroic Age, into the bright, misty morning of legend and literature,

> *And hear, like ocean on a western beach,*
> *The surge and thunder of the Odyssey.*

Roger Lancelyn Green

The Gods and
Goddesses of Ancient Greece

GREEK	LATIN
Cronos	Saturn
Rhea	Cybele
Helios	Sol (The Sun)
Eos	Aurora (The Dawn)
Selene	Luna (The Moon)
Zeus	Jupiter or Jove
Poseidon	Neptune
Hades	Pluto or Dis
Demeter	Ceres
Hestia	Vesta
Hera	Juno
Persephone	Proserpine
Ares	Mars
Dionysus	Bacchus
Hermes	Mercury
Hephaestus	Vulcan
Athena	Minerva
Artemis	Diana
Aphrodite	Venus
Asclepius	Aesculapius
Heracles	Hercules or Alcides

Apollo, Pan, and Hecate are the same in both

CHAPTER I

The Coming of the Immortals

What forms are these coming
So white through the gloom?
What garments out-glistening
The gold-flower'd broom?

First hymn they the Father
Of all things; and then
The rest of Immortals,
The action of Men.

MATTHEW ARNOLD: *Empedocles on Etna*

1. The Coming of the Immortals

IF ever you are lucky enough to visit the beautiful land of Greece you will find a country haunted by more than three thousand years of history and legend.

The towering mountains slope steeply into the bluest of blue seas, and between the mountains lie valleys green and silver with the leaves of a million olive trees; golden with corn in the early summer, and then brown and white as the hot sun dries all up until the wide rivers become tinkling streams wandering in great courses of grey and yellow stones.

In winter and early spring the mountains are clothed with snow; mist hides the higher lands, and the rivers are roaring torrents racing down into the great gulfs and bays which break up Greece into little divisions as surely as the mighty mountains do.

As you wander through Greece in the late spring you are back in those ancient days the moment you leave the towns behind. Up on the green slopes below the towering heights of the great mountains, of Parnassus or Taygetus or Cithaeron, you can sit and dream yourself back into the time when you might expect to meet an Immortal on the mountain, in the olive-groves, or in the lonely valleys.

Far away a shepherd pipes to his flock, magic notes stealing up through the warm silence; surely that is Pan, half-goat, half-human, who guarded the shepherds of old?

Among the olive leaves stand the broken columns of temples, grey, or white, or golden-yellow; every one has a tale to tell – a legend, a story, or an actual history.

Over the blue sea, with its streaks like purple wine, lie islands dotted away into the distance; and they too have each a tale to tell. It may be Delos, perhaps: no one lives on it now, but the ruins of cities and temples, harbours and theatres, cluster from the shore to the hilltop on which Apollo the Shining One and his sister Artemis the Maiden Huntress were born. Or it may be rocky, rugged Ithaca, from which Odysseus sailed to the siege of Troy, and found again after ten years' wandering over strange and dragon-haunted seas.

With all the breath-taking beauty of Greece round about them, it is hardly wonderful that the ancient Greeks felt that the mountains and the valleys, the woods and streams, the very sea itself, were peopled with Immortals. There were wood nymphs among the

15

Zeus   Dionysus

trees and water nymphs in the rivers – fairies of human size who did not die and had powers which mortals do not possess. There were sea nymphs too – mermaids, though not all of them had tails – and strange sea-beings, who might be cruel and fierce even as the sea was fierce and cruel when the storms arose. And the sea must have a king, more powerful even than the nymphs, the Immortal called Poseidon who might come up through the waters in his chariot drawn by white horses, waving his trident – the three-pronged spear which was his sceptre, or sign of power.

On land also there were Immortal powers. Apollo, shining like the sun, who was also the lord of music and poetry; Artemis the huntress who guarded all wild things; fierce Ares the warlord, whose terrible shout might ring across the field of battle when the spears were flying and the swords of bronze or iron clanged on the shields and helmets; Athena, Immortal Lady of Wisdom; the kind Mother Goddess, Demeter, who caused the corn to grow and the young lambs to be born, with her lovely daughter Persephone who had to spend half the year in the kingdom of the dead when dark winter was spread over the earth.

Hera   Aphrodite

Then there was Aphrodite, Immortal Lady of Beauty and Love, with Eros her son, who shot the invisible arrows that made a young man or a girl fall in love; there was Hephaestus, more skilled than any mortal man in working with bronze and gold and iron, whose forge was beneath the island of Lemnos, with a volcano as his furnace chimney; there was Hermes of the winged heels, swift messenger, more cunning than any human; there was Dionysus who gave such power to the grapes that they could be brewed into wine to be a joy and a comfort to mankind; and there was the quiet Hestia, Lady of the Home and Guardian of the Hearth – for the hearth was the heart of the home in the days when fire was difficult to make.

All these, and more, were the Immortals, and their powers were great. But they too must surely obey laws and have a ruler set over them – and this was Zeus, the King of Heaven and of Earth, who wielded the thunderbolt, and was father of Mortals and of Immortals; and his Queen was Hera, Lady of Marriage and Guardian of Children. Zeus had power over all Immortals, though he seldom exercised it over his brothers, Poseidon, Lord of the

Sea, and Hades, Lord of the Dead, whose kingdom of shadows was thought to be beneath the earth.

The Greeks called these Immortals the 'gods', and worshipped them, making sacrifices to them at their particular shrines: Zeus at Olympia, Apollo at Delphi, Athena at Athens, and so on. When they began to tell the stories about them they had very little idea of what gods should be, and quite naturally pictured them as very like themselves, but much more powerful, more beautiful, and more free. Nor did it seem wrong to them to imagine that gods and goddesses could be cruel, or mean, deceitful, selfish, jealous or even wicked, according to our ideas, and as they themselves would have thought if ordinary men and women had done as the gods did.

Another trouble was that the Greeks in each of the little kingdoms and cities, and in the islands, made up different stories more or less without knowing what was being told over the sea, or beyond the mountains. Then, later, when minstrels travelled from place to place, and writing became more common, and people began to meet those from other parts of the Greek world, they found that many of the stories did not agree.

'Hera is the wife of Zeus,' the people of Argolis would say. 'Nonsense!' the Arcadians would answer. 'He married Maia, and they had a son called Hermes.' 'What are you talking about?' the people of Delphi or Delos would protest. 'The wife of Zeus is called Leto, and they had two children called Apollo and Artemis.'

Well, there was only one thing for it: they had to agree that Zeus must have had several wives! But Hera, as the most important of the Immortals, was obviously the real Queen of Heaven – and, as a woman would be, she was jealous!

In the earliest days the Greeks themselves often had several wives, as the people of Egypt did, and as the Turks and the Indians did until quite recently. In Greece, however, there was usually one real wife, and the others were captives taken in war, who were treated more and more as mere slaves; well looked after, but obliged to do just as they were told.

So it was not difficult to think of Zeus or Apollo behaving in much the same way as such a King of Athens as Theseus: and of course, over in Asia, kings always had many wives. That was where Troy was, so naturally King Priam had fifty sons, and Hecuba, the Queen of Troy, was simply his chief wife.

Each of the little Greek kingdoms, or city-states, had its own royal family; and each royal family liked to trace its descent back to one of the gods. It was much the same in England a thousand years ago: Alfred the Great was said to be descended from Odin, who held just the same place among the Saxons and the Danes as Zeus did among the Greeks. Indeed, if we believe the old writers of the Middle Ages, our own Royal Family, right down to the present Queen herself, can trace its descent from Odin on the one hand, and from Antenor who was the cousin of Priam of Troy, on the other!

Certainly Hera had some reason to be jealous – and she was very jealous indeed, or so the stories tell us – of Zeus's mortal wives. He had one in nearly every kingdom, just as sailors were said to have a wife in every port!

When the Greeks began to tell stories of the gods and goddesses, they had not become very civilized, so the legends seemed quite normal and credible to them. But as time went on, and the Greeks thought and learned more and more, some at least of them began to wonder about many of the stories: they began to realize that there was only one real God, and that he was good – better than any man could be.

Surely, however, this God must be Zeus: therefore Zeus himself must have become better and better, and have learnt by suffering until he understood what Mercy really meant.

Then the story-tellers realized that this fitted in rather well with the oldest of the stories about the gods. For in the very early days, before Zeus came, there were other gods – terrible creatures who were hardly people at all – who were as cruel and as dreadful as a tempest or an earthquake, as a tidal wave or an erupting volcano. These, in the earliest stories of all, those made by savage ancestors ages before, were the children of the Sky and the Earth. They were Giants and Titans, terrible ogres and trolls with many hands, or snake-like tails; and the most terrible of them was called Cronos, the father of the real gods, of Zeus, Poseidon, Hades, and of the goddesses Hera, Hestia, and Demeter.

We need not try to imagine what Cronos was like. The Greeks who invented the stories about him cannot have been very sure. His name means Time – but it was only the Romans who began to picture him as kindly old Father Time, with his scythe and his hour-glass.

The original Cronos was horribly different. He had a scythe, indeed, or rather a sickle – but he used it to cut pieces off his father Uranus, or Sky!

'You may be our ruler now!' Sky told him. 'But your children will treat you just as you have treated us and worse. They will bind you in a terrible prison, and one of them will rule instead of you!' And what Sky said, Earth said also, and Cronos knew that Earth cannot tell lies.

'We'll see about that!' roared Cronos, and he began to swallow his children as soon as they were born – just as Time swallows up the years, one after another.

First he swallowed Hestia, and then Demeter and Hera, and after them Hades and Poseidon.

This was too much for his wife, Rhea, although she was much the same kind of creature as Cronos; and as soon as her youngest son, Zeus, was born, she hid him away in a cave on the island of Crete.

'Where is the child?' demanded savage Cronos, and Rhea gave him a great stone wrapped in baby-clothes – and he swallowed that, thinking it was Zeus.

But Zeus was safe enough in Crete, guarded by the mountain nymphs, the children of kindly Mother Earth.

When he was fully grown, Zeus sought counsel of the good Titaness Metis, or Thought, who gave him a magic herb which he put into Cronos's wine. It made Cronos very sick, and up came the swallowed children, still very much alive, and all very angry.

The stone came up too, and you may see it to this very day just where it fell, at Delphi. Beside it is another stone which Zeus placed there to mark the centre of the earth: for he let loose two eagles, one from either end of the world, and they met exactly over Delphi.

Then for ten years Zeus, with his brothers and sisters, fought against Cronos and the Titans, and at last beat them, with the aid of the Cyclopes. These were giants with only one eye each, which was in the middle of the forehead. They made thunderbolts which Zeus showered down on his foes; and they made the trident with which Poseidon stirred up the sea to drown his enemies. They made a helmet of invisibility for Hades, who, when he wore it, could creep up unseen behind the Titans.

When the war was ended, Zeus shut up Cronos and the Titans in a fiery prison under the earth called Tartarus; and in after days the souls of the wicked were sent there to suffer with them.

Zeus and his brothers then cast lots to see which should rule the air, which the sea, and which under the earth: and so Zeus became the King of Heaven, Poseidon ruled the waves, and Hades the realm of the dead.

Then there was peace, and Zeus caused the palaces of the gods to be built: but whether their golden home was on Mount Olympus in the north of Greece, or on some cloud-mountain high up in the heavens, the Greeks were not quite certain.

After this Zeus began to restore the bruised and battered earth, for the Titans had thrown great mountains about, and brought desolation wherever they went.

Not all the Titans had taken part in the war, for the stories say that Helios, who drove the chariot of the Sun, was a Titan, and so was Selene, the Moon, and so too was Ocean, the very sea itself. And there were Metis, or Thought, Themis, or Justice, and Mnemosyne, or Memory, the mother of the Nine Muses, who lived on Mount Helicon. The Muses, of course, attended to the Arts – History, Lyric Poetry, Comedy, Tragedy, Dancing, Love-Poetry, Hymns, Epic, and Astronomy – and they were the special companions of Apollo.

One of the Titans who were imprisoned in Tartarus was Iapetus. He had three sons, two of whom helped Zeus in many ways. The third son, the only one who *looked* like a Titan, was Atlas, who fought against Zeus, and for a punishment was made to stand on top of Mount Atlas in North Africa and hold up the sky on his shoulders.

The two helpful sons of Iapetus were Prometheus and Epimetheus; and the first of these was one of the most important figures in all Greek myth.

CHAPTER 2

Hermes and Apollo

There through the dews beside me
    Behold a youth that trod,
With feathered cap on forehead,
    And poised a golden rod.

With lips that brim with laughter
    But never once respond,
And feet that fly on feathers,
    And serpent-circled wand.

A. E. HOUSMAN: *The Merry Guide*

2. Hermes and Apollo

BEFORE the great war with the Titans there had been men on the earth, and that time was the Golden Age when the corn grew without ploughing or sowing, and all the animals lived on fruit or grass.

The Golden Age came and passed, for no children were born, and the men and women did nothing but eat and drink, and wander about the lovely garden of the world.

Then came the men of the Silver Age, and with them came wickedness and evil, because of Cronos and the Titans; and they were destroyed utterly from the earth and were imprisoned with their wicked makers in Tartarus.

But when Zeus sat throned in Olympus, and the great war was over, he called to him the good Titan Prometheus.

'Go,' he said, 'and make Man out of clay. Make him in shape and form like the Immortals, and I will breathe life into him. Then you shall teach him such things as he needs to know, so that he may honour the Immortals and build temples for us. And after a little time he shall die and go down to the realm of my brother Hades, and be subject to him.'

Prometheus did as he was told. He went to a place in Greece called Panopeus, not many miles to the north-east of Delphi, and from the red clay he fashioned Man. Then Zeus gave life to the clay men, and left Prometheus to teach them all things needful.

'You may give such gifts as are suitable,' Zeus said, 'but you must not give them fire – for that belongs to the Immortals. If you disobey me in this matter, your fate shall be more terrible than that of all the other Titans put together!'

After this Zeus went away into the rocky land of Arcadia in the south of Greece and dwelt there for a while with the Star Maiden, Maia. They lived in a cave on the beautiful Mount Cyllene, and there a marvellous child was born, whose name was Hermes.

None of the Immortals knew where Zeus had gone, nor what he was doing: but Apollo learnt, and in a strange way.

Apollo owned a herd of the most magnificent cattle, and they were guarded for him by Helios, the Titan who drove the chariot of the Sun, and who could see all that happened on the earth during the day.

One morning he sent a message to Apollo: the cows had vanished! Last night they were grazing peacefully in a green valley of Arcadia, and today there was not a trace of them to be seen.

Full of rage, Apollo set out across Greece in search of them, uttering terrible threats against the thief, and promising wonderful rewards to anyone who could find the cattle.

In Arcadia he met a band of satyrs, who were wild wood-dwellers, left over, perhaps, from the Golden Age. Now they were inclined to be stupid and cowardly, full of mischief, and out to have a good time at all costs. They had pointed ears and little horns on their heads, and their leader Silenus was fat and foolish.

'We'll find your cows!' puffed Silenus. 'You trust us, Lord Apollo, we're always ready to help. Our eyes are sharp – and we're afraid of nothing!'

'Good!' said Apollo in his lordly fashion. 'Find my cows, and I will reward you well!'

Apollo went on his way, and the satyrs began their search up and down the valleys of Arcadia.

After much search, they found the cows' hoof-marks: but to their great surprise the tracks all pointed directly *towards* the grazing-ground from which they had been stolen!

'They're mad! They're bewitched!' cried Silenus at length. 'And some terrible creature must have driven them: look at his footmarks!'

The satyrs crowded round and stared at the traces of the cattle-thief which were large and round and blurred, with neither toes nor heels, but strange scratches and lines criss-crossing one another.

As they stood talking, a sound came to them out of the hillside, a new and wonderful sound which at first filled them with terror. It was the sound of music, the rich, sweet strains of the lyre, which is like a zither or small harp.

After much discussion and many attempts on the part of Silenus to run away and leave the other satyrs to face the monster, they all began to make as much noise as they could just outside the cave from which the music came – and *from* which the tracks of the cows led.

'He'll come out! He'll come out!' yelled the satyrs. 'And he'll be so frightened of us that if he's the cattle-thief, he'll fall down with terror as soon as he sees us!'

Hardly had they spoken, when the door of the cave opened slowly. Silenus got ready to run away, and the satyrs followed his example. But instead of any fearsome monster, there came out of the cave a beautiful mountain nymph.

'Wild creatures,' she said in her sweet, gentle voice, 'why are you making this noise, and frightening all of us who dwell in this pleasant land? I heard your mad shouting, the stamp of your feet in front of my cave, and on the hillside above it, and I came out to know why you disturb a poor nymph like this.'

26

'Do not be angry, beautiful nymph,' begged Silenus. 'We do not come here as enemies, meaning to hurt you. But that sound, that wonderful sound of strange music which excites us so – what is it, and who is making it?'

'Come, that's better,' smiled the nymph. 'You will learn by gentleness what you would never discover by force. Then know that I am Cyllene, the nymph of this mountain, and that I am the nurse to a son of Zeus, and the Star Nymph, Maia. His name is Hermes, and he is truly a wonderful child! He is only six days old, and yet he grows at an amazing speed. As for the sound you heard, it was the child playing a strange thing which he has made out of a dead creature which made no sound at all when it was alive!'

'A dead creature!' cried Silenus. 'Not a cow, by any chance?'

'What nonsense you talk!' said Cyllene scornfully. 'The dead creature was a tortoise: Hermes has used its shell, that's all. He's made a wonderful new musical instrument by stretching a piece of ox-hide across it, and then stringing it with cow-gut. . . .'

Cyllene paused, realizing that she had said too much, and Silenus exclaimed triumphantly:

'There you are, he *is* the thief who has stolen Apollo's cattle!'

'Do you dare to call the son of Zeus a thief!' protested Cyllene. 'I tell you it's nonsense! A baby less than a week old doesn't go stealing cows! And I'll swear, by any oath you like, that there isn't a single cow in the cave.'

'Well, let's see this child, anyhow,' demanded Silenus, and Cyllene had no choice but to go and bring Hermes.

Meanwhile Apollo, searching far and wide, came to the further side of Mount Cyllene, and found there strange tracks just as the satyrs had found. And while he was puzzling over them, he came upon an old man called Battus, and pointing to the tracks he questioned him:

'There have been cows passing this way, though the tracks lead mysteriously to the grazing-ground from which they have been stolen. Tell me, old man, have you seen them, and do you know where they are?'

Battus, not recognizing Apollo, replied:

'My son, I am old and I cannot see very well. But what I saw lately has surprised me exceedingly. Last night I was digging in my vineyard when the sun went down: and I was still there after blessed Selene had driven the Moon-chariot up into the sky. And in the silvery, shimmering light I saw, or thought I saw, a child driving a great herd of cattle. Sometimes he drove them backwards, and sometimes he pulled them after him by their tails;

and he was for ever darting about them like a gleam of quick-silver. Yet on his feet he wore strange shoes made of plaited osier twigs: you can see the round marks of them over yonder.'

Apollo thanked old Battus, and hastened on, following the hoof-marks backwards now that he knew how they had been driven. Very soon he found the cattle penned into a great cave; and though he was glad to have discovered them, his brows darkened with anger when he saw that two of them were missing.

Penning the cattle in the cave behind him, Apollo followed the tracks across Mount Cyllene, and on the further side came upon the satyrs who were still questioning Hermes outside Maia's cave.

'Lord Apollo!' cried Silenus excitedly. 'Here's the thief who stole your cows! This boy here! He's the son of Zeus, so he says: but he's a thief none the less. We've tracked two of the cows to this cave, and he has in his hand a piece of the skin of one of them!'

Apollo saw then that there would be trouble, so he hastily thanked Silenus and his satyrs, gave them their reward, and sent them away.

Then he turned upon the little boy who sat, smiling innocently, in the sunshine, playing with his lyre, and said:

'Child, tell me quickly where my cattle are, or I shall deal severely with you, and fling you down into Tartarus – even if you are indeed the son of Zeus.'

'Brother Apollo,' answered Hermes, looking up at the shining Immortal with big, wondering eyes, 'why do you speak to me so harshly? And why do you come here seeking for cattle? I have not seen them: how should I even know what cows look like? I am only a baby still: I do not care for anything but sleep, and warm milk; to lie wrapped in a warm cradle, or to play with toys such as this in my hand. But if it pleases you, I will swear an oath by Styx, the black River of Death, for I am an Immortal even as you are, and I know that Immortals cannot break that oath. Listen: by Styx I swear that none of your cows are in this cave, and that I have not set eyes on the thief who stole them!'

Then Apollo smiled at the cunning of the child Hermes, and said:

'Surely after this your name shall be Prince of Robbers! But your clever story does not deceive me, so come quickly to Olympus, and if Zeus our father has returned, we will lay the case before him.'

He made as if to seize the child by the scruff of his neck, but before he could do so, Hermes laid his fingers gently upon the strings of his lyre and as the heavenly music swelled up, Apollo's hand fell to his side, and he stood still in amazement and delight.

The infant Hermes, Zeus and Apollo

Very soon, as he listened, he forgot his anger, and thought no more about his cows. His only desire was to make such music himself, and he stretched out his hands to Hermes:

'Give me the lyre!' he cried, 'and I will forgive you for the theft of my cattle, and for the two cows which you have killed. Give me the lyre, and swear that you will not steal from me again, and I will give you also my wand and make you the Herald of the Immortals, and the guide of souls down the steep ways of death.'

As Apollo was speaking, Zeus drew near and heard all that he had said.

'It shall be so!' he cried in his voice of thunder. 'Swear the oath, son Hermes, and give the lyre to Apollo. Then shall he be the Lord of Music and of all sweet songs and the Nine Muses shall follow him and do him honour. And you, Hermes, shall be our messenger, right welcome in the golden halls of Olympus, and kindly disposed to the mortals upon earth.'

The oath was sworn, and Apollo took the lyre and went gladly on his way to Mount Helicon, where the Muses awaited him. When he grew tired of singing, he crossed to Parnassus, the next mountain, which became his especial dwelling-place; and he slew the great serpent called Python who lived in a cave at lovely Delphi on its lowest slope. There, later on, stood the most famous of all the temples of Apollo in Greece, and there was his oracle at which the priestess spoke the truest prophecies of the future in all the known world.

Hermes remained for a time in Arcadia; but he did not stay many days in the cave on Mount Cyllene, though Zeus lingered there with lovely Maia. Just as he had grown to boyhood in six days, so in a very brief space of time he was full-grown, and ready to seek a wife.

He had not far to search, for in a valley nearby a nymph, Dryope, tended her sheep, and Hermes loved her at first sight. But Dryope was shy, frightened of the shining youth who came wooing her, and she declared that she would only marry a shepherd.

Hermes went away, but returned in disguise, bringing with him a flock of sheep – which, doubtless, he had stolen as easily as he had the cattle of Apollo. For a long time he grazed his sheep in the rich valleys, and met Dryope there from time to time, so that they became friends, and at last she consented to marry the supposed shepherd.

All went well for them in happy Arcadia, where the Golden Age seemed still to linger. But when Dryope's baby was born, she took one look at the child, and fled away shrieking. For the little creature had the legs and horns of a goat, and was born with a beard on his chin. All the same he was a noisy, merry, laughing child, and Hermes took him in his arms with delight, wrapped him in the soft skins of the wild hares, and carried him to Olympus.

Zeus had just returned, and he welcomed Hermes, and smiled at the strange child. All the other Immortals were pleased too with the merry little creature and they named him Pan and bade Hermes take him back to Arcadia. That was to be his chief dwelling-place, and there he was to attend to the flocks and herds, and to all wild things. When he grew older, Pan cut himself reeds in the river, and made the syrinx, the Pan-pipes, on which he played with a strange and mystical sweetness.

Zeus had little time to see how the son of Hermes would fare, for he had not been back in Olympus for long, when, looking out over the world after sundown, he beheld little sparks of light in many places; and in the daytime he saw smoke rising from the houses of newly-created men.

Then he knew that Prometheus, the good Titan, had disobeyed his orders and given fire to mankind.

CHAPTER 3

The Story of Prometheus

Lo, a god in the anguish, a god in the chain!
 The god Zeus hateth sore
 And his gods hate again,
As many as tread on his glorified floor,
Because I loved mortals too much evermore.

AESCHYLUS: *Prometheus Bound* (Translated by E. B. Browning)

3. The Story of Prometheus

AFTER he had formed men out of the clay of Panopeus, and they had received the breath of life from Zeus, Prometheus set to work to make them something more than mere living images of the gods.

For man as first created was little better than the beasts, a poor creature, who did not know how to think or how to use the things which he saw and felt round about him. He lived in caves, ate herbs and raw meat: and when he was wounded or hurt, he died because he knew nothing of medicine or surgery.

But Prometheus, the good and kind, taught men all the arts and crafts of life. He taught them how to build houses and make tools; how to plough the earth and sow the corn, how to reap it when it had grown, to thresh out the bright grains and grind them between flat stones. He showed them how to catch and tame some of the wild creatures: the dog to guard their houses and go hunting with them; the horse to draw their chariots, and the ox to pull the plough; the sheep to yield wool, and the goats milk which might be made into cheese.

It is said that Prometheus also gave men the power of speech, taught them the names of all things and even how to write and read.

But it was slow work, since fire, the greatest aid, was missing. Without it meat must still be eaten raw, and tools could be made only of stone and wood; bread could not be baked, and houses could not be warmed in winter.

Prometheus looked up at the sun, coursing across the sky in the golden chariot which Helios drove, and he sighed deeply. For he could read the future, and, though much of it remained dark to him, what he could see he knew would surely happen.

Then he called to him his brother Epimetheus, who was as foolish, thoughtless, and improvident as he was wise, thoughtful, and fore-sighted.

'My brother,' he said. 'You have helped me so far, and now you live as a man among men to carry on my work. You know how well I love the men whom we have made and taught – and yet you, who see only the outward aspect of everything, do not realize how deep such a love as mine can be. Listen! I must give fire to mankind, the last and greatest of gifts. But if I do so, I shall incur the terrible wrath of Zeus. . . . Yet even that I will endure – for so it is ordained. But I beg you to guard mankind to the best of your power, and to be very careful when I am no longer with you. Above all things, beware of any gift from Zeus.'

Then Prometheus bade farewell to his brother, and set out for Olympus, carrying with him the stalk of a fennel plant, as long as a staff and hard as wood, but hollow and filled with a white pith which would burn slowly and steadily like the wick of a candle.

At the foot of Olympus he was met by Athena, the Immortal daughter of Zeus, Lady of Wisdom, who had helped Prometheus in his labours for mankind. There was a strange story told of her birth, which shows that her father Zeus might have taken after the terrible Cronos.

For while Zeus was still at war with the Titans, he married Metis, daughter of the friendly Titan, Ocean, and Prometheus came to him and said:

'Mighty Zeus, if Metis bears you a child, it will be stronger and wiser than you, its father!'

Then Zeus, who knew that whatever Prometheus prophesied was certain to be true, was much alarmed. Metis had all the terrible powers of the Titans, and at that time Zeus was not yet armed with his thunderbolts; but he thought of a clever plan, or maybe Prometheus thought of it for him.

'Lady Metis,' he said, 'I know that you have the wonderful power of turning yourself into any creature you please. I can well believe that you could become a great and magnificent animal such as a lioness or a she-bear; but surely it is beyond your power to turn yourself into so small and worthless a creature as a fly!'

'Beyond my power, is it?' cried Metis, forgetting her usual prudence, 'I'll show you!' And in a moment she had turned herself into a fly. Zeus smiled, caught the fly – and swallowed it.

That was the end of Metis, and by swallowing her Zeus added all her wisdom to his own, also her power of shape-shifting. But some months later a terrible pain shot through his head, and grew worse and worse, until he cried out in agony for Prometheus to help him.

Prometheus took his axe and split open the head of Zeus, knowing that an Immortal cannot die, and being himself the master of the art of healing.

Then a great wonder was seen, for from the head of Zeus sprang Athena the daughter of Metis, fully grown and clad in shining armour. She had the wisdom of Metis also, but had no wish to surpass her father Zeus. Her wisdom was of a gentler kind, so that she became the teacher of such arts as spinning and weaving, and also of good and wise government. But she had some of her mother's fierceness also, as she proved by joining in the battle at her father's side, and slaying the Titan Pallas, whose skin she flayed off to make her cloak and whose name she added to her own, so that all who were unjust might fear the terrible voice of Pallas Athena. She could be jealous too, as she proved when the mortal maiden Arachne boasted that her skill in weaving was greater than Athena's, for, not content with proving her superiority by a contest, Athena turned the foolish girl into a spider – to weave cobwebs and useless gossamer.

But Athena was always friendly to Prometheus, and interested in his work for mankind; and so when she knew that he had decided to give them fire, she led him by the secret paths to the summit of Olympus.

As day drew to an end, Helios drove up in his shining chariot, and Prometheus, hiding by the gateway, needed but to stretch out his fennel-stalk and touch the golden wheel. Then, the precious spark concealed under his cloak, he hastened down the mountain side, and away into a deep valley of Arcadia where he heaped up a pile of wood and kindled it.

The first people upon earth to see the wonderful new gift of fire were the wild satyrs who dwelt in the lonely valleys. Slowly and shyly they gathered round the edge of the glade in which Prometheus had lighted the first camp-fire; and gradually they drew nearer and nearer.

'Oh the lovely thing!' they cried as they felt the warmth. 'How beautifully it dances; how warm, and gentle, and comforting this new creature is!'

'Oh, how I love it!' cried Silenus. 'It shall be mine, mine! See, I will kiss the lovely creature, to prove it!'

With that he knelt down and tried to kiss the tallest and brightest tongue of flame. The look on his face was so comical as the flame scorched him and burnt his beard, that Prometheus sat back and roared with laughter.

But he had more serious work in hand, and when day dawned he began to teach men the uses of fire. He showed them how to cook meat and bake bread; how to make bronze and smelt iron; how to hammer the hot metals into swords and ploughshares and all the other cunning crafts of the smith and the metal-worker.

Now that fire had come upon the Earth, it could be kindled there whenever it was needed. So Prometheus, with the help of Hermes, invented rubbing-sticks and taught men which woods to use and how to twirl the hard piece in the soft until fire was kindled by the friction.

So mankind came into its true inheritance: cities began to grow up, and men to practise all the arts and crafts for which Greece was soon to become famous.

But Zeus, as soon as he became aware that his command had been disobeyed and the gift which he withheld had been stolen and given to men, summoned Prometheus before him.

'Titan!' he cried fiercely. 'You have disobeyed me! What is there to prevent me from casting you down into Tartarus with your brethren, and destroying these vile insects, these men, to whom you have given gifts reserved for the Immortals alone?'

'Lord Zeus,' answered Prometheus quietly, 'I know what is to come, and how cruelly you will punish me for all I have done. But there are two things you cannot do: no Immortal may take away the gift an Immortal has once given – so you will not deprive men of fire now that I have made it theirs. And I am certain that you will not destroy mankind, when I tell you that a man – your son, born of a mortal woman – will save you and all of you who dwell in Olympus in that future day when Earth will bring forth the Giants, meaning to be revenged for the overthrow of the Titans. This I tell you, and you know that my words are true: no Immortal will be able to slay a Giant, but a man will slay them, if he be strong and brave enough. And I will tell you this also: at a certain time in the future you may fall as your father fell.'

Then the wrath of Zeus was terrible. In a voice of thunder he bade his son Hephaestus, the Immortal whose skill was in the working of metals, take Prometheus and bind him with fetters of brass to the great mountain of Caucasus on the eastern edge of the world.

'There you shall lie,' he cried in his cruel rage, 'for ever and ever as a punishment for your daring and disobedience. The snows of winter will freeze you, and the summer sun will burn you: and your fate shall be a warning to all who would disobey!'

Then sorrowfully Hephaestus took Prometheus, and at his command his two servants, the demons Might and Force, chained him to the rock with fetters that he could not break.

But as Hephaestus was about to leave him there, Prometheus said:

'Zeus, that cruel tyrant, will fall as Cronos fell, unless he can find out how to avert his doom. And how to do that, I alone know!'

Hephaestus reported these words, and Hermes was sent to offer Prometheus his freedom if he would tell the secret.

'If you do not at once disclose what you know,' said Hermes, 'Zeus will torture you until you do so. He will send a fierce eagle who will visit you every day and devour your liver: and every night

'He will send a fierce eagle who will visit you every day and devour your liver'

your liver will grow again so that next day your agonies may be repeated.'

Still Prometheus would not say how Zeus could avoid the fate which hung over him, and, though the eagle did as Zeus had threatened, still he would not tell. But at times his screams echoed over the haunted cliffs and chasms of Caucasus, so that none dared to approach.

Meanwhile Zeus, a prey to fears for the future, and still made cruel by terror, sought how he might plague mankind so that the gift of fire might not make them too happy.

Now at first men had full knowledge of their own future, and Zeus, not knowing that Prometheus, with his great foresight, had taken this power from them, decided to make them immortal also, so that when he had worked his will on them and set free sin and care in the world, they might go mad with terror knowing the sorrows and sufferings which lay in store for them.

He went cunningly to work, visiting men in disguise and asking who had given them the gift of fire.

And men betrayed their benefactor, Prometheus, with cruel thoughtlessness. This gave Zeus his excuse.

'I will reward you,' he said, 'for telling me what I wanted to know, by giving you a jar of nectar, the drink of the Immortals, which keeps them for ever young.'

The men who received this precious gift were overjoyed; but with the usual folly and laziness of mankind, they put it on the back of a donkey and drove it before them towards a place where they meant to keep it in safety. Presently they came to a spring of clear water bubbling from the rock, and when they had refreshed themselves, they sat down to eat at a little distance, leaving the donkey to graze nearby.

Soon the donkey felt thirsty too, and went over to the spring for a drink. But now there was a cunning snake guarding it, who spoke to the donkey with crafty words.

'If you touch my spring, I will bite you, and you will die in agony from the poison.'

'I am dying already – of thirst,' protested the donkey. 'So please let me drink a little of the cool spring water.'

'Well,' said the guileful serpent, 'I'll make a bargain with you. Give me the wine in the jar on your back. It's warm, and nasty, and donkeys don't like wine, anyway. If you give it to me, I'll let you drink as much water from my cool, refreshing spring as you please.'

'Agreed,' cried the donkey eagerly, and the exchange was made – and that is why snakes renew their youth every year, casting off the old skin and appearing as young and shining as ever.

When Zeus discovered that men could no longer foresee the future, he was rather pleased that the snake had cheated the donkey: for he knew that in the days to come many serpents would bite both men and asses, and that snake-bite produces a worse fever of thirst than anything.

Meanwhile he was busy on a surer punishment for Man: he was making the first woman. Her name was Pandora, which means 'all-gifted', for all of the Immortals helped to endow her. Clever Hephaestus shaped her out of clay, and lovely Aphrodite gave her beauty, while Hermes taught her cunning and boldness, and Athena dressed her in lovely clothes. Zeus breathed life into her, and then Hermes led her down to earth and brought her to Epimetheus, the thoughtless brother of Prometheus, who lived now more or less as a man among men.

When Epimetheus saw the beauty of Pandora he forgot his brother's warning against accepting any gift from Zeus, and fell in love with her at once. Very soon they were married, and they had a daughter called Pyrrha, who married Deucalion, the wisest and most virtuous of all the first men whom Prometheus had fashioned out of clay.

But meanwhile Pandora brought all the evil upon mankind which Zeus had planned.

In the house of Epimetheus stood a golden box which Prometheus had left there with strict orders that no one was to open it. Epimetheus told his wife this, but she was so curious and inquisitive that life did not seem worth living until she knew what treasure it was that her husband was hiding from her.

So one day when he was out, Pandora crept quietly to the golden casket and lifted the lid. Then with a rush and a cry out came all the ills which beset mankind – diseases, and sorrows, hate, jealousy, lies, theft, cheating, and a hundred others.

Terrified at what she had done, Pandora slammed down the lid. But she raised it again quickly when a little voice cried: 'Let me out too! I am Hope!'

For Prometheus had placed Hope there when he shut up the evil things, so that mankind might not suffer quite so much if Zeus had his way.

CHAPTER 4

How Zeus and Hermes Went Visiting

The gods are angry: we shall never be
Now as of old, when far from all men we
 Dwelt in a lonely land and languorous,
Circled and sundered by the sleeping sea.

Yea, the Olympians then were wont to go
Among us, visible godheads, to and fro.

J. W. MACKAIL: *In Scheria*

4. How Zeus and Hermes Went Visiting

TIME went by and men settled down all over the earth as if it had always been theirs. And Zeus was pleased with what he saw as he looked down from Olympus, and busied himself setting the rest of the world to rights after the desolation made by the Titans.

Of course it was to Greece that he gave most of his attention, though he did not neglect the islands of the Aegean Sea which separates Greece from Asia Minor, nor that part of the mainland beyond which is called Troy.

When he was tired with his labours, Zeus would go southwards to the land of the blessed Ethiopians, men of the Silver Age who had not learnt the wickedness of the Titans, and who often entertained the Immortals at their banquets.

But the evils which Pandora had let loose from the golden casket found their way surely enough into the hearts of men, and some even in Greece became almost as wicked as those of the Silver Age whom Zeus had destroyed before Prometheus made man as we know him out of clay.

Rumours of wickedness beyond belief came to Zeus, and he began to wonder whether he could destroy the people of the Bronze Age and make yet another race of men: but without Prometheus to help him, he hesitated. At last he decided to see for himself, and so he called to him his son Hermes and said:

'Let us take upon ourselves the form and likeness of men and go down into the land of Greece and seek entertainment as if we were poor travellers. And if we find that men are not fit to live upon the beautiful earth, I will destroy them utterly.'

Hermes, who loved mankind and had helped Prometheus, replied:

'Father Zeus, let us not be over hasty. If we visit three households, and find that two out of the three merit destruction, then let mankind perish. But if we find virtue and kindness in even two, however wicked the third may be, then spare the good. But bring whatever doom you like upon the wicked.'

This pleased Zeus, who had grown less cruel than in the days when he sent Prometheus to his terrible doom and made Pandora to be a plague to all mankind.

He agreed to what Hermes suggested, and the two Immortals began their wanderings in the land of Arcadia, Zeus disguised as an old man and Hermes as his grandson.

Now at that time the King of Arcadia was Lycaon, a fierce, savage man given to all manner of evil. He had fifty sons, most of them as bad as he was, and like him they were cannibals.

Zeus and Hermes entered King Lycaon's palace, and at first he refused to give them food, and even threatened to kill them. Hermes, so young and handsome, would make him an excellent feast; perhaps it was this which made him change his mind.

Certainly he bade Zeus sit down at his table: perhaps he already considered Hermes a prisoner being fattened up for a future banquet. Suddenly Lycaon realized that there was no fresh meat ready for that day; but this did not trouble him overmuch, since he had one son, Nyctimus, who was not as wicked as the rest, and always refused to eat human flesh. On this day he had dared to tell his father that to eat one of his guests was the wickedest thing a man could do.

'You're only fit for stewing!' snarled Lycaon; and so Nyctimus was killed, jointed and put in the pot.

When this hideous meal was placed on the table, Zeus the all-seeing knew at once what the dish was which was set before him. Filled with rage he sprang to his feet, and a great light shone round him as Lycaon cowered away, realizing in a moment of terror that his guest was none other than the King of the Immortals.

'Wretch!' cried Zeus. 'All that I have heard of you is true! You are not fit to be a man! Go forth into the wilderness and haunt the lonely mountains and dangerous valleys: be a wolf, and your impious sons with you!'

Then Lycaon tried to answer, but all he could utter was the howl of a wolf. He tried to fall upon his knees, only to find that he was already on all fours. So he fled away into the forests of Arcadia with his sons behind him, a wolf at the head of his pack.

Zeus restored Nyctimus to life and bade him rule justly and well. Then he and Hermes, once more in disguise, continued on their way.

'You see,' said Zeus presently. 'Men are as wicked as I thought. Is there need of further search?'

'Remember your promise,' answered Hermes. 'And this time, let us seek hospitality of a poor man: perhaps we may find a virtue among the humble which is lacking to a king such as Lycaon.'

So they went on across the world, passing at will over sea and land, and came in the evening to a mountain top near Tyana in Phrygia. Here stood a little cottage thatched with straw, and the walls made of reeds and clay. There were no servants in this house,

44

indeed its only inhabitants were an old man and his wife whose names were Philemon and Baucis.

Poor though they were, these two welcomed the travellers kindly, made up the fire with their last dry faggot, put on the pot to boil, and cut up their only joint of smoked bacon which hung from the beam.

They prepared a bed for their guests, the only bed in the house, and heaped all the rugs they possessed upon it. Then they laid the table and set the supper before the two strangers.

Besides the meat there were olives and cheese; eggs roasted in the warm embers, and what little store they had of dried figs, dates, and nuts. Old Baucis, her hands trembling with age, served the meal, while Philemon placed two wooden cups upon the table and poured into them wine from the only jar that remained to him.

All this they did with simple kindness, talking to their guests and making them welcome, without the slightest idea that they were anything but human travellers as poor as themselves.

But when Philemon came to refill the cups which he had seen his guests drain to the dregs, he found them both still full of wine – and of wine so sweet and fragrant that the delicious scent of it filled the whole cottage. Then he fell on his knees before his guests.

'Noble sirs,' he cried, holding up his hands in prayer, 'surely you are blessed gods come down from Olympus! Pardon us, I beg you, that our entertainment has been so poor, and the food so meagre. Indeed, we would have done better, if we possessed better: but we have given you all we had.'

Then Zeus smiled kindly on the two old people, and said:

'You have guessed truly: we are Zeus and Hermes, come down to test mankind – and in you we find nothing to blame. Come now, and see what we propose for you!'

He led the way out of the cottage, and scarcely had they left it when it began to grow and change as they watched it. The rough sticks which held up the roof turned into columns of white marble; the thatch grew yellower and yellower until it shone with pure gold, and the dark earthen floor grew hard and smooth with many-coloured mosaic.

'And now,' said Zeus, 'what gift do you desire for yourselves?'

Then Philemon and Baucis spoke together for a few moments, after which Philemon turned and said:

'Of all things we desire most to be your priest and priestess in the beautiful temple which you have made. And this also we beg, that since we have lived our lives together in such perfect harmony and happiness, we may both die at the same moment.'

45

'All this I grant,' cried Zeus, and the thunder rolled across the sky in token of his gift. 'And, whatever may chance to the wicked among men, here on this sacred mountain top you will be safe. Moreover I make you young again: live your lives as virtuously as you have done, and when death comes, both of you on the instant shall be turned into trees that you may still stand here and bow your heads before my temple.'

So saying Zeus turned away from Baucis and Philemon, and set out once more with Hermes, in the direction of Greece.

Soon they came to wooded Thessaly in the north of Greece, and here Zeus turned to Hermes and said:

'Son of Maia, we have found a virtuous and holy couple living in Asia, but here in our own land of Greece Lycaon the impious man-eater, the wolf-king. This our last visit will save or destroy mankind!'

Now it may be that Hermes knew, and led the way, or it may be that Zeus was anxious for an excuse to spare some at least of the race of men: but certain it is that the house in which they next sought shelter was that of Deucalion, whom Prometheus had made from the clay of Panopeus, and his wife Pyrrha, the daughter of Epimetheus and Pandora.

They found these two everything that they could wish: kindly and pious, honouring the gods, living blameless lives, and practising diligently all the arts which Prometheus had taught.

'Now,' said Zeus, when he and Hermes had tested Deucalion's hospitality and found that a King of Thessaly could be as simple and kindly as an ancient peasant of Phrygia, 'now I will return to Olympus, and let loose a great flood over the earth. All those who are not fit to live shall drown in that flood, and I will see to it that any who save themselves by climbing to the tops of mountains are worthy of life – and I fear there will be few indeed of them. As for you, noble Deucalion, make haste and build a ship; place a roof over the top of it, store food and clothes in it, and then enter it with your wife and children. In this ship you will be safe, and I will guide it to the land over which I purpose that you and your children shall rule.'

Then Deucalion did as he was bidden, and brought to the task all the skill which Prometheus had taught him. Soon the ship was finished, and as soon as he and Pyrrha were safely inside it, Zeus let loose the rain.

For nine days and nine nights the rain poured down upon the earth; and Poseidon stirred up the waves with his trident so that the sea flowed in over the land as well.

46

All was desolation: houses lay in ruins beneath the waters, the corn rotted and turned black, and the fishes swam in and out among the branches of the trees. Only the sea-peoples, the nymphs and the dolphins, were happy, swimming about among the mountain-tops, and diving down to explore drowned cities beneath the waves.

At last the waters began to fall, and the ship came to rest on a slope of Mount Parnassus, near Apollo's shrine at Delphi. Praising the gods for their deliverance, Deucalion and Pyrrha stepped on shore and lay down to sleep.

In the morning a voice spoke to them out of the deep earth beneath Apollo's temple, which was now hung with sea-weed and encrusted with shells:

'Deucalion and Pyrrha! Father Zeus does not mean to stamp out utterly the race of men. Therefore go down into the valley before you, cover your heads with your cloaks, and cast behind you the bones of your mother!'

For a long time they were puzzled by this command, for each of them had a different mother, and both were dead. But at last Deucalion hit upon the right answer.

'Surely,' he said, 'our mother is the Earth, for out of earth were men formed by our maker Prometheus. And the bones of Earth must be the stones.'

So they went down into the river valley, covered their heads, and began to throw stones backwards over their shoulders. And presently as they threw they heard a murmur behind them, a murmur that swelled and swelled until at last they could restrain themselves no longer.

They turned round, and there was a multitude of men and women. And as they gazed they saw the last few stones which they had thrown swelling, changing, growing soft and rising up into human shapes: the men from the stones which Deucalion had thrown and the women from those which fell behind Pyrrha.

In this way the land of Greece was re-peopled, and very soon new cities sprang up from the ruins of the old; the fields yielded rich corn once more, and the olive groves shimmered silver in the sunlight.

The children of Deucalion and Pyrrha, with those who had survived the flood by climbing to the mountain-tops, became the kings and queens of the various states of Greece; and the most famous of them, whose name was Hellen, gave his name to the whole country, which is often called Hellas to this very day, and its people the Hellenes.

47

*'Animals of every kind came leaping and tumbling
out of the ground'*

Zeus was pleased with mankind now that the more evil of them
had been destroyed, and he and the other Immortals wandered
often through the lovely land of Hellas, and some married mortal
brides whose children became kings and princes.

'This is the Age of the Heroes,' decreed Zeus, 'and the men in
it shall be stronger and the women more beautiful than their descendants in times to come.' For Zeus remembered the prophecy
of the Titan Prometheus, that when the Giants came to attack
him and the other Immortals, they could only win the war if there
was a mortal man strong and brave enough to fight at their side and
kill the Giants when the Gods had overthrown them.

So Zeus planned, hoping that the greatest hero of all would
be born in time to help him. The Heroic Age lasted until the
youngest son of that hero had grown old and died, together with
those heroes who fought at Troy, of whom the last was Odysseus.

But, without the wisdom of Prometheus to guide him, Zeus
made a mistake which very nearly caused his doom and wrecked
the world. For when Deucalion and Pyrrha had made men and

women by casting stones over their shoulders, Zeus, eager to make Greece a pleasant dwelling-place for the heroes, laid a command upon Earth.

'Bring forth animals!' he commanded, for all animal life had perished in the great flood, though the birds and the reptiles had been able to survive it.

Earth did as she was bidden, and animals of every kind came leaping and tumbling out of the ground, squeezing up between the rocks, and pushing their way upwards just as a mole does. But she laughed to herself, deep down in the caverns where the Titans were imprisoned. For besides the animals, she made the Giants – though they did not come out of their caves for a long time yet to do battle with the Immortals. But in addition to the Giants, Earth produced the most fearful monster ever seen, who was called Typhon.

CHAPTER 5

Typhon the Terrible

The lyre's voice is lovely everywhere;
In the courts of gods, in the city of men,
And in the lonely rock-strewn mountain-glen,
In the still mountain air.

Only to Typhon it sounds hatefully;
To Typhon only, the rebel o'erthrown,
Through whose heart Etna drives her roots of stone,
To imbed them in the sea.

MATTHEW ARNOLD: *Empedocles on Etna*

5. Typhon the Terrible

TYPHON, the last of the Titans, was born out of the Earth in Asia Minor, far away from the sight of Zeus. Earth hid him as long as possible in a great dark cave in a place called Cilicia, that he might be full-grown before Zeus discovered him.

But when Typhon came to full size, there was no hiding for him anywhere in the world. Of all creatures ever known upon the earth, he was the biggest and most frightful.

He was so tall that as he walked far out in the sea the waves came only a little way above his knees; and when he stood upon the dry land, the stars became entangled in his hair. He was terrible to look at, for from his shoulders grew a hundred heads, with dark, flickering serpent tongues and flaming eyes. Each head uttered from its fearsome mouth a voice of its own: some spoke in words that men could understand, but others bellowed like bulls, or roared like lions or howled like hunting wolves. From this monster's shoulders grew dragons' wings; and his hands were so strong that he could lift mountains with them.

As soon as he was grown to his full height, Typhon came striding suddenly across the Aegean Sea towards Greece, roaring with rage like a thousand hurricanes. Straight for Olympus he came, for the one thought in each of his hundred heads was to destroy the Immortals and rule in their place.

Then there was terror and panic in heaven, and to save themselves the Immortals fled away into the land of Egypt where they disguised themselves by assuming the heads of animals or birds so that Typhon might not know them. The Egyptians made statues of them and gave them new names: Artemis with a cat's head they called Bast; Dionysus with the ram's head became Osiris, cowheaded Demeter became Isis, and so on with the other Immortals.

But Zeus did not flee: he stood up on Olympus to do battle with his fearful enemy, and hurled a thunderbolt at him.

Typhon laughed at thunderbolts, and catching the next one Zeus threw he hurled it back, and after that a whole cascade of rocks and mountain-tops.

Zeus dodged them, and snatched up the great sickle made of adamant with which in the beginning of time Cronos had maimed his father the Sky. With this weapon, harder and sharper than the sharpest iron, he attacked the monster, and the whole earth shook and quaked as they fought. Long and fiercely the battle raged; but Zeus was the stronger, and soon Typhon was bleeding from many wounds.

But as they rolled on the ground, wrestling and struggling together, Typhon made one last tremendous effort and wrenched the sickle from Zeus, while he twined the snaky coils of his body round him and held him prisoner for a moment. Then with a few swift blows Typhon cut off the immortal sinews from Zeus's arms and legs, leaving him lying on the slope of Olympus, powerless to move.

Typhon also was sorely wounded and bleeding from many cuts, but he managed to crawl down into a deep valley in the wild land of Thrace in northern Greece, and hid the sinews in a cave. Then he rested outside in the sun, guarding the sinews, and waiting until his wounds healed and his strength came back to him.

Meanwhile Hermes and Pan came quietly across the world in search of Zeus, and found him lying on the mountain-side, unable to stir, powerless to defend himself if Typhon returned to the attack.

They thought of many schemes to save him, and at last Hermes devised a plan:

'We need some simple human to help us,' he said. 'Typhon is an Immortal himself, so that he would recognize either of us, however well we disguised ourselves.'

Then Zeus remembered that Prince Cadmus was at this moment wandering among the hills of Thrace in search of his sister Europa.

For it happened that a little while before the coming of Typhon, Zeus had visited the land of Phoenicia, to the north of Palestine, in the shape of a wonderful white bull with horns of gold.

The Princess Europa had been playing on the sea-shore with her companions, and she was delighted with the beauty of the white bull. At first she was afraid, but it came to her in such a friendly way, and let her stroke it, that soon she was treating it almost as a pet. She twined garlands of flowers for its horns, and then, much daring, climbed on to its back for a ride. The white bull was gentleness itself: he walked carefully up and down the beach, and then began to splash through the little waves as they broke on the sandy shore. At first Europa was wild with delight, but her excitement changed suddenly to fear when the bull moved into deep water, and began to swim out to sea.

She screamed vainly for help, and clung desperately to the golden horns; but the bull brought her safely across the sea to the island of Crete. There Zeus resumed his ordinary shape, and told her that her children should rule in this beautiful island, and so well and so wisely that after their death two of her sons would be made judges of the souls of the dead in the realm of Hades.

But meanwhile, in Phoenicia, the King, Europa's father, called his three sons to him and said:

'Go north and south and west in search of your sister, and do not return without her, or you shall die!'

That was why the eldest of them, Prince Cadmus, was wandering through the valleys of Thrace in northern Greece when suddenly the two Immortals met him.

'Do not be afraid, Prince Cadmus,' said Hermes, 'we bring you a message from Zeus. You shall be king of a great city in Greece, and your children shall be famous. Zeus will be your friend, and heap good things upon you and yours. . . . But now he himself is in terrible need, and you can help him.'

They disguised Cadmus as a shepherd, and Hermes built a little house for him not far from where Typhon was. Pan, the kindly goat-footed Immortal who has charge of all shepherds and their flocks, lent Cadmus some sheep, and gave him also his wonderful pipes, which play sweeter, more magical tunes than any made by mortal hands.

And when Hermes had instructed him in all that he must say and do, Prince Cadmus, in his disguise, went wandering down the valley playing upon the pipes of Pan, with the sheep and lambs gambolling and frisking about him. Presently he came to where Typhon was lying on the soft grass in front of his cave. Typhon heard the music, and made no attempt to harm the simple shepherd who could breathe through the pipes such sweet and wonderful sounds.

'Do not be afraid of me, shepherd,' rumbled the monster, 'but play and let me hear sweeter music still, so that I may forget my pains and grow whole more speedily. And when I am lord of heaven and earth I will reward you royally.'

So Cadmus set the pipes of Pan to his lips once more and played the wild, sweet notes such as come from no other pipes in the world. And Typhon felt that never in his life had he heard anything so wonderful.

'Play! Play again!' he cried eagerly as Cadmus paused for breath.

'So you like the tune of my pipes,' said Cadmus. 'If only you could hear the music of my lyre, you would not even remember the pipes! Why, Apollo himself does not play upon the lyre so sweetly as I do.'

'Then play on the lyre, whatever that is,' grunted Typhon.

'Alas,' said Cadmus cunningly, 'I cannot do so any more. For

55

when I played more sweetly than Apollo himself, that jealous master of music snatched the lyre from my hands and broke all the strings. See, here it is; and unless I can find fresh sinews with which to string it, I can never again draw from it the most beautiful music in the world.'

Suspecting no evil of this simple young shepherd who played so enchantingly, Typhon crawled painfully into his cave and presently returned carrying the sinews of Zeus.

'Here,' he rumbled. 'Take these! String them to your lyre, and play me to sleep!'

Cadmus took the sinews and placed them carefully in the hollow of the lyre under the stretched cow-hide which made the sounding-board.

'I will take these back to my cottage,' he said, 'and fit them in place tonight, so that tomorrow I may delight you with the lyre's melody. It is a slow and delicate task and will take time. But now let me play you a lullaby on the pipes.'

Then, without giving Typhon time to think, Cadmus played on the pipes of Pan a lullaby so soothing and so filled with the drowsy whispers of slumber that all his heads began to nod and his two hundred eyes to close. Soon he lay there asleep, his snores murmuring up the valley like distant thunder on a summer's night, and Cadmus crept swiftly away.

Beyond the hills Hermes and Pan were waiting for him, and while Hermes took the sinews and made haste to carry them to Zeus, Pan led Cadmus swiftly south, away and away until he came to the sea shore where his ship was waiting for him.

Zeus fitted the sinews back into his arms and legs once more, and in a moment his strength returned to him. He leapt into his chariot, caught up a handful of thunderbolts, and rode out to do battle again with his terrible enemy.

Typhon, still bleeding from his earlier encounter with Zeus, fled away this time in terror and, pelted with thunderbolts, he fell down at last and lay grovelling in the sea not far from Italy.

Then Zeus caught up the island of Sicily and flung it upon him. And there he lies imprisoned for ever under the roots of Mount Etna. Sometimes he still writhes, and cries out in fury, sending his fiery breath up through the volcano and with it streams of burning lava which lay waste the fair fields and vineyards of Sicily.

But meanwhile Prince Cadmus was sailing over the blue sea towards Delphi, for so Pan had told him to do, since by the command of Zeus he must seek for Europa no longer, but make ready to found a kingdom of his own.

Presently, when he had finished with Typhon, Zeus sent a storm which blew Cadmus's ship out of its course, away to the eastward, until on the tenth day it came to the enchanted island of Samothrace.

On this island stood a palace made of gold, with marble pillars and floors of precious stones. It was surrounded by the loveliest garden in the world, filled all the year round with every sort of flower and fruit, always in season.

Hephaestus, the Immortal Smith, had built this palace by the command of Zeus as a home for Harmonia, the daughter of Ares and Aphrodite; and there this fairy princess lived, with the nymph Electra to look after her, and Electra's children to guard her from all enemies. And the eldest of these children was Dardanus who later became the first king of Troy.

Electra welcomed Cadmus to her beautiful home and entertained him and his companions for many days. The lovely Harmonia walked in the fragrant gardens with the handsome young prince, and very soon they fell in love with one another, just as Zeus had intended.

Then one day Hermes came to Samothrace and said to Electra:

'Cadmus and Harmonia love one another, and Father Zeus, remembering his promise to the brave prince who did him such notable service in his battle with Typhon, has decreed that they be man and wife. So bid them set sail in the swift ship, with all their followers and attendants, and pass over the sea to Delphi as Zeus bids: for there the oracle of Apollo will tell Cadmus where to found his city.'

Electra did as she was told, and very soon the ship, with white sails set, was dancing over the blue waves, leaving behind an island which was no longer enchanted, now that Harmonia had left it.

They sailed over the summer seas among the jewel-like islands of the Aegean. They passed round stormy Cape Malea at the south of Greece – but the kind sea nymphs guided them past all the treacherous rocks, and a gentle wind wafted them speedily on their way.

At last they came up the lovely Gulf of Corinth, anchored the ship in a land-locked bay, and went up to Delphi the beautiful on its green and grey hillside beneath the yellow cliffs of Parnassus.

There Apollo spoke the will of Zeus through his oracle:

'Cadmus!' said the voice out of the steaming shadows of the dark cleft beneath the temple. 'Cadmus! You left your distant home to search for the white bull of Zeus. Seek it no longer, but

'Build a city with seven gates and call it Thebes!'

follow where a cow shall lead; and where that cow sinks to rest, build a city with seven gates and call it Thebes!'

Cadmus did as he was told; and down in the valley below Delphi he found a cow grazing. As soon as it saw him coming it raised its head, lowed gently, and set off up the valley. Up the steep pass at the top it went, past the dark junction of three roads, and down the hillside beyond into the most fertile plain in all Greece.

When it came to the place appointed, it sank down to rest, and Cadmus knew that his quest was accomplished. It had stopped on a low ridge of land with a little valley on either side; and there Cadmus built his citadel, with walls and a palace and temples.

When the palace and the walls round the citadel were complete; and Cadmus had killed the dragon which lived below the hill, and had marked out fields and rich corn lands for his followers, he held his wedding to Harmonia.

58

To that wedding feast came all the Immortals from Olympus. Zeus himself sat at the head of the table, with Hera beside him; Ares and Aphrodite were there, of course, to give away their daughter as bride to the brave prince who had won her. Hermes and Pan were there, and Apollo to make music with his heavenly lyre while the Nine Muses sang the marriage hymn, and Immortals made merry with mortal men and women.

When the feast was ended the Immortals returned to Olympus, and only once again, as shall be told, did they come to the wedding of a mortal man.

Cadmus and Harmonia lived happily all their lives; and when the time came for them to die, Zeus carried them away to the Elysian Fields where it is always spring. There they dwell for ever unchanging, with the shades of those men and women whom Zeus has chosen for this immortality.

CHAPTER 6

The Adventures of Dionysus

Semele dared a wish, – to see;
That her eyes might equal be
With her heart and lips and ears:
Night on perfect night she pled.
Sudden lightning drank her tears,
Life and sweetness: she lay dead.

T. STURGE MOORE: *Semele*

6. The Adventures of Dionysus

AFTER the struggle with Typhon, Zeus began to look out more and more anxiously for the hero who was to help him defeat the Giants. If Earth could still produce a monster like Typhon, the war with the Giants might be much nearer than he thought!

It may have been due to something which Prometheus had said, or to some half-knowledge of his own, but Zeus became certain that the hero would be born at Thebes.

So when Cadmus and Harmonia had built their city of the seven gates, with the aid of the musicians Amphion and Zethus (at the sound of whose lyre the stones moved of themselves to make the walls) Zeus took good note of their children.

The eldest of these was Autonoe; but when she married, her only son, Actaeon, came to a tragic end. He insulted Artemis, the Immortal Huntress, boasting one day when he found her bathing in a lonely pool on Mount Cithaeron that he was a better huntsman than she would ever be. In her anger she turned him into a stag, and he was hunted by his own hounds, who caught him and tore him to pieces without knowing what they did.

Next came Ino, who married Athamas king of a city not far from Thebes, who already had two children, Phrixus and Helle. Their mother was Nephele the Cloud Maiden; and after they were born, she flew back to heaven, and Athamas never saw her again. When Ino had children of her own she hated these two who were not quite as other mortals, and soon showed herself to be a cruel and wicked stepmother. She dared not kill them herself, but by parching the seed-corn secretly she caused a famine, and then bribed the messenger who was sent to Delphi to ask the oracle why no crops grew that summer. She told him to bring back word that the land was under a curse which would only be lifted if Phrixus was sacrificed by his father.

Athamas was very sad when he heard this, but dared not disobey the oracle, which he believed was the voice of Apollo. So on the appointed day all the people gathered round the altar of Zeus on which Phrixus was to die by his father's hand.

But Nephele the Cloud Maiden would not desert her children like this. At her request kindly Pan gave her a magic ram with a fleece of pure gold; and as Athamas raised his sword to perform the sacrifice, it flew down and took Phrixus and his sister Helle on its back, and carried them away.

Over land and sea it went, bearing them in safety, but as it crossed from Europe into Asia it swooped down suddenly, and Helle tumbled off and was drowned in the narrow sea which, after her, is called Hellespont to this very day.

The ram flew on with Phrixus until it came to the land of Colchis near the world's eastern end where Aeetes the Wizard was king. There he lived in safety, and when the ram died, its golden fleece was hung up in a magic grove with a watchful dragon to guard it until the day when the Argonauts should come for it.

In Thebes only Ino was sorry that the two children had been saved, and punishment came to her before long.

Her next sister, the third daughter of Cadmus, was the lovely Semele; and her Zeus decided to marry himself. As her mother Harmonia had been the daughter of two Immortals, Ares and Aphrodite, he felt that their son should be a being of more than mortal powers.

Now when Hera, the Queen of Olympus, discovered what Zeus was about, she became very angry, and her jealousy knew no bounds. She was also afraid that if Zeus and Semele had a son, he might be made an Immortal of greater power and glory than her own sons, Ares and Hephaestus.

She made up her mind to destroy Semele and the child. So one day she disguised herself as an old woman and went to call on her. She spoke kindly at first, and after a while asked who her husband was. But when Semele told her that it was Zeus himself, the old woman laughed.

'Are you sure of that?' she asked. 'May it not be some ordinary mortal man who is deceiving you by pretending to be Zeus? I'm sure he does not visit you clad in the shining glory that Zeus wears on Olympus when he sits at the golden table beside his Immortal wife, Queen Hera!'

Semele was troubled by this, and next time Zeus came, she said:

'You made me a promise when we were married, that you would grant me one wish, whatever it might be.'

'I did,' answered Zeus, 'and I swear by Styx that you shall have it!'

'Then come to me in the same glory that you wear among the Immortals,' begged foolish Semele. 'Then I will know that you are Zeus indeed, and that you are not ashamed of having a mortal wife.'

Zeus sorrowed bitterly; but he could not break his oath, though he realized that it was Hera who had tricked him like this.

He rose to his feet, raised his hand, and in a moment was transfigured with light so bright and so fierce that, being mortal, Semele could not bear it. She fell back with a shriek, and died – shrivelled up by the shining glory of Zeus.

But he took the child, whom he named Dionysus, and after caring for him for a little while, he told Hermes to look after him and guard him from Hera's jealousy.

At first Hermes entrusted him to Ino and her youngest sister Argave, telling them something of the truth, and commanding them to keep secret who he was, and for greater security to pretend that he was a girl.

So Dionysus grew safely to boyhood in Thebes, unknown to Hera. But at length he was betrayed by Ino and Argave, and Zeus only just saved him by turning him into a little goat which Hermes carried off to Mount Nysa in Thrace, where the kindly water nymphs, daughters of the river Lamos, took care of him.

Ino was punished for this and for her earlier wickedness. She went mad and leapt into the sea, carrying her own son in her arms; but the sea nymphs took them, and they lived ever after among the waves, and atoned for the evil which Ino had done during her life on earth, by bringing help to storm-tossed sailors.

Meanwhile Dionysus grew to manhood in the cave on Mount Nysa, and made friends with Silenus and the satyrs, who vowed to follow him wherever he went. For Dionysus discovered how to make wine out of the grapes which grew on Mount Nysa, and the satyrs were the first creatures to taste this new and wonderful drink, and to grow intoxicated by it.

It was after his first drunken feast that Silenus fell asleep in the garden of King Midas, who treated him so kindly that Dionysus promised him any gift he might ask.

'Let everything I touch turn into gold!' cried greedy Midas eagerly, and Dionysus granted the wish with a merry twinkle in his eye.

Home went Midas and had very soon turned his house into gold, and his garden also with all its trees and flowers. But when he found that even food and drink turned to gold as soon as he touched them with his lips, he realized what a fool he had been, and he sought out Dionysus and begged him to take back his magic gift.

Midas did not learn wisdom by this experience, and not long afterwards he angered Apollo, who gave him asses' ears for refusing to recognize good music when he heard it.

Meanwhile Dionysus had gone out into the world to teach mankind how to grow grape-vines, and how to make the grapes into wine. He had many adventures on the way, travelling even as far as India whence he returned in a chariot drawn by tigers. On one occasion, for example, he only escaped from his enemies by turning a river into wine, which sent them all to sleep after they had attempted to quench their thirst at it.

When at length he came to Greece, Dionysus found several kings who were anxious to prevent him from teaching their people how to make wine. The reason they gave was that, like the satyrs, many women, who were called Maenads, followed Dionysus, and these often deserted their husbands and children to go dancing away on the lonely hillsides.

One of these kings was called Lycurgus, and he drove Dionysus into the sea, where the sea nymphs rescued him and the loveliest of them all, Thetis, entertained him in her coral caves.

Lycurgus suffered for what he had done, since when he tried to cut down the vine which Dionysus had planted, he cut off one of his own feet instead.

Meanwhile Dionysus came up again out of the caves of Thetis, but on the wrong side of the sea, and hired a ship to carry him across. Now it chanced that the sailors were wicked pirates from Tyre who were in search of handsome young men to sell as slaves, and to them Dionysus seemed a fine prize indeed. For he was tall and shapely, with a fair skin and rich, dark hair falling upon his strong shoulders and over his cloak of deep purple.

When they were well out to sea, the pirate captain told his men to bind Dionysus with ropes and put him down in the dark hold of the ship. But when they tried to do so, the ropes fell again and again from his hands and feet as soon as they had been tied.

Then the helmsman cried:

'We are mad to do this! It must be one of the Immortals whom we are carrying in our ship – it may be Apollo, or Poseidon, or great Zeus himself. Let us set him free and bear him with all honour over the waves to Greece, lest he grows angry and is fearfully avenged upon us.'

The captain was furious.

'Madman yourself!' he shouted. 'You look after your own job, and we'll attend to this fellow. He'll fetch us a fine price in Egypt or in Sidon, depend upon it!'

Then they hoisted the sails and sped away over the dancing waves with a fair wind behind them.

But soon strange things began to happen: first a sweet smell of wine rose from the hold of the ship, and a stream of it coursed across the deck. Then, while the sailors stood still in amazement,

'Grapes grew in great, dark bunches down either side of the sails'

the mast and spars of the ship began to put forth leaves and long, waving tendrils. Grapes grew in great, dark bunches down either side of the sails, and the thole-pins between which the long oars rested grew up into vines clustered with flowers.

When the pirates saw all this, they cried out to the helmsman to turn the ship and steer for Greece with all the speed he could. But their remorse came too late, for even as they turned towards Dionysus to beg his mercy, he changed into a fierce lion and came bounding along the deck towards them.

With shrieks of terror, they sprang over the sides into the sea – and were changed immediately into dolphins. All except Achaetes the helmsman, who sat rooted to his seat with terror. Then Dionysus returned to his usual shape, and spoke to him kindly:

'Do not be afraid, good Achaetes, you counselled your evil companions to treat me as they should, and you have found favour in my heart. Know that I am Dionysus, son of Immortal Zeus, and that I travel to the land of Greece bearing the gift of wine to be a comfort and a joy to all mankind.'

So Achaetes steered the ship, and the winds blew it over the waves until they came to Athens. There Dionysus was kindly received and his gift was welcomed, though his host Icarius suffered a sad fate by mistake. For he offered wine to his friends and they, having drunk too much of it and feeling its strange effects for the first time, cried out that Icarius had poisoned them.

In their fear and anger they killed him and threw his body into a well, where his daughter Erigone found it with the help of his faithful dog – and hanged herself for grief. Zeus saw what had happened, and set all three among the stars, where you may see them to this day as the constellations of Virgo, Arcturus, and Procyon the Little Dog.

But Dionysus continued on his way, and came at length to Thebes where he had been born. There no one knew him, and Pentheus, son of Argave, who was now king instead of his grandfather Cadmus, shut him up in a stone prison and swore that he would kill him.

Once again, however, the powers of Dionysus triumphed. Vines grew up between the stones of the prison walls so that they fell to the ground, and Dionysus went free. Pentheus was mistaken for a lion by a wild band of Maenads, amongst whom was his mother Argave, and they caught him and tore him to pieces.

All these and many more deeds as strange and wonderful were told of Dionysus; and men honoured him and said that he must be one of the Immortals. Yet he had one more adventure to face before he could take his seat on Olympus, and this was the strangest and one which befell no other Immortal. For he came to the land of Argos towards the south of Greece, and there King Perseus came against him fully armed.

Perseus was also a son of Zeus, and the greatest of the heroes of Greece except one, and for a little while Zeus had thought him the hero for whom he sought.

So when Perseus drew his sword against Dionysus, all the Immortals gathered in the clouds to watch so terrible and fateful a battle. The end of it was that Perseus smote Dionysus a mortal blow: for thus only could the anger of Hera be appeased. But whether Dionysus also killed Perseus at the same time is not known for certain, since some say that Perseus was murdered shortly afterwards by Megapenthes whose father, Proteus, he had turned to stone with the Gorgon's head.

As he died, Dionysus leapt into the Lake of Lerna by which they had fought: for this lake had no bottom, and led to the Realm of the Dead where Hades ruled over the souls of mortals. In this way Dionysus shared the fate of all mankind, though Zeus had decreed that he should become an Immortal and sit on Olympus.

In the Realm of Hades, Dionysus made his way to the throne where that dread King sits with pale, sad Persephone beside him – Persephone, the daughter of Demeter, who longs ever for the light of day and the sight of the fair spring flowers on the green hillsides.

For in the early days of the world dark Hades looked upon Persephone, the Divine Maiden, and loved her: but she would have none of him, as indeed he knew full well. So one day, as she danced with her maidens in the fair fields of Enna in Sicily, the earth opened suddenly and Hades rode out of the gulf in his dark chariot drawn by black horses, caught up Persephone in one strong arm, and plunged down again into his gloomy realm.

The earth closed behind them so quickly that Persephone's maidens scarcely knew what had become of her. And Demeter also sought her in vain over the wide earth, where spring came no more and all was black winter, until she paused to rest by the well at Eleusis near Athens. There the daughters of King Celeus found her sitting alone and desolate. To them she seemed no more than a sad old woman; but they welcomed her to their father's simple palace and strove to comfort her as best they could. Demeter dwelt with them for many months. But the spring never came and no corn pushed its green shoots through the barren earth.

At last Zeus sent Hermes the swift messenger down to the Realm of Hades to bring back Persephone. And when she came to her sorrowing mother the corn came with her all over the earth, and spring was born anew with green leaves and flowers glowing in the sunshine.

But cunning Hades had persuaded Persephone to eat six seeds of the pomegranate before she left the Land of the Dead; and consequently she could not avoid spending six months of each year with him – the six months when bleak winter reigns.

So now she sat beside Hades, ready to urge mercy, as this strange, bright son of Zeus knelt before their throne and addressed his prayer to her sombre lord.

'King of the Dead!' cried Dionysus, 'by the will of Zeus, who is my father, I do not remain here as your subject, but rise presently through the earth and take my place with the other Immortals. But it is my desire to take my mother Semele with me: and I beg of you to release her from death so that she may accompany me.'

'That cannot be,' answered Hades in his slow, solemn tones, 'unless you give me in exchange for your mother, your best beloved who now lives upon the earth.'

'I will certainly do that,' said Dionysus, and he swore it by the River Styx, the oath which no Immortal may break.

'Good,' said Hades, and bound himself by the same oath to release Semele. 'Now for your best beloved!'

'My best beloved is here!' cried Dionysus, and he struck the thin rod, or thyrsis, which he carried in his hand into the barren ground. At once it took root, sent out leaves, and grew great clusters of grapes.

'The vine is my best beloved!' he exclaimed in triumph.

Then Hades nodded his head, and Semele was given up to her son.

At the command of Zeus a chasm then opened in the earth, so deep and mysterious that no bird ever dared fly over it, and through this Dionysus passed up to Olympus, leading his mother by the hand. There the other Immortals welcomed him, and even Hera smiled and forgot her jealousy.

CHAPTER 7

Perseus the Gorgon-Slayer

Led by Athena I won from the grey-haired terrible sisters
Secrets hidden from men. . . . They showed me the perilous pathway
Over the waterless ocean, the valley that led to the Gorgon.
Her too I slew in my craft, Medusa, the beautiful horror:
Taught by Athena I slew her, and saw not herself, but her image.

CHARLES KINGSLEY: *Andromeda*

7. Perseus the Gorgon-Slayer

PERSEUS was not the hero for whom Zeus waited, though when he was born Zeus may not have been sure about it: prophecies were uncertain things, or why should he think that the hero would be an Argive from Argolis? This was the fertile triangle of land through which the river Inachus flows down to the blue bay of Nauplia, and in it the sons of men built three fair cities, Argos, Mycenae, and Tiryns, aided by the Cyclopes, those giant servants of Zeus who had each but one eye, in the centre of the forehead. The huge stones which they raised to form the city walls may be seen, still in place, even to this day.

In Tiryns lived King Acrisius, who had one child only, a lovely girl, called Danae. Being very anxious to have a son to succeed him, Acrisius sent to ask the oracle of Apollo what he had done that this was denied him. His question was not answered; instead the oracle warned him that his daughter would have a son who would kill him.

'We'll see about that!' cried Acrisius, and, vowing that Danae should never marry, he shut her up in a tower at Tiryns which was plated all over with brass so that it shone in the sun like gold. The plates have gone from it today, but you can still see the brass nails embedded in the stone which once held them in place.

But Zeus visited Danae in a shower of golden rain, and spoke with her out of the shining mist, and they had a son called Perseus who was born there in the prison-tower at Tiryns.

When Acrisius heard that, in spite of all his precautions, he had a grandson, he was filled with anger and fear, and these passions made him cruel. He would not believe that Zeus was the child's father, but said that it was Proteus, his brother, whom he hated, who had stolen the key of the brazen tower and married Danae in secret.

He had a great wooden chest made, and he set Danae in it with the baby in her arms, and pushed it out on to the rippling waters in the Bay of Nauplia.

'It would be a terrible crime to kill my daughter and my grandson,' he said, 'and the Immortals would send a curse upon me. No, I am merely dispatching them across the sea – and if the waves chance to fill the chest and make it sink, I am not to blame!'

Away floated the chest over the blue sea and out of sight of land; and presently the waves began to rise and the wind to blow, and

73

Danae wept with fear and clasped the baby Perseus close in her arms.

'Oh, what a fate is yours,' she sobbed, 'and yet you do not cry but sleep as peacefully as ever, feeling no terror of the dreadful place in which we are. You do not fear the heaving sea, nor the salt spray on your hair. . . . Oh, perhaps it is because you know that Father Zeus will protect us. . . . Then sleep on, sweet babe, for the waves swell only to rock your cradle, and I will pray to Zeus that we may come safely to land.'

All night the chest floated over the sea, and in the morning it was washed up on the shores of the island of Seriphos where Polydectes was king. And there Dictys, the king's brother, who was a fishermen, found Danae and her child, and took them to his home and looked after them.

Perseus grew up, a strong and noble youth skilled in all manner of things from the craft of the fisherman to the use of the sword. In time King Polydectes heard of them, and fell in love with Danae; but she would not marry him, for he was a cruel and wicked tyrant. At length he decided to take her by force; but this he dared not do because Perseus was always there to guard her.

So he devised a scheme to remove Perseus without incurring any blame for killing him. He held a great feast to which he invited the young men of Seriphos, including Perseus, and they all came bringing rich gifts to the King.

But Perseus had nothing to give, and he alone came empty-handed, so that all the young men mocked him, until his cheeks burnt with shame.

'I'll bring a finer present than any of you!' he cried fiercely.

'That cannot be,' said cunning Polydectes, '*unless you bring me the head of Medusa the Gorgon!*'

'That I will!' shouted Perseus, 'I'll bring it, or die in the attempt!'

And with that he rushed out of the palace amid the loud laughter and jeers of Polydectes and his friends, and went down beside the quiet sea to think what he should do.

While he sat there, deep in thought, two Immortals came to him: Athena, tall and stately in her shining helmet, with her polished shield upon her arm; and Hermes with kindly laughter in his eyes, slim and quick of limb, with the winged sandals on his feet.

'Do not grieve, Perseus,' said Hermes, 'for, by the will of Zeus, we are come to help you. See, here I lend you the sharpest weapon in the world, that very sickle of adamant with which Cronos wounded the Sky, and which Zeus used in his battle with Typhon. No lesser blade will smite the head from Medusa the Gorgon.'

'And I,' said Athena in her calm, sweet voice, 'will lend you my shield with which I dazzle the eyes of erring mortals who do battle against my wisdom. Any mortal who looks upon the face of Medusa is turned to stone immediately by the terror of it: but if you look only on her reflection in the shield, all will be well.'

'Rise now,' said Hermes. 'Your mother will be safe until your return, for the good fisherman, Dictys, will protect her – and you have far to travel. First you must visit the Grey Sisters and learn from them how to find the nymphs who dwell at the back of the North Wind: they will lend you all else that you may need, and will tell you how to find the Gorgons, and how to escape from the two who are immortal, when you have slain Medusa.'

So Perseus hastened away, his heart beating with excitement at the thought of the high adventure which was his, and the great honour which the Immortals had done him.

He came, as Hermes had instructed him, to the lonely cave in the dark north where the three daughters of the Titan Phorcus lived, the Grey Sisters who had been born old women with grey hair, and who had only one eye and one tooth between them.

Perseus stepped quietly up behind them as they sat near the mouth of their cave; and as they passed the single eye from one to another, he took it from an outstretched hand, and then cried aloud:

'Daughters of Phorcus, I have your eye! And I will keep it and leave you for ever in darkness if you do not tell me what I wish to know.'

The Grey Sisters cried aloud in alarm, 'Give us back our eye, and we will swear by Styx to tell you truthfully all you ask. But do not leave us for ever in this terrible darkness!'

So Perseus learnt the way to the magic land at the back of the North Wind and, returning the eye, hastened on his journey.

When he reached the lovely garden of the northern nymphs, he was welcomed kindly by them, and he rested for a long time in the paradise where they dwelt, for ever young and happy.

But at length he said: 'Fair nymphs, I must hasten away to kill the Gorgon Medusa and carry her head to wicked King Poly-dectes. Tell me, I beg of you, where the Gorgons live, and how I may kill Medusa.'

'We will lend you the Shoes of Swiftness,' answered the nymphs, 'so that you may escape from Medusa's terrible sisters. And we will lend you this magic wallet in which to carry away the head. There is but one thing wanting, and that is the Cap of Hades, the dog-skin cap which makes its wearer invisible.'

Then one of the nymphs went swiftly down to the Realm of Hades, for she had been Persephone's favourite companion on earth, and could visit the Queen of the Dead whenever she wished, and return at will.

She brought back the Cap of Darkness, so that Perseus now had all things needful, and was ready for his dreadful task.

He bade farewell to the kind nymphs, and set out on the way which the Grey Sisters had told him, and he came at last to the stony land of the Gorgons. As he drew near to where they lived, he saw all about in the fields and on the roads, the statues of men and beasts which had been living creatures until turned to stone by the deadly glance of the Gorgons.

Then he saw the three terrible sisters lying asleep in the sun with the snakes which grew instead of hair writhing about the head of Medusa, and the dragon-scales which covered her sisters' heads. They had white tusks like pigs and hands of brass; and great golden wings grew from their shoulders.

Wearing the Cap of Darkness, and stepping cautiously, Perseus drew near, looking only at the reflection in Athena's polished shield. Then he trembled indeed as he saw the terrible face of

Medusa

Medusa pictured on the bright surface; but he did not draw back. Still looking only at the reflection, he drew the adamantine sickle and cut off the terrible head at a single blow. Then, quick as could be, he picked it up and dropped it into the wallet which the nymphs had given him.

But the hissing of the snakes on Medusa's head woke the other two Gorgons, who could not be killed, and they sprang up, eager to avenge their sister.

Perseus leapt into the air and sped away on the Shoes of Swiftness as fast as he could go. After him came the Gorgons, screaming with rage, but Perseus fled away and away out over the dark ocean, south, ever south until his terrible pursuers were lost in the distance behind him.

Then Perseus turned east and flew over Africa, across the great empty desert where there was no green thing, and no drop of water. As he went the blood soaked through the magic wallet and dripped behind him, and wherever a drop touched the thirsty sand, it became a green oasis.

Night came, and in the morning as he flew over the seashore he beheld what at first he thought was a wonderful statue of a fair girl hewn from the rock just above sea level.

Swooping down, Perseus found that it was no statue but a living maiden chained naked to the face of the rock, with the little waves creeping up to her feet.

'Chained maiden!' said Perseus gently. 'My heart bleeds for you!'

'Who speaks? Who is it pities poor doomed Andromeda?' she cried wildly.

Perseus had forgotten that he still wore the Cap of Invisibility. Now he removed it swiftly, and hovering above the waves he said: 'Lovely Andromeda, why are you chained here?'

Then, weeping bitterly, she told him how her foolish mother, Cassiopea, had offended the sea nymphs by her ridiculous boastings, and they had sent a monster to ravage all the sea coast, until King Cepheus, her father, chained her there as a sacrifice, hoping thus to satisfy the creature's fury.

'If I can save you, will you at least remember me?' asked Perseus, who had fallen in love with Andromeda at first sight.

'Do not make me weep, dreaming of deeds that can never be done!' she sobbed.

'Deeds that men deemed impossible have been accomplished, none the less,' he answered. Then he turned quickly away, for he had noticed a ripple in the sea drawing nearer, ever nearer.

Perseus, still hovering just above the waves, got ready, and in a few moments the monster raised its head above the water and opened wide its fierce jaws. Then, while Andromeda screamed, and her parents on the cliffs above wept and prayed, Perseus drew the Gorgon's head from his wallet and held it in front of the savage eyes. And the monster sank back still and cold and silent, a long ridge of jagged stone.

Then Perseus returned the head to the magic wallet, cut Andromeda's chains with the adamantine sickle, and carried her in safety to the cliff top.

There was great rejoicing at the rescue of Andromeda, and King Cepheus readily agreed that Perseus should marry her. So there Perseus stayed for many days, and there was a noble feast at his wedding. But as they sat at the great table, the door was flung suddenly open, and a great man strode in followed by a band of desperadoes, all armed with drawn swords.

'Yield up Andromeda to me!' shouted the leader of this band, who was a prince named Phineus. 'She was promised to me, and unless I get her, I'll slaughter every man here, burn the city and carry off the women to be my slaves!'

Then Perseus strode down the hall until he stood in front of Phineus, and taking out the Gorgon's head he turned him and all his followers to stone on the instant.

Not long after this, Perseus and Andromeda set sail for Greece, and came at length to the island of Seriphos. Here he found that his mother Danae had been made a slave by Polydectes, while Dictys, his kind friend, languished in prison.

Leaving Andromeda on the ship, Perseus went alone up to the palace and found Polydectes sitting at meat with the same band of followers who had jeered at him once before.

'Well, here is that landless boaster, Perseus!' cried the king scornfully, while the others laughed and jested at him. 'Have you, by any chance, brought me the present you promised?'

'Yes,' answered Perseus quietly. 'I come, according to my promise, bringing the Gorgon's head.'

'Boaster and liar!' jeered Polydectes. 'Do you think to frighten us with empty words? Show us this wonder – if you can.'

Perseus answered nothing, but pulled the Gorgon's head out of the wallet and held it up for all to see. And afterwards the stone lumps which had once been men were dragged out and left on the hillside.

That evening Hermes came to Perseus and received back from him the sickle and the shield and with them the cap, the shoes, and the wallet. He also took the head of Medusa, which Athena set in the centre of her shield to strike terror into the hearts of the Giants when the long expected invasion should take place.

After this Dictys became King of Seriphos, and married Danae, while Perseus and Andromeda set sail for Argolis. But on the way he stopped at Larissa and took part in the great games which the king of that land was holding.

Perseus distinguished himself greatly in these; but when it came to throwing the round iron disc, he hurled it so hard that it struck an old man who sat watching, and killed him instantly. This, it turned out, was Acrisius, who had left Tiryns in fear that Perseus, on his return, would kill him and so fulfil the oracle.

Sorrowing deeply, Perseus went on his way, and he and Andromeda ruled over Argolis for many years and had numerous children. Among these were Electryon and Alcaeus. The first of these became the father of Alcmena and the second was the father of Amphitryon. These two cousins married, and went to live in Thebes. And there was a third son called Sthenelus, who late in life had a son called Eurystheus, who ruled over Tiryns and all Argos.

Perseus perished after his battle with Dionysus, and Zeus set him among the stars, with Andromeda beside him: but the son of his grand-daughter Alcmena was destined to be the hero who was to surpass all others in strength and mighty deeds, and who was to help Zeus in his war with the Giants. For this child was Heracles, whom the Romans call Hercules.

CHAPTER 8

The Birth of Heracles

The lay records the labours, and the praise,
And all the immortal acts of Hercules.
First, how the mighty babe, when swathed in bands,
The serpents strangled with his infant hands.

VIRGIL: *Aeneid* (Translated by John Dryden)

8. The Birth of Heracles

ELECTRYON, the son of Perseus, had an only daughter called Alcmena, whom he promised in marriage to his nephew Amphitryon. All his sons were killed while fighting a band of robbers who had stolen his great herd of cattle, and Amphitryon was to marry Alcmena and become king of all Argolis when the cattle were recovered and the dead princes revenged.

Amphitryon began by repurchasing the stolen cattle for a large sum of money, which he suggested that Electryon should pay.

'I'll pay no money to regain my own cattle!' shouted Electryon. 'If you've been fool enough to buy back stolen property, you yourself must suffer the consequences of your folly.'

In a moment of temper at this rebuff Amphitryon flung away the club with which he had been driving the cattle, and by an evil chance it struck a horn of one of the cows, rebounded, and killed Electryon.

After this, Sthenelus, youngest son of Perseus, banished his nephew Amphitryon from Argolis on a charge of murder, and ruled in his place.

Amphitryon fled to Thebes, and Alcmena went with him:

'I know you only killed my father by accident,' she said, 'so I will still marry you: but on one condition. You must first punish the robbers who killed my brothers.'

At Thebes, King Creon was now ruler. He had come to the throne after the banishment of the famous King Oedipus who saved Thebes from the terrible Sphinx. The Sphinx was a monster, with a lion's body, eagle's wings, and a woman's head; she sat on a great rock near the city and asked everyone who passed to answer a riddle. And what she asked was this:

'What creature, with only one voice, has four legs in the morning, two at midday and three in the evening; and yet is weakest when it has most?'

All who failed to answer the riddle, she ate immediately, and no one found the correct answer until young Oedipus came to Thebes. He replied:

'The creature is a man. For as a child, in the morning of his days, he goes on all fours and yet is weakest. In the middle of his life he walks upon his two legs, and is strongest; but in old age he needs the aid of a stick, and so three legs support him.'

At this the Sphinx screamed with fury, and cast herself down

The Sphinx

from the rock and was killed. Then Oedipus ruled well and wisely at Thebes, until a curse fell upon the land because of crimes which he had committed unintentionally, and he wandered away as a blind beggar, leaving his uncle Creon as king.

When Amphitryon came to Thebes he found that another curse had descended on that unlucky city. For the Teumessian Fox, which was as large and savage as a wolf, had been sent by Dionysus to plague the land, catching children and carrying them away to its lair, as a punishment for the things he had suffered in Thebes.

Now this was an enchanted fox which nobody could catch, for it ran faster than the fastest creature in the world.

'If you can rid us of the Fox,' said Creon, 'I will lend you an army to take vengeance on the robbers.'

Amphitryon agreed to this, for he knew of a magic hound which was fated to catch whatever it pursued. With the help of Artemis, he was able to borrow this dog, and he set it upon the trail of the Fox. The uncatchable was being chased by the inescapable; but Zeus saw what was happening, and made haste to turn both fox and dog into stone. Then Amphitryon set out to punish the robbers (with the aid of Creon's men) and Alcmena got ready to marry him the moment he returned victorious.

But the time was growing short now. Already the Giants were stirring under the dark northern hills, and still the hero was not born who was to save both men and Immortals. Zeus looked about him anxiously, and on a sudden realized that the time had come. For the hero, he believed, was to be born in Thebes – and was also to be a member of the royal family of Argolis, descended from Danae whom he had visited in the shower of gold.

Alcmena, the grand-daughter of Perseus, dwelt at Thebes,

waiting but for the return of Amphitryon to be her husband: surely here indeed was the mother of the hero?

Alcmena was the loveliest woman alive at that time, though her beauty could not compare with that of Helen, who would be born not many years later. She was taller than other women, wiser and more noble. Her face and her dark eyes seemed like those of Immortal Aphrodite herself; she was good and virtuous, one who would always be true to Amphitryon.

This being so, how was Zeus to marry Alcmena? For long he pondered, and a pang of regret passed through his heart as he thought how he must cheat her. Yet it had to be done, for the hero must be born, to free mankind from many evils and the Immortals from the unconquerable Giants.

While Zeus pondered, Amphitryon overcame the robbers, punished them thoroughly for what they had done, and set out rejoicing for Thebes, having sent a messenger before him to bid Alcmena make ready for the wedding.

Then Zeus came down swiftly from Olympus, and by his powers put on the very shape and voice and likeness of Amphitryon. He arrived at Thebes, dusty from travel, and Alcmena welcomed him without any shadow of suspicion, and the wedding was celebrated that very evening.

That night was the longest the world has known, for by command of Zeus the Sun Titan, Helios, did not drive forth his flaming chariot next day, and Hermes visited the Silver Lady, Selene, begging her to linger in her course across the sky with the pale Moon in her cloud-washed boat. Kindly Sleep lent his aid also, making mankind so drowsy and sending them such sweet dreams that no one suspected that this one night was the length of three.

Whether Amphitryon was overtaken by sleep or not, he failed to reach Thebes until the rosy-fingered morning was awake in the east – Eos, who harnesses the golden horses to the chariot of the Sun. He came straight to Alcmena, but maybe Zeus met him on the way and told him of what had chanced: for it was long before she knew that she was doubly wedded on that triple night.

The months passed, and the time drew near when the child was to be born, and Zeus, certain that he would be the hero destined to save the Immortals, could not contain his satisfaction.

'Today,' he told the other Immortals as they sat on their golden thrones on Olympus, drinking nectar and eating ambrosia – the wine and food, made only in heaven, which keeps those who partake of it for ever young and fair to look on. 'Today,' repeated Zeus with a sigh of pleasure, 'there will be born a boy, a descend-ant of Perseus, who will be lord over all the people of Argolis.'

He would have said more, but jealous Hera interrupted quickly, saying:

'Of Argolis? Of the land which is my special care? Well, so be it! But swear an oath now that what you have said will surely happen.'

Surprised, but anxious to please her, Zeus swore the unbreakable oath by Styx, the black river of Hades, and changed the subject quickly.

Hera hastened in triumph to Argos, accompanied by her daughter Eilithyia, who presides over the birth of children. By witchcraft she had made sure that Alcmena's son, Heracles, was not born until *next day*, but that his cousin Eurystheus, the son of King Sthenelus, was born instead, much earlier than was expected.

While these things were happening on earth, Zeus sat happily on Olympus chatting with Ate, another daughter whom Hera had instructed to keep him occupied while she and Eilithyia were busy in Argolis and Thebes.

When she returned to Olympus she cried in triumph:

'Now your promise is performed, great Zeus, for Eurystheus, grandson of Perseus, has just been born at Tiryns – and today is ended!'

In his fury, Zeus seized Ate by the hair and flung her out of heaven:

'Go and wander over the earth!' he cried, 'and stir up trouble among men! Wherever you go there shall be wars and troubles, caused by you!'

Ate landed in Phrygia, near the city of Troy, which became the scene of the greatest war in all the history of ancient Greece.

But Zeus could not break his oath, so it came about that Heracles became the slave of Eurystheus in after years.

In the meantime, he was born a day late in Thebes, and with him a twin brother, the son of Amphitryon, who was named Iphicles, and who came into the world an hour later than Heracles – but very far indeed behind him in courage.

When they were no more than ten months old, Heracles performed his first feat of valour.

It happened on a summer's evening when Alcmena had bathed the two babies, given them their milk and rocked them to sleep in a cradle made out of a big bronze shield which Amphitryon had brought back as a prize from his campaign against the robbers.

'Sleep, my little ones!' crooned Alcmena. 'Sleep softly, and pass safely through the dark night and into the gentle morning, my twin babes!'

Darkness fell, and all the house grew still. But at the hour of midnight Hera sent two monstrous snakes with scales of azure blue, to slay the infant Heracles. Writhing and curling along the ground they came, shining with a strange, baleful light, and spitting deadly venom.

But when they drew near the children (for all the doors flew open before them), Zeus caused the babes to wake. Iphicles, seeing the serpents curling up to strike with their cruel fangs, screamed with fright, and kicking off his coverlet rolled out on to the floor.

Heracles, however, sat up smiling in the brazen shield, and grasped a snake in either hand, gripping them by their necks and keeping the poisoned fangs well away from him. The serpents hissed horribly, and twined their cruel coils about the child. But Heracles held on, squeezing and squeezing with his tiny hands, trying to throttle them with his strong little fingers.

Then Alcmena heard the screams of Iphicles and, running to the room, saw the unearthly light flickering through the open door which she had closed so carefully.

'Arise, Amphitryon!' she cried. 'Do you not hear how loud our younger child is wailing? Do you not see the light flickering on the walls? Surely some terrible creature has come into the house!'

Amphitryon sprang up, seized his sword, and rushed into the nursery, with Alcmena close behind him carrying a lamp.

There they found Heracles grasping a dead snake in either hand, shaking them fiercely, and crowing with delight. But Iphicles lay on the floor, his eyes wide with terror, too scared even to cry any more.

Proudly the baby Heracles showed the serpents to Amphitryon and Alcmena, then flinging them from him, snuggled down once more and went quietly to sleep.

In the morning Alcmena, feeling that there must be something strange about her child Heracles, went to consult the ancient prophet Tiresias, the wisest man in Thebes.

Strange things were told of Tiresias, who was blind and who had already lived three times as long as any ordinary man. It was said that when he was a boy two enchanted snakes turned him into a woman, and that a year later they made him a man again. And that once, when Zeus and Hera had an argument, Hera saying that Zeus had a much better time than she did, they had consulted Tiresias, who replied that it was nine times as pleasant to be a woman as to be a man.

Hera was furious at this, and struck Tiresias blind in that instant. Zeus could not undo what another Immortal had done, but he gave Tiresias the gift of prophecy and decreed that he should live for more than three generations.

'Tell me what all this means,' Alcmena begged Tiresias, when she had related the adventure with the serpents. 'It is not natural that a child of ten months should do all that Heracles has done. So tell me the truth, I beg, even if you see much suffering and sorrow in the future for me and mine.'

'Be of good cheer, grand-daughter of Perseus,' answered the old prophet solemnly, 'for your son is destined to be the most famous mortal who ever trod the soil of Greece. He shall rid the land of monsters, and do many labours of which poets will tell in song and story for ever. Many things shall he suffer also and the long enmity of Hera, Queen of the Immortals, who sent those serpents against him. But in the end he shall stand beside the Immortals in their direst need, and afterwards shall become one of them and sit on Olympus for ever. For know that he is the hero, the son of Zeus, whose coming was foretold at the beginning of the world by Prometheus, the good Titan.'

Then Tiresias went on to tell Alcmena what had happened on her wedding-night, and how she was in reality the bride of Zeus, and the most honoured among mortal women, to be the mother of Heracles.

After this Heracles grew quickly and in safety, well tended by Alcmena and her husband, who was not in the least jealous of Zeus.

At first Heracles learnt all the gentle arts: how to sing, how to play sweetly on the lyre and how to read and write. Then Amphitryon taught him how to drive a chariot skilfully; and he learnt also the use of sword and spear, and the whole art of boxing and wrestling. None could throw a dart more truly than Heracles, and of all archers he was the best, sending an arrow further than any other mortal, more swiftly, and with deadly aim.

It was plain to see, even when he was young, that Heracles was the son of an Immortal. For he was a head taller than any other man, and broad in proportion, while his eyes flashed fire.

But his temper was very violent, and when he was still only a boy he killed Linus who was teaching him to play the lyre. For Linus struck him angrily one day when he played a false note, and Heracles struck back so violently with the instrument which he held in his hand that Linus fell dead immediately.

Heracles was pardoned for this deed; but Amphitryon, fearing lest such a mischance might happen again, sent him away from Thebes, to tend the cattle on Mount Cithaeron. And here Heracles increased in strength and skill; and at last he drew near to manhood.

CHAPTER 9

The Choice of Heracles

First, then, he made the wood
Of Zeus a solitude,
Slaying its lion-tenant; and he spread
The tawniness behind – his yellow head
Enmuffled by the brute's, backed by that grin of dread.

EURIPIDES: *Heracles* (Translated by Robert Browning)

9. The Choice of Heracles

WHILE Heracles was guarding the cattle of Amphitryon on the lonely slopes of Mount Cithaeron, and was still ignorant of his high destiny, a strange thing befell him.

As he sat alone on the hillside one day, wondering if he was fated to be a cow-herd all his life, or whether it would not be better to become a wild robber of the mountains, he saw two lovely maidens coming towards him. One of them was dressed in simple white, and had modest, downcast eyes and a calm, gentle face from which seemed to shine both goodness and wisdom; but the other wore bright colours, and came striding along, glancing boldly about her – now admiring herself, and now looking to others for admiration. She was decked with rich jewels, and her face was artfully touched with paint and with powder.

As they drew near to Heracles, the second, as if anxious to forestall her companion, pushed eagerly ahead and spoke to him:

'Dear Heracles,' she said, 'I see that you have reached the age when you must choose what kind of life yours is to be. So I have come to urge you to take me as your friend and let me guide you on your way. I promise that if you do I will lead you by the easiest and most delightful paths. You shall taste every pleasure, and no troubles or toils shall come near you. Your life shall be passed in the pursuit and enjoyment of pleasant things, with no labour of body or mind, except to please yourself without any thought for the cares of others.'

She paused, and Heracles asked: 'Lady, tell me your name.'

Then she answered softly: 'Heracles, those who love me call me Happiness, but my enemies, it is true, have another name which I do not care to mention.'

Meanwhile the modest maiden had come up, and now she spoke:

'I too, noble Heracles, am come to offer you a way of life. I know of what a worthy line you come, that you are descended from Perseus the Gorgon-slayer, and are yourself the son of Zeus. I know how well you have learnt all the accomplishments necessary for the path which I trust that you will take in my company. Follow me, and you will do great deeds and leave a name which will never be forgotten. But you cannot win what is glorious and excellent in the world without care and labour: the gods give no real good, no true happiness to men on earth on any other terms.

If you would bring happiness to others and be remembered in Greece, you must strive for the service of Greece – as you well may with your strength and your skill, if you do but use them rightly. As for my companion, who is called Vice and Folly and other such names, do not be misled by her: there is no pleasure and no happiness like those which you earn by strife and labour and with the sweat of your brow.'

'Do not believe this foolish girl, who is called Virtue!' interrupted Vice hastily. '*My* way to happiness is short and pleasant; hers is hard, and long, and the end is doubtful.'

'Come, Heracles,' said Virtue quietly, 'choose which of us you will follow. Her path leads through easy, worthless pleasures that grow stale and horrible and yet are craved after more and more. But follow me through toil and suffering to the great heritage which Zeus has planned for you.'

'Lady,' cried Heracles, 'I choose your path! Tell me how to set my foot on it, and I will not turn back however hard it prove, and whatever I have to endure on the way.'

'You have chosen worthily,' she said in her calm, gentle voice. 'And for the beginning – look yonder! What is it that disturbs your cattle so?'

Heracles looked across the valley, and saw a great yellow lion leaping down the slope with open jaws towards the cows, who fled this way and that, lowing piteously in terror.

With a shout of fury Heracles sprang to his feet and went charging down the valley and up the other side. But by the time he got there, the lion had gone, and one of the cows lay dead.

'I'll kill that lion, or perish in the attempt!' cried Heracles angrily, and he turned back towards the two strange maidens – but there was no one to be seen.

Heracles returned to Thebes for his brother Iphicles who took charge of the cattle, and he himself set out to trail the lion to its den. He did not succeed in this, however, and after a night and a day on Cithaeron he came down into a distant valley where dwelt King Thestius with his fifty beautiful daughters.

He was welcomed at the palace, and there he stayed for fifty nights entertained kindly by the fifty lovely princesses who took it in turns to attend upon the young man, who spent each day hunting upon the mountain.

After fifty days Heracles at length tracked the lion to its lair, a cave in a dark, evil-smelling crevice of the rocks. Armed with a great club of olive wood cut roughly from a tree which he had torn up by the roots, Heracles strode boldly into the cave.

Heracles

The great yellow lion came at him, roaring horribly, and Heracles retreated so as to have more light. In the entrance to the cave he stood at bay, and as the lion leapt, he struck it on the head with the club, bringing it to the ground, where it stood, trembling all over while its head swayed from side to side from the force of the blow.

Heracles struck once more, and the great beast lay dead before him. Then he pulled a knife from his belt and tried to skin it, but the hide was too tough. In vain he sharpened the knife on a stone, and even tried with the stone itself. It was only when he had cut out one of the terrible claws that he had an instrument keen enough for his task.

When the skin was off, Heracles dried and cured it carefully, and wore it ever afterwards tied over his shoulders and round his waist, with the scalp over his head like a helmet, so that it served both as clothing and armour.

On his way back to Thebes, Heracles met with a messenger from a certain King Eriginus, who was on his way to collect tribute from the Thebans whom he had conquered in war some years before this and robbed of all their weapons and armour.

Heracles was furious when he heard what the messenger wanted, and insulted him so grossly in his rage that King Eriginus sent a band of armed men to Thebes demanding that Heracles should be given up to him for punishment. Creon, King of Thebes, was ready to do this, for the Thebans had nothing with which to fight.

Heracles however gathered together the young men and armed them with the sacred trophies which hung in the temple of Athena. He taught them quickly how to use these weapons, and then led them against the company of men sent by King Eriginus, whom they defeated and drove out of Thebes.

Full of rage, Eriginus gathered an army and set out to destroy the city, but Heracles ambushed them in a narrow mountain pass and defeated them almost single-handed, killing the king and most of his captains. A quick march over the hills with his band of Theban youths gave Eriginus's little city into their hands, and the inhabitants were themselves forced to bring tribute each year to Thebes.

Amphitryon was killed in the battle, but Alcmena found a good second husband at Thebes, and lived there quietly for the rest of her life.

King Creon was so grateful for what Heracles had done – and so afraid lest he might think of seeking revenge for his willingness to give him up to Eriginus, that he made haste to offer him his daughter Megara in marriage.

The wedding was celebrated with great rejoicings, and Heracles settled down with every hope of becoming King of Thebes when Creon died.

So several years passed, and Heracles had three sons whom he adored, and for whose future he planned great things.

Now, living quietly in Thebes, Heracles did no deeds of valour, nor did he free Greece from any plagues; and Zeus was troubled, seeing that the hero was not fitting himself for his great task.

Hera was troubled also, though for a very different reason.

'What of your oath?' she cried to Zeus one day. 'You swore that Eurystheus of Argolis should rule over all the natives of that land, and yet Heracles, the greatest of them, dwells safely in Thebes, and will soon become King of the city which Cadmus built.'

Then Zeus answered: 'Hera, Queen of Olympus, do not be jealous any longer. Fate holds many troubles in store for Heracles, but what good will it do if he lives merely as a captain in Argolis, second only to Eurystheus?'

'I would have him as slave to Eurystheus!' cried Hera viciously.

'That I will grant,' answered Zeus. 'Let him serve that cowardly lord of Argolis, performing ten labours for him, the hardest that can be devised, and if he survives them, then grant him his freedom.'

'I agree to that,' said Hera, 'for I will help Eurystheus to choose the tasks which Heracles must perform. But how shall we contrive to bring this servitude about? Force is useless against him, and if Eurystheus tries to make him his slave, Heracles will certainly kill him, come what may.'

Zeus sighed; then he answered sadly:

'Hera, my Queen, it shall be as you wish. Send madness upon Heracles so that, unknowing what he does, he may commit murder and be driven as an exile from Thebes. Go, see to it!'

Zeus nodded his head, and as Olympus shook to confirm his words, Hera sped gleefully on her way. But at a word from Zeus, Athena followed quietly to help Heracles as far as possible.

Now that morning the sons of Heracles and their cousins, the children of Iphicles, were engaged in martial exercises on the plain of Thebes, with other boys and young men of the city.

Heracles sat on a hillside watching them, his bow on his back and a quiver full of arrows by his side. Suddenly a dark shadow crossed the sun, and a low, evil moaning drew near and seemed to pause above his head. Then Heracles staggered to his feet, his eyes rolling wildly and foam starting from his lips.

'Enemies are upon us!' he cried. 'Eurystheus of Argolis comes to take us prisoners and make us his slaves! I will not suffer it! Alone I will save Thebes and protect my beloved children from servitude!'

In his madness, he fitted an arrow to his bow, aimed and loosed it with such skill that his eldest son sank dead upon the plain. Then, while the boys fled away shrieking with terror he sent arrow after arrow screaming after them, until all three of his sons lay dead, with two of Iphicles' as well.

He would have done worse deeds, but Athena came at this moment, and seeing how quickly and how fatally the madness had worked, she took up a great stone and cast it at Heracles, laying him stunned and insensible on the ground. In this state he was bound and carried to Thebes where, Creon being too old to interfere, Lycus, a pretender to the throne, declared himself king and banished Heracles for murder.

When the madness had left him Heracles in his misery and despair shut himself up in a dark room and refused to see or speak to anybody. No one dared to come near, until at length King Thestius visited him by command of Zeus, and told him that he must go to Delphi and ask Apollo how he was to atone for the terrible things he had done.

Then Heracles roused himself, gathered the lion skin about his shoulders, took the club in his hand and departed from Thebes for ever: for now his children were dead, and his wife Megara had died of a broken heart.

When he came to Delphi, the voice of the oracle spoke to him out of the dark chasm beneath the temple:

'Heracles, son of Zeus, the time has come for you to begin the labours which will make you famous ever more, and which will fit you for the great purpose for which you were born. Go now to Eurystheus, who rules over Argolis, in his high citadel of Tiryns, and serve him faithfully in the tasks which he shall set you, doing him no harm nor striving to wrest the kingdom from him. At the last it may be that Zeus will raise you to Olympus and give you a place among the Immortals.'

So Heracles set out for Argolis, accompanied only by his nephew Iolaus, a son of Iphicles who refused to desert him.

CHAPTER 10

The Beginning of the Labours

Are ye the same that in your strength of yore
Strangled the Nemean lion, from whose roar
The herdsmen fled as by the Alastor crossed;
Smote Lerna's Hydra, smote the Centaur host . . .
The boar on Erymanthus: and in Hell
The Hound Echidna-born, untamable . . .
All these and other Labours have I won.

SOPHOCLES: *Trachiniai* (Translated by Gilbert Murray)

10. The Beginning of the Labours

EURYSTHEUS, the cowardly weakling who had become King of Argolis after Amphitryon was banished, lived in the mighty fortress of Tiryns, whose great walls had been built by the Cyclopes, and whose narrow gateway led beneath the brazen tower in which Acrisius had kept Danae prisoner.

He was delighted when Heracles arrived and gave him Apollo's message.

'Well, you're a fine great, hulking fellow!' he cried insolently. 'Be sure that I'll work you hard, though I doubt whether you'll be able to perform any of the labours which I have in store for you. As a beginning, off you go up the valley and over the hills towards Corinth. Halfway there, turn left into the mountains, and bring me back the dead body of the Nemean Lion.'

Now this lion had fallen from the moon, and was ravaging the lands all round Nemea. Nobody could kill it, for it was invulnerable, its hide so hard that neither iron nor bronze nor stone could pierce it.

Heracles set out, and near Nemea he met a shepherd who told him which way to go.

'But you've no hope of killing the Lion,' the shepherd warned him. 'He has ravaged the land all about his lair, and nobody dares to go near him. Still, I'll make a sacrifice to Zeus, and perhaps he will at least give you an easy death.'

'Wait thirty days,' said Heracles shortly, 'and if I have not returned by then, offer your sacrifice – but not to Zeus – to me, as a dead hero!' Then he went on his way, armed with his club, his bow, a quiver full of sharp-tipped arrows, and a great sword by his side.

For a long while he searched in vain, but at last one evening he discovered the den of the fearsome Lion, which had two entrances and was strewn with the bones of men and cattle.

Heracles waited nearby, and presently the great tawny beast came prowling up the hillside, its mane streaked with the blood of its latest kill and its tongue licking its great bearded chin.

Setting an arrow to the string, Heracles drew it to his ear and loosed. The swift shaft hummed to its mark, but the sharp point rebounded from the Lion's flank and fell harmlessly to the ground.

With a cry of rage, Heracles drew his sword and charged, lunging with all his strength at the Lion's chest as the huge creature reared up on its hind legs to strike at him with its mighty claws.

But the tempered iron bent as if it had been lead, and the Lion, though it fell backwards, then crouched for a spring, roaring horribly.

Suddenly Heracles remembered the lion which he had slain on Cithaeron, and taking his club in both hands he dealt this one a smashing blow on the head. The Lion stood dazed for a moment, then fled to its lair, where it turned, snarling, to wait for its adversary.

Realizing that no weapon could kill it, Heracles rushed into the cave with his cloak wrapped round one arm, and seized the Lion round the neck with the other. Then they rolled and wrestled on the ground, over and over, the Lion's struggles growing ever weaker and weaker, until at last it lay dead, throttled by the mighty arm about its neck. Before it died it made one final effort and bit off one of Heracles's fingers.

When the beast was dead, and he had rested and recovered from the battle, Heracles flung the body across his shoulders and strode off towards Tiryns. On the way he found the shepherd getting ready the sacrifice, which he was quite certain would need to be offered to the ghost of the dead hero.

Heracles laughed when he saw what was happening. 'I'll join you in your prayers,' he cried jovially, 'but we'll make them to great Zeus, the giver of victory. You cannot sacrifice to a living man!'

Then he returned to Tiryns, and flung down the grizzly carcass before Eurystheus, who squeaked with horror and indignation.

'Take the nasty thing away!' he commanded, 'and never dare to come into the city again, if you return from any more labours. But the next one will not be accomplished so easily. Go and kill the Lernean Hydra!'

The second labour was much more dangerous and difficult than the first, for the Hydra was a great serpent, with nine heads, which lived in the marshes of Lerna not far from Argos. It was so venomous that its very breath was deadly and it was the terror of the whole district.

Accompanied by Iolaus, Heracles drove down to the edge of the marsh in his chariot, and there Athena appeared to him.

'When you draw near to the Hydra's lair,' she said, 'you must make it come out by shooting fiery arrows into the cave. But when you fight, take care to hold your breath, for its very smell is deadly. Remember also that the centre head is immortal!'

Heracles thanked Athena, and did as she advised. After crossing the marsh and reaching the hillock of firm ground on which the

Hydra lived, Heracles bade Iolaus light a fire, and then tying blazing bundles of grass to his arrows he shot them into the cave.

Out came the Hydra, hissing fiercely; and holding his breath, Heracles leapt forward and shattered the nearest head with a blow of his club. But what was his horror and consternation when from the bleeding neck sprang out two new heads, each as fierce and deadly as the old! To make matters worse, a gigantic crab came scuttling out of the marsh and seized Heracles by the foot.

With a roar of rage, he crushed the crab with a single blow of his club, and shouted to Iolaus to light a torch and come to his assistance. Iolaus obeyed bravely, and as Heracles crushed each head of the Hydra with his club, he burnt and seared the shattered neck so that no new heads could grow from the bleeding stumps.

When at last the battle was over, Heracles cut off the immortal head with his sword and buried it under a gigantic rock, where doubtless it lies safely to this day. Then, having dipped his arrows in the Hydra's blood, which was deadly poison, he returned to his task-master.

'You have cheated!' cried Eurystheus, when he heard all the story. 'Iolaus helped you, and your labours must be performed

Heracles and the Lernean Hydra

by you alone. This one does not count, so you have still nine to accomplish. Off you go now, and for the next one bring me the Hind with the Golden Horns!'

This creature was a wonderful reindeer, sacred to Artemis, who had once seen five of them away in the distant north and, capturing four by her fleetness of foot, tamed them and harnessed them to her chariot. The fifth hind wandered free in the hills of Arcadia, by the lovely river Cerynites, and no one dared touch it, knowing that it belonged to Artemis.

Heracles did not wish to harm this beautiful creature and, though it was the swiftest of all deer, he chased it on foot for a whole year. On this quest he journeyed to the land at the back of the North Wind, wandered there in the great, sweet-smelling pine forests, and came back into Greece, still pursuing the Hind. At length he overtook it in Arcadia, as it drew near to its usual dwelling-place.

As he was bringing it towards Tiryns, Artemis, the Immortal Huntress, met him in anger and cried:

'Rash mortal, how dare you seize and carry away my Hind? Surely there is no reason why I should not immediately slay you with one of my golden arrows?'

Then Heracles answered humbly, telling her that it was not of his own will but at the command of Eurystheus that he was carrying the Cerynitian Hind to Tiryns. Artemis smiled when she heard the story of his quest, and her anger departed from her.

'Go, and show my Hind to your master,' she said, 'but be sure that you do it no harm, and that you return it to my sacred grove on the hills above the Cerynitian river – otherwise Eurystheus will feel my anger!'

Heracles delivered her message faithfully, and Eurystheus lived in terror until the Hind with the Golden Horns had been returned to its Immortal owner.

'Now,' he said, with a sigh of relief when this was done, 'bring me the Erymanthian Boar, and bring it alive, in case Apollo makes any fuss about it, as I believe it has something to do with him.'

This boar was, indeed, said to be the very one which killed Adonis, the beautiful youth who was the favourite of Aphrodite. She, in a moment of anger, blinded Erymanthus, a mortal son of Apollo, because he saw her bathing, and in revenge Apollo sent the Boar which gashed Adonis in the thigh, and killed him. When Adonis had died in her arms, Aphrodite wished to be revenged on the Boar, and had it brought before her tightly bound, though indeed it came willingly.

'Vilest of all wild beasts!' cried Aphrodite, 'was it indeed you who gashed the thigh of my beautiful Adonis?'

'I did it,' answered the Boar, 'but not out of any hatred. For when I saw Adonis, I loved him and ran to kiss him, even as I had seen you do. In my devotion I forgot about my sharp tusks, and one of these it was that wounded him.'

Hearing this, Aphrodite forgave the Boar, and set it free to wander on Erymanthia, where in time it became so fierce and savage that no one dared go near it, or live on the slopes of the mountain.

Yet Heracles set out undaunted, and on the way met with a centaur called Pholus. These centaurs were men only to the waist, below that they had the body and legs of a horse. Some of them were very wise, for, though not immortal, they lived to a great age; but the wisest of all was Chiron.

Pholus entertained Heracles hospitably in his cave, setting roast meat before him. But he foolishly opened a jar of wine which Dionysus had left in the cave, and the wild centaurs who lived nearby, attracted by the smell, came crowding round, drank the strong wine, and were so maddened by it that they attacked Heracles. He was forced to shoot several of them with his poisoned arrows, and to drive the rest away. One of them, called Nessus, never forgave Heracles, but swore vengeance upon him, which he carried out in a strange fashion many years later.

After the battle Pholus picked up one of the arrows, marvelling that so little a thing could kill so great a creature as a centaur. As he examined it, the arrow slipped from his fingers and pricked him in the foot; and the poison of the Hydra on its tip was so strong that he died in a few minutes.

Heracles grieved sorely when he saw that the kindly centaur was dead, and buried him with all honour before continuing on his way in search of the Boar, which he caught by chasing it into a deep snow-drift, plunging in after it, and tying its legs firmly together.

When he arrived at Tiryns with the Boar and flung it down for inspection, Eurystheus was so terrified that he jumped into a large brass pot and hid at the bottom of it, gibbering with fear, until Heracles took the creature away. He flung it into the sea and it swam away to Italy, and its tusks were preserved ever after in the temple of Apollo at Cumae.

As soon as the coast was clear, Eurystheus emerged from his jar, and sent Heracles off on his next labour.

'I won't have any more dangerous animals brought back this

time!' he declared. 'But I've thought of a thoroughly nasty job for you, and one that's absolutely impossible. Go to King Augeas over at Elis – he has the biggest herd of cattle of any man in Greece, thousands of them. Clean out his stables in a single day; they are rather dirty, as they've not been touched for thirty years!'

Off went Heracles, determined to accomplish this labour too, however unpleasant and difficult it might be, and after careful examination he hit upon a scheme.

But first of all he went to King Augeas and, without saying anything about Eurystheus, declared:

'I'll undertake to clear your cattle-stables, yard and all, in a single day, while your cows are out on the pasture, if you'll promise to give me a tenth of your herd in payment.'

Believing that what he offered was quite impossible, Augeas agreed to the bargain and swore solemnly to fulfil his side of it if the task was performed.

Heracles at once knocked holes in either end of the great stable-building, and by digging a short channel turned the courses of the rivers Alpheus and Peneus which flowed close by, so that both streams ran in through one gap and out through the other.

The strong current of water cleared out the thirty years' accumulation of dung in a very short time, and Heracles had turned back the rivers into their normal beds and rebuilt the gaps in the stable walls before the herds were driven home in the evening.

Augeas, however, refused to fulfil his side of the bargain, and Heracles had to return some years later to punish him. He did not reap any reward from Eurystheus either, who said that this labour did not count, since Heracles had worked for hire, and packed him off to chase away the Stymphalian Birds.

These were the property of Ares: they had brazen claws, wings, and beaks, could moult their feathers at will – which sped down like sharp arrows – and ate human flesh. Athena advised Heracles not to go near them, for, so sharp were their beaks, that by flying straight at a man they could pierce even the hardest armour. But she lent him a pair of brazen castanets, which Hephaestus had made specially, and he went up onto a mountain overlooking the deep pool of Stymphalus, which was surrounded by dense woods.

When Heracles clashed the castanets the noise, helped by the echo, was so terrible that the Birds flew up in fear, and fled shrieking and clapping their wings to the distant island of Aretias, where Heracles was to meet them again when he went voyaging with the Argonauts.

As they fled he was able to bring down several of the Stymphalian Birds with his deadly arrows, and these he took back in triumph to Eurystheus.

'That was a poor exploit!' the latter scoffed, kicking the dead birds contemptuously. 'No one could be afraid of harmless little creatures like this: I wish I'd known before I sent you after them. However, off you go now, and bring me the Cretan Bull.'

Heracles turned without a word, strode down to the harbour at Nauplia, and took ship to the beautiful island of Crete, where King Minos welcomed him warmly and entertained him in his great palace at Knossus with its many stairs and passages, its strange, short columns with broad tops and narrow bases painted vivid reds and blues, and the running water and sanitation which were unknown anywhere else in the ancient world.

Minos gladly gave Heracles permission to take the Bull. 'It is causing havoc all over the island,' he told him. 'The fault is mine, I'm afraid. Poseidon sent it to me out of the sea so that I might offer up a worthy sacrifice, but, in my greed and folly, I kept it myself and substituted one of my own bulls. After that it went mad, and now no one can do anything with it.'

Heracles, however, was a match for any mad bull. He captured this one without any difficulty and carried it away to Greece. When he reached Tiryns he let the Bull loose, and Eurystheus only just got into his jar in time, and crouched there gibbering with fear for several days.

But the Bull, after failing to find Eurystheus, fled away north, crossed the Isthmus of Corinth, and came to Marathon, beyond Athens. Here it found the pastures green and lush, and decided to stay there, killing anyone who came near it.

Unfortunately one of its first victims was a son of Minos, who happened to be visiting Athens, and Minos would not believe that he had been killed by the Bull. So he invaded Athens, and only made peace when King Aegeus agreed to send an offering of seven youths and seven maidens every year to be devoured by the Minotaur, a monster half bull and half man which lived in the Labyrinth, a maze at Knossus which the clever craftsman Daedalus had made.

For twenty-seven years the Cretan Bull plagued the people of Marathon, and the Athenians regularly sent the tribute of youths and maidens to Minos, until Theseus came to Athens. But meanwhile Heracles was waiting in Tiryns for Eurystheus to recover from his fright; and when at last he did, the new labour which he had devised for him was to journey north to Thrace and bring back the horses of King Diomedes.

'Only be sure you tame them before they reach Argolis,' insisted Eurystheus, 'for they are terrible creatures, which are fed only on the flesh of men!'

So Heracles set out; but on his way a strange adventure befell him, when he stopped to visit the young Prince Admetus of Pherae in Thessaly.

CHAPTER II

The Story of Admetus

Oh, a House that loves the stranger,
  And a House for ever free!
And Apollo, the Song-changer,
  Was a herdsman in thy fee;
    Yea, a-piping he was found
    Where the upland valleys wound,
To the kine from out the manger
  And the sheep from off the lea,
    And love was upon Othrys at the sound.

EURIPIDES: *Alcestis* (Translated by Gilbert Murray)

11. The Story of Admetus

In the days when Heracles was still living happily at Thebes, there was a beautiful princess called Alcestis who was the daughter of Pelias, King of Iolcus. She was so beautiful that many princes came to ask her hand in marriage and Pelias, who did not wish to anger the rest by choosing one of them, said that he would only give her to the man who could yoke a wild boar and a lion to his chariot and drive safely round the racecourse.

Of all the young princes, Admetus of Pherae was the bravest and most handsome, and Alcestis loved him alone. But her father would not let them marry unless Admetus fulfilled the condition which he had made.

Now just before he came to woo Alcestis, a strange herdsman had come to him and begged to serve him for one year without wages. Admetus readily agreed to this, and being a good and amiable prince he treated his servant kindly and well. The herdsman served faithfully, and the herds of Admetus grew and prospered in the most remarkable way: for not one of his livestock died or was killed by wild beasts during that year, and all the cows had twin calves, and gave cream instead of milk.

One day, when the year was nearing its end, Admetus went up on to Mount Othrys to seek his herdsman, and saw a strange sight. In a green valley shaded by pine trees the herdsman sat playing on his pipes more sweetly than any mortal minstrel; and as he played the streaky golden lynxes and the tawny-coated lions, drawn by his music, came and rubbed their heads against him, while the shy fawns danced and frisked in and out of the shadows, fearing neither the lions nor the man who piped to them so magically.

Admetus stood at the edge of the glade overcome with awe and wonder, and seeing him the herdsman smiled, and said:

'Prince Admetus, do not be afraid nor surprised at what you see, for now that my servitude is almost ended I can tell you that I am none other than Apollo, the immortal son of Zeus. Listen, and I will tell you how it comes about that I, an Immortal, am servant to a mortal man.

'My son Asclepius, whose mother was the mortal woman Coronis, by my will and with the aid of wise Chiron the centaur, became the greatest healer and the most expert in the knowledge of medicine that the world has known. So skilled did he become that at length he discovered how to bring the dead to life – if only he could use his arts at the very moment of death. But Hades, Lord of the Dead, found that on account of my son's skill few new subjects were being added to his kingdom, and he accused Zeus of cheating him of his share in the bargain which was made between them at the beginning of the world.

'Then Zeus bade his servants the Cyclopes forge a thunderbolt, and when it was made he hurled it at Asclepius and struck him dead. In a moment of rage I seized my bow and arrows and slew those of the Cyclopes who had made the thunderbolt. Filled with righteous fury, Zeus would have cast me down into Tartarus; but my mother, the divine Leto, begged for my pardon, and Zeus decreed that I must become the slave of a mortal master for one year.

'So I came to you, Admetus; and I have not regretted my choice. For you have proved a fair and kindly master, and I will reward you in any way I can.'

When Admetus heard this, he remembered the condition on which Alcestis was to be won, and begged Apollo to help him, for he knew what a power he had over the wild beasts.

'I will certainly assist you in this,' Apollo assured him. 'But you must journey to Thebes and seek a young man called Heracles who will help in the taming of the lion and the boar.'

Admetus did as he was told; and with such assistance it was not long before he was driving in triumph to Iolcus behind his strange steeds, and bringing Alcestis back to Pherae as his bride.

The wedding was celebrated immediately, but in his excitement Admetus forgot to offer the usual sacrifice to Artemis. To punish him, she hid away Alcestis and in her place left a hissing coil of snakes.

Apollo made haste to appease his sister, and not only restored Alcestis to her anxious husband, but as a reward to Admetus arranged that when Death came for him he need not obey that fearful summons if any other would consent to die in his place.

This was highly irregular, but Apollo managed it by making the Three Fates drunk with sweet wine. These were the three weird sisters whose task was to spin the thread of a man's life and cut it off at the proper time.

The time came sooner than was expected: Hades sent his messenger, Death, to the palace at Pherae, and Admetus turned anxiously to the only people likely to help him, his aged father and mother.

'You are old,' he said, 'you have lived long and enjoyed all that life has to offer. There is nothing for you to look forward to now except the pain, illness, and slow death to which old age comes.'

But neither of them was willing to face death in his place, and indeed his father answered angrily: 'I have no call to die! You say I have not many days to live, whatever happens: all the more reason for taking special care of myself and enjoying them as fully as possible! As for you, I call you a mere coward, seeking for someone else to die instead of you!'

But Death was waiting; and when Alcestis heard how Admetus could be saved, she gave herself up in his place, so great was her love, and nothing he could say would change her determination.

So, while Admetus and the whole household mourned and wept, Alcestis said goodbye to her husband and her children, and feeling herself grow weaker and weaker, lay down on her bed and died.

It was just at this moment that Heracles, on his way north in search of the horses of King Diomedes, arrived at the palace, and being an old friend of Admetus, knocked at the door and asked for hospitality.

Admetus honoured Heracles more highly than any of his friends, and moreover among the Greeks hospitality was one of the most sacred duties of a good man. So he welcomed Heracles into the palace, saw to it that he had a good meal with plenty of wine, and told him nothing about what was happening.

'But surely you're in mourning?' objected Heracles. 'Is it your old father? Or your mother who has died?'

'They both live yet,' answered Admetus.

'Is it then some relation?' asked Heracles, who did not even think that it might be Alcestis.

'It's a foreign woman, not related to me in blood,' said Admetus carefully.

'Well, if that is all,' replied Heracles, much relieved, 'I'll accept your hospitality, though I know it's burdensome when guests come to a house of mourning.'

'Whoever had died,' said Admetus firmly, 'you should still find a ready welcome here. The guest chamber is far away from the place of mourning, so we will not distress you with any sounds of grief.'

Only half satisfied, Heracles, who was weary after his long journey, settled down to supper, ate well, and drank a large quantity of wine.

Meanwhile Admetus and the mourners left the palace, carrying the body of Alcestis on a bier towards the burial ground at some distance from the city.

They were hardly out of sight when Heracles came striding

out of the guest-room, a wreath round his head, singing lustily. There he met the house steward, an old man who was devoted to Alcestis, and could not restrain his tears.

'How now!' cried Heracles jovially. 'What's all this about? Some foreign woman dead, and all the household glum and sullen! That's not the way to welcome a guest, particularly not your master's old friend and comrade in arms. Your master and mistress are both alive and well, so all this mourning seems rather excessive!'

'Alive!' sobbed the old steward. 'Man, have you not heard?'

'Why yes, your master told me. A foreign woman, he said.'

'Oh, foreign by birth, certainly. . . .'

'What is it? Some real grief which your master has hidden from me?' Heracles was beginning to grow suspicious. 'Speak, I command you!'

'Yes,' answered the steward, awed by the fierceness of his tone. 'A real grief indeed: the Princess Alcestis has died.'

'Alcestis? And he welcomed me in and feasted me?' Heracles was overcome.

'He held it shame to turn you away,' answered the steward.

'So.' Heracles stood in deep thought. 'For my friend, who has treated me so nobly,' he said at last, 'I will dare anything. . . . Where lies the tomb? Where shall I find Alcestis now?'

The steward told him, then fled back into the house while Heracles, flinging his lion-skin about him, strode away over the steep hillside.

Admetus had already returned to the palace by a longer way round when Heracles reached the graveyard, so that he had the place to himself.

But he was not quite alone, for there, standing by the tomb was a dark-robed figure which, being half an Immortal, Heracles was able to see. The tomb was open, and the figure was bending over the body of Alcestis with a drawn sword in his hand, about to cut off a lock of her hair.

'Stay, Death!' cried Heracles in his great voice. 'What do you there?'

The tall, solemn figure rose slowly and turned his dark, baleful eyes upon Heracles.

'I come for mine own,' he answered in a cold, hissing voice. 'Once this grey sword of mine has touched the hair of any mortal, that soul belongs to Hades, my lord and master.'

'Will you not this once release your victim?' asked Heracles. 'You know how and why she has come into your power: surely the lady of your lord, the divine maiden, Persephone, would willingly send back to earth the soul of a wife who has died, so young and so lovely, to save her husband?'

There was some truth in this, and the dark servant of Hades paused in thought. Then, with a grim smile, he laid down his sword:

Heracles wrestling with Death

'Heracles,' he said, 'I know you well, you whose mighty deeds are spoken of even in the dark Land of the Dead. So come now, I will wrestle with you for the soul of Alcestis: many men have fought against Death, but none has ever conquered him!'

Heracles flung off his lion-skin and advanced unarmed to grapple with his dark adversary. Then there was such a wrestling match as had never been known before, or is likely to be seen again. To and fro they reeled and struggled, the cold arms of Death locked round Heracles and his icy breath coming in great gasps.

But Heracles had him round the waist, and his mighty arms closed tighter and tighter until he felt Death's ribs cracking in his grip. At last Death admitted himself beaten and departed to his own place, moaning direfully. But Alcestis sat up in the tomb, and when Heracles took her by the hand she stepped out and followed him, walking like one in a dream.

Casting a veil over her face, Heracles led her back to the palace, and found Admetus plunged in grief, blaming himself most bitterly that he had ever let Alcestis die for him.

'I have returned,' said Heracles, 'to ask a favour of you. I am going on a wild and hazardous adventure: will you guard this woman for me until my return? Let her be a handmaiden in your house.'

But Admetus would not have her: she reminded him too much of Alcestis. So Heracles soon gave up his little trick and told his friend the whole truth.

'She will not speak for three days,' he warned Admetus. 'She has dwelt with Death, and cannot come back to this world all in a moment. But do not fear: she is no ghost but Alcestis herself, and in a little while will be as if she had never taken your place when Death came for you.'

Full of gratitude, Admetus begged his friend to stay and feast with them, but Heracles shook his head.

'I have feasted,' he said. 'Now I must be on my way: there is but little rest for me in this world.'

He turned resolutely and went north, ever north until he came to the wild land of Thrace. There Diomedes welcomed him kindly: but Heracles knew that it was only a pretence, since it was this savage king's custom to throw his guests to the four terrible horses, who would immediately devour them.

Next day, with the help of a groom belonging to Diomedes, Heracles managed to steal the four horses, and even to harness them to a chariot, though they had never before known bit or bridle.

But the groom then betrayed him to Diomedes, who followed him with a band of men. Heracles, when he saw them coming, left the groom to hold the horses, and broke down a stretch of the sea wall. It was high tide, and the great waves came pouring through, and washed away most of the Thracians.

King Diomedes, however, he captured and carried back to the chariot. There, finding that the horses had already eaten the treacherous groom, he threw the wicked king to them as well, and they devoured him also.

After this Heracles drove off at full speed, and whether it was through eating their master, or whether he managed to tame them on the way, certain it is that when they reached Tiryns, Eurystheus had no need to hide himself in his brass jar.

The horses were quite tame now, and Eurystheus dedicated them to Hera. But they continued to be the strongest and most fearless horses in all Greece; and several of their descendants were used in the war against Troy.

As for Heracles, he was given no rest from labour: for Eurystheus sent him off again immediately – this time to bring back the belt of Hippolyta, the Queen of the Amazons, which his daughter greatly desired to possess. This belt was the gift of Ares, the Lord of War, to the bravest of the Amazons, who were a race of warrior women, trained to the use of arms and skilled particularly in casting the javelin and shooting with the bow.

They allowed no men in their wild land on the south coast of the Black Sea; and they kept their husbands in the next country, visiting them only for one month in every year.

To reach this land Heracles had to go by sea. So he gathered together a band of adventurers, and set sail for Troy and the Hellespont.

CHAPTER 12

The Wanderings of Heracles

> ... Now he goes
> With no less presence, but with much more love,
> Than young Alcides when he did redeem
> The virgin tribute paid by howling Troy
> To the sea monster ... Go, Hercules!
> Live thou, I live:– with much, much more dismay
> I view the fight than thou that makest the fray!

SHAKESPEARE: *The Merchant of Venice*

12. The Wanderings of Heracles

HERACLES sailed from Nauplia in Argolis with nine companions, amongst whom were two young heroes named Peleus and Telamon, who were both to win great fame in days to come.

After several adventures on the way, they came into the Black Sea and arrived in the land of the Amazons. They prepared for war, but to their surprise Queen Hippolyta came down to the harbour to visit them in a friendly manner, and even offered to give Heracles the belt as soon as he explained why he had come.

But Hera, who had an eye on what Heracles was doing, felt that this was far too easy a victory for him. So she disguised herself as an Amazon warrior and went hastening to the fortified citadel.

'Amazons, come swiftly!' she cried. 'There is a ship in the harbour filled with men, vile pirates, who have captured our queen and will carry her off to sell as a slave in Greece or Troy!'

The Amazons needed no second summons. Out they came like bees when their hive is disturbed, and with fierce cries rushed down to the shore and attacked Heracles and his companions.

Terrible was the battle that followed: great were the deeds done that day by Peleus and Telamon; but it was Heracles with his unerring arrows who slew the leaders of the Amazons, and at length captured Melanippe, the Queen's favourite sister. When he threatened to kill her unless they gave him the girdle and let him sail away in safety, they obeyed Hippolyta and marched back to their city in great sorrow, while Heracles set sail for Greece in triumph.

On the return journey, as they sailed down the coast of Troy, a strange adventure befell them. As they passed near a pleasant inlet of the sea the sound of weeping came to their ears. Following the voice, and rowing gently, they found a lovely girl chained to a rock by the side of the water – just as Perseus had found Andromeda many years before.

Halting the ship close by, Heracles spoke to her:

'Maiden,' said he, 'who are you, and why are you chained here?'

'Alas,' she sobbed, 'I hang here, waiting a terrible fate, through no fault of my own. I am called Hesione, and my father is Laomedon the King of Troy. It is said that the great Immortals Poseidon and Apollo came to him, by the will of Zeus, as workmen, and with their own hands built the walls of Troy city. King Laomedon swore to pay them well; but when the work was done, he broke his oath, refusing to pay anything and threatening to sell his two workmen as slaves, after cutting off their ears, if they did not immediately depart from Troy. Then the two Immortals revealed themselves, and in their anger Apollo sent a pestilence which has devastated the country, and Poseidon sent a sea serpent which comes at high tide to prey upon the people. So Laomedon has bound me here as an offering, for he hopes that my life will buy Poseidon's forgiveness.

'Noble sir, you seem a mighty man, skilled in arms: I beg you to save me from the serpent. For very soon he will come!'

Then Heracles beached his ship, and on the shore King Laomedon met him.

'What will you give me,' asked Heracles, 'if I kill this monster and save your daughter and your land?'

'If you save my daughter, you may have her as your wife,' answered Laomedon, 'and if you kill the monster, I will give you the magic horses which Zeus gave to my grandfather Tros when he took Ganymede to Olympus.'

Now Ganymede was a handsome young prince of Troy whom Zeus had chosen to be cup-bearer to the Immortals and assist his daughter Hebe in waiting on them as they feasted on golden Olympus. So he sent a great eagle to carry Ganymede up to heaven; and he gave Tros in exchange two magic white horses which could run over the sea or the standing corn as lightly and as swiftly as the wind.

Heracles agreed to this, and when the Trojans had built him a low wall by the sea-shore, he crouched down behind it to lie in wait for the monster.

Scarcely was he ready, when far out to sea he saw a line of white foam, and heard a strange roaring which drew nearer and nearer. Then he saw the monster itself, its eyes flashing and flickering beneath the blue-grey film of its eyelids, and its three rows of mighty teeth gleaming in its huge mouth. It came with head and neck raised high above the water and the long coils of its scaly body curling and rippling in great arches.

Heracles lay behind his wall until the great sea serpent reared up its head over the shore, roaring and hissing with rage. Then Hesione shrieked with terror and, as the serpent turned to seize her, Heracles leapt up on the wall, uttering a fierce war cry, and began loosing swift arrows at the creature's head and neck.

The serpent minded them no more than a mountain minds the rain drops which beat on its rocky sides; but when Heracles, seeing how useless the arrows were, dropped his bow and began pelting the monster with great rocks and boulders, it turned away from the screaming maiden and came towards him, roaring with rage, its huge mouth wide open.

Then Heracles cried to Zeus for help and, drawing his sword, leapt straight into the serpent's mouth, just avoiding the three rows of razor-sharp teeth, and charged down its throat, hacking and hewing with his sword.

The serpent screamed horribly and, while all the watching Trojans cried aloud with terror and pity, it closed its jaws and plunged down under the waves. But they saw that its great coils were twisting and writhing beneath the water, and before long it lay dead on the sand. Then the water was suddenly red with blood, which bubbled above the corpse, and Heracles rose to the surface, gasping for breath, having cut his way out through the serpent's side.

Telamon and Peleus cheered loudly, and guided the ship quickly towards him. He clambered on board, and they rowed to the rock where Hesione was still tied, and cut her bonds.

Then they brought her to the shore, and King Laomedon met them, already planning treachery in his evil heart.

'Come to my city,' he said, 'so that we may feast after this mighty exploit. Then you may rest safely, and sail away tomorrow carrying my daughter and the magic horses.' But he intended to murder them all that night as they slept.

Heracles, though he suspected nothing, replied:

'I cannot stay now, King Laomedon, for my labours must be accomplished. But I will return to claim my reward, never fear. So keep the horses safely for me, and keep my bride to be also.'

Then he set sail, and after several more adventures arrived safely at Tiryns, where Eurystheus received the belt of the Amazon Queen for his daughter, and sent Heracles straight out again – this time to fetch back, without either asking or paying for them, the cattle of Geryon, who was said to be the strongest man in the world. This ogre had been born with three heads and six arms and hands, but only one body from the waist downwards. He lived on the mysterious island of Erythia in the Atlantic Ocean beyond the Straits of Gibraltar.

Heracles set out on this expedition alone, and journeyed overland through Italy, France, and Spain, slaying many wild beasts and other monsters on the way, until he came to the straits separating Europe from Africa.

Here he set up two great stone pillars, one at Gibraltar and the other at Ceuta: and the straits were called the Pillars of Hercules by the Romans in consequence.

As he laboured to raise the pillar on the African coast, the heat was terrific and Heracles, half crazed by the sun's tropical glare, set an arrow to his bow and loosed it with all his strength in the direction of the Sun-chariot, which the Titan Helios was at that moment bringing down towards the western ocean.

Helios was so amused by the audacity of this struggling mortal that he not only veiled his beams immediately, but lent Heracles his magic goblet of pure gold, shaped like a gigantic water-lily.

In this Heracles crossed to the island of Erythia, using his lion-skin as a sail. On reaching the shore his first care was to moor his strange boat in a concealed inlet: then he climbed a hill in the centre of the island to spy out the land. He had scarcely reached the summit, when a great dog came rushing at him open-mouthed, only to meet his end from a single blow of the deadly club.

As he descended in the direction of the pastures where he could see the beautiful red cattle grazing, Heracles was attacked by the herdsman, whom he killed also, but only after a fierce fight. Heracles then drove the cattle towards the shore, but before he reached it the ogre Geryon came rushing towards him, brandishing various weapons in his six huge hands, and shouting threats of terrible vengeance.

Heracles knew that he was no match for so powerful a monster if they came to hand-grips; so, quick as thought, he discharged three arrows, one through each of the ogre's three throats: and that was the end of him. Then he drove the cattle into the magic goblet, sailed back to Spain, and having returned his strange vessel to Helios with many thanks, began the weary task of driving the herd overland all the way back to Greece.

On the way many adventures befell him. Once in the south of France near where Marseilles now stands, he was attacked by a large army of warlike natives. He fought and fought until all his arrows were spent, and then it seemed that his end had come, for the ground was soft with not a stone in sight. In despair, Heracles prayed to Zeus, who took pity on him and rained down stones from above, thus supplying him with ample ammunition. That great plain covered with smooth round stones may be seen to this very day.

On another occasion Heracles camped for the night in a valley among seven low hills where now stands the city of Rome. He did not know that a fire-breathing troll called Cacus lived in a huge cave under Mount Aventine, nor did he realize in the morning that this creature had come down during the night and stolen several of the cattle. For Cacus had carefully blotted out all the footmarks, and the mouth of his cave was hidden by a great door of solid rock which slid down in grooves.

But just as Heracles was setting out in the morning, he heard a cow lowing somewhere in the hillside: for Cacus had very foolishly taken one of the cows who had a calf, and left the calf with the herd.

Heracles at once counted the cattle, found that some were missing, and set out to deal with the thief. Before long he found the door of the cavern, but Cacus, realizing that he was discovered, hastily broke the chains and balances which should have raised it, and even Heracles could not lift the enormous block of stone without them.

Three times Heracles strove to stir it, and three times drew back, gnashing his teeth with rage. But after the third attempt, as Cacus laughed triumphantly within, Heracles saw that there was a crack in the hillside above the cave. He climbed up to it, set his heels in it and his back against the hill itself, and pushed with all his might. The crack slowly widened, and then with a sudden roar the whole side of the hill slid away and a great mass of rock went crashing down into the river at the foot.

But Heracles landed on the floor of the cavern, which was now open to the light of day for the first time, and rushed to attack Cacus. The troll immediately filled the hollow with smoke which he belched out of his mouth; but Heracles plunged valiantly into the thick of it, guided by the flames which Cacus was breathing, and caught him by the throat. Very soon the fight was over, and Heracles, singed and choking from the smoke, dragged the troll's body out into the open. Then he gathered the missing cattle and continued on his way.

One more strange adventure befell him as he drew near to the north of Greece, for Hera sent a giant gadfly which stung the cattle and scattered them far and wide. Heracles pursued them relentlessly, and at length, having retrieved nearly all of them, he lay down to rest in a cave somewhere in the hills of the country now called Bulgaria, on the west coast of the Black Sea.

It was cold and stormy, and Heracles slept long and heavily after his laborious search for the cattle. But in the morning he found that the horses which drew his chariot had mysteriously disappeared.

In a great fury he wandered far and wide until at length he came to another cave in which he found a mysterious creature. She was like a woman from the waist upward, but below that was a scaly snake. He looked at her in wonder, but asked nevertheless:

123

Heracles and the snake-maiden

'Strange maiden, have you seen my horses?'

'Yes,' she replied, 'it was I who took them in when they strayed this way. But I will never give them up to you, unless you wed me, according to the custom of this country. Here we are married when we have kissed thrice; and the marriage lasts only for as long as we both wish it.'

There was no help for it, so Heracles kissed the snake-maiden three times, and lodged in her cave for three days.

At the end of that time she gave him back his horses, and before leaving he strung the spare bow which he carried with him and gave it to her, saying:

'Lady, I prophesy that you will have three sons: let the one who can draw this bow as I do, come and seek me if he wishes for assistance in winning his fortune. But if he does not come, then let him, and no other, rule over this land after you.'

In due time it all fell out as he had prophesied: neither the eldest son or the second son could draw the bow, but the third was able to pass the test of strength, and he became the first king of the Scythians.

Heracles set out once more, and this time he reached Greece safely with the cattle.

As he was crossing the isthmus of Corinth, a giant bandit who had taken possession of the place and stopped all travellers to rob or kill them, held him up:

'Hand all those cattle over to me!' he cried, 'and you shall pass in safety.'

'Never,' replied Heracles briefly.

Then the bandit picked up a huge rock and hurled it at him. Heracles dodged the great whirling mass, and picking it up flung it back with such good aim that the bandit never again molested travellers.

So Heracles came to Tiryns and handed over the cattle to Eurystheus.

'Now!' he cried, 'I have accomplished the ten labours which you set me, and spent more than eight years of my life in doing so: at last I may go free!'

'Not so,' answered Eurystheus, 'for you know that two labours do not count. Iolaus helped you to kill the Lernean Hydra, and you cleaned the Augean Stables for hire. So Hera commands that you perform two further labours. Go now and bring back three golden apples from the Garden of the Hesperides!'

Once again Heracles bowed to his fate and with a weary sigh turned his back on Tiryns and set off once more.

CHAPTER 13

The Golden Apples, and the Hound of Hell

Round and round the apples of gold,
   Round and round dance we;
Thus do we dance from the days of old
   About the enchanted tree;
Round, and round, and round we go,
While the spring is green, or the stream shall flow,
   Or the wind shall stir the sea!

After PINDAR: *Tenth Pythian Ode* (Translated by Andrew Lang)

13. The Golden Apples, and the Hound of Hell

HERACLES set out wearily on his eleventh labour without any idea of where the golden apples were to be found. But Zeus was watching him, since he had a special deed for him to perform which as it turned out, did more to save both mortals and Immortals than any help which Heracles could give in the coming war with the Giants.

For all this while Prometheus the Good Titan had been lying chained to Mount Caucasus in punishment for disobeying Zeus by bringing fire to mankind. And the great eagle still came every day to devour his liver, which still grew again every night: but in spite of all his suffering, Prometheus still refused to tell Zeus of the danger greater than that of the Giants which was threatening him.

Nevertheless, Zeus had grown merciful with time. If Prometheus had suffered in body, Zeus had suffered in mind – for he knew that at any moment he might make the mistake Prometheus had prophesied, and which only Prometheus could prevent.

So when Heracles came into the land of Illyria and begged the nymphs who lived there to tell him how he might find the golden apples, they replied that, by the command of their father, Zeus, he must journey on, to Mount Caucasus, and ask Prometheus.

The way was long and dangerous, but at length Heracles came to the great mountain above the world's end. Climbing by chasm and crevasse, by steep glissade and slippery glacier, he came to the great cliff-face on which the Titan was chained. And as he clambered up beside him, the great eagle swooped down to its horrible feast, and the mighty Titan screamed aloud in his agony.

But Heracles, with a shout of rage and pity, fitted an arrow to his bow, drew it to the head, and loosed it with all his might. The great eagle flew up, transfixed by the arrow, and plunged down into the waves of the Black Sea, thousands of feet below.

'Who are you, rash mortal?' asked Prometheus slowly.

'I am Heracles, the son of Zeus,' was the answer. 'And I come here by his command, to free you. For Zeus forgives you for your great crimes against himself, and asks your pardon for the torture to which he has put you. Nevertheless, he bids me say that, since his great decrees cannot be broken altogether, you must wear a ring on your finger for ever as a token that you are still bound in fetters of metal.'

Prometheus nodded his head and smiled.

'You are the hero of whom I prophesied,' he said. 'Your hand shall strike down the Giants and save Olympus from ruin. But that you would come to set me free, I did not know, for a prophet cannot foretell his own future. Come, strike off my fetters and let me girdle my finger with that ring; and in memory of my sufferings I declare that mankind shall ever after wear rings in token of this day.'

Heracles set to work; and while he hacked and twisted at the brazen fetters he told Prometheus of his quest and asked him about the golden apples of the Hesperides.

'They grow on the tree which Mother Earth gave to Hera as a wedding present,' said Prometheus, 'and that tree is in a magic garden on the world's western verge, beyond the mountain on which my brother Atlas stands for ever supporting the starry sky on his shoulders. The dragon Ladon curls round that tree, and in the garden dwell the immortal daughters of Hesperus, the Warden of the Evening Star, which is also the Star of the Morning; and he is the son of Atlas. Ask Atlas to assist you: for no mortal may enter that garden without great danger; and he has built a high wall round it that cannot be climbed.'

Many other things Prometheus told to Heracles, so that when his work was ended he went on his way with bowed head, thinking of the greatness and nobility of the mighty Titan, helper of mankind.

Once again Heracles met with many adventures as he traversed the earth on his quest: but there is not time now to tell how he fought with Cycnus the son of Ares, slew him and wounded even the Immortal Warlord himself; nor how in Egypt the cruel King Busiris who sacrificed all strangers came to find himself bound and offered up on his own altar; nor even of his adventures with the King of Ethiopia. But as he traversed Libya on his way to Mount Atlas, his strength was put to the proof in the most dangerous wrestling match of his whole career. For there dwelt the savage Antaeus, a giant son of Earth, who challenged all strangers to wrestle with him; and when he had killed them with his mighty hands, he used their skulls to decorate the temple of Poseidon. He lived in a cave and slept on the bare earth; and he would rob the lionesses of their cubs and eat them raw for his supper.

Heracles needed no second bidding when Antaeus challenged him to wrestle. He flung off his lion-skin, anointed himself all over with oil, and stood ready. Antaeus did the same, but in place of oil he covered himself from head to foot in dust.

The Garden of the Hesperides

Then they seized hold of one another, arms twisting with arms, bending and swaying backwards and forwards, striving to reach each other's throat with their clutching fingers. Heracles proved the stronger, and with a mighty effort flung the almost fainting Antaeus to the ground.

But then an amazing thing happened. The moment Antaeus touched the earth all his weariness passed from him, and he sprang to his feet with a shout of triumph, as fresh and strong as at the beginning of the battle.

Astonished, Heracles closed with him once more, and with a great effort flung him to the ground again. Up jumped the young giant with his strength and vigour again renewed, and Heracles exclaimed:

'A son of Earth, are you? I might have guessed from whence you drew your strength! Come on again, and this time I'll see to it that we fight standing: if fall you must, fall upon me, and see what sort of vigour I can impart to you!'

Again they wrestled, and this time Heracles exerted his great strength and lifted Antaeus above his head, held him there in spite of all his struggles, and did not lower him even when he grew weaker and weaker. But at last he took him in his arms, still careful that not so much as a toe touched the ground, and hugged him to death as a bear might.

Flinging aside the corpse of his cruel foe, Heracles continued on his way, and came soon to the great mountain, the highest in the known world, on top of which stood Atlas the Titan, holding up the sky lest it should sink down again upon the earth as it had done in the beginning of the world.

'I come to you for help, great Titan,' cried Heracles when he had climbed to the peak on which Atlas stood. 'Your brother Prometheus advised me to ask your assistance: I am Heracles, and I come for three of the golden apples to deliver to my task-master, Eurystheus of Tiryns, who loads me with labours by command of Immortal Hera.'

'Heracles, son of Zeus,' answered Atlas, 'I was warned long ago of your coming by wise Themis, sister of my Titan father. I will do what you wish if you will perform two great deeds to assist me. While I am away you must take my place and hold the sky upon your shoulders; and before you do this, you must slay the dragon Ladon who guards the tree; for even I may not touch the fruit while he lives.'

Heracles looked down beyond the mountain, towards the Western Ocean, and saw far below him the lovely Garden of the Hesperides.

There were the cool glades and the silver leaves of Paradise, and in the midst the great tree shining with the golden fruit, while three lovely nymphs, the daughters of Hesperus, danced and sang in the dappled sunlight.

Then he saw the dragon curled about the tree, a monster longer than any he had slain, its scales shining with gold and blue. He drew an arrow from his quiver, fitted it to his bow, and shot with so unerring an aim that it pierced the dragon's throat. The creature uncurled from the tree and glided away into the bushes there to die slowly and strangely, for its tail was still alive several years later when the Argonauts visited the spot.

When Ladon the dragon had gone, Atlas shifted his mighty burden on to the broad shoulders of Heracles, and stretching himself with a great sigh of relief, he hurried off in the direction of the Garden.

The hours passed slowly for Heracles as he stood there holding up his gigantic burden, and he felt weary and ill at ease as the light faded and the stars began twinkling in his hair. All through the long night he stood there, supporting the sky, and in the morning he could have shouted for joy when he saw Atlas striding up the mountain carrying three golden apples in his hand.

But his heart sank suddenly when the Titan stood still at a little distance and looked at him with a cruel gleam in his eyes.

'Here are the apples,' said Atlas. 'But I will take them to King Eurystheus myself. I have been through great dangers to obtain them, it is only fair that I should have a sufficient respite from my burden. You cannot know what joy it is to walk the earth again, and feel no longer that heavy weight upon my shoulders.'

'You do indeed deserve your holiday,' answered Heracles, thinking quickly, 'and I wish you all joy of it, though I look forward to your return, for this is certainly a very heavy load. But when you set it upon my shoulders, I thought it was to remain there only a few hours, and I paid little attention to how it was placed. Now you, who have supported it so long, must be an expert sky-carrier: can you teach me how to arrange the burden most easily?'

'I can indeed,' replied the slow-witted Atlas, 'you should hold it like this – let me show you.'

He dropped the golden apples, and stepping forward eagerly, took the sky on his shoulders once more, explaining as he did so what was the easiest way to hold it up.

Heracles watched carefully.

'You know,' he said gravely, 'you do it so much better than

133

I . . . I think I'd better leave it to you, and myself take those golden apples to Eurystheus. Every man to his own task!'

With that he set off down the mountain, leaving Atlas to lament the loss of his only chance of freedom.

When he reached the sea coast, Heracles took ship for Greece and after a long voyage was landed at Lindos on the island of Rhodes. He was so ravenously hungry after the journey that he killed the first ox he came upon, and roasted a great dinner for himself. But the owner of the ox stood on the lovely hillside where the castle of Lindos stands today, and cursed the stranger for an hour without stopping.

Heracles paid for the ox when he had eaten it. But in after days when the people of Lindos honoured Heracles as an Immortal, they always invoked him with curses instead of prayers in memory of his visit to their land.

Heracles went on his way to Tiryns when his hunger was satisfied, and delivered the golden apples to Eurystheus. That cowardly king was afraid to receive them, in case Hera should take vengeance on him, and said:

'I'll make you a present of them. You deserve them after so much trouble! You've only one more labour to perform, and if you return safely from that, I expect you'll need the golden apples!' He sniggered cruelly, for the final labour was to be the hardest and most dangerous of all – no less than to descend into the Realm of Hades and bring back Cerberus, the three-headed Hound of Hell.

When Heracles heard this, he turned away in despair, and left Tiryns, still carrying the golden apples.

But Zeus again was watching over him, and sent Athena and Hermes to his help. First of all Heracles gave the apples to the Goddess, who handed them over to Aphrodite to take care of for the time being. But when, later, Athena returned them to the Garden of the Hesperides, she took pity on Atlas and showed him the Gorgon's head – and he became the topmost peak of stony Mount Atlas with great thankfulness.

Meanwhile the two Immortals led Heracles to the great cave at Taenarum, not far from Sparta, and down into the gloomy depths of the earth until they came to the underworld which was bounded by the black River Styx. Here Athena waited, while Hermes went on with Heracles, for it was one of his offices to lead souls down to Hades.

At the River Styx the dark old ferryman, Charon, was waiting with his boat. He was only allowed to ferry dead souls across that stream, and they paid him one coin, called an 'obol', which was always placed ready in a dead person's mouth. He would have refused to take this living passenger, but Heracles scowled at him so fiercely that he did not dare: and he was punished afterwards by Hades for his cowardice.

On the other side Heracles found himself in the grey, twilit land of the dead, where ghosts flitted about moaning and gibbering.

The first he met was the Gorgon Medusa, and when he saw that terrible shape, he fitted an arrow to his bow; but Hermes reminded him with a smile that she was only a harmless ghost, killed by Perseus.

Heracles saw many terrible sights in the Realm of Hades, for he crossed the fiery river of Phlegathon and entered Tartarus, the prison where the Titans lay, and where the wicked are punished.

He saw, for example, Ixion on his flaming wheel, the wicked king who had broken faith with Zeus; and Tantalus who stood up to the neck in cool water and yet could not quench his burning thirst since the water went away as soon as he stooped to drink. Also he saw Sisyphus, thief and murderer, whose doom was to roll a stone to the top of a hill down which it always rolled just as he neared the summit; and the daughters of King Danaus who murdered their husbands and had to fill for ever a cask which had a hole in the bottom.

Only one of the souls in torment was Heracles allowed to free; and that was Ascalaphus, who had given Persephone six pomegranate seeds when Hades first carried her down to his kingdom. If she had not eaten these, she could have returned to earth for ever: but since she had eaten in the realm of the dead, she was forced to return there for six months every year. So Demeter in fury placed a heavy stone on top of Ascalaphus. Heracles was allowed to roll it away, and Ascalaphus was turned into an owl instead.

At last Heracles came to where Hades and Persephone sat in state, and he told them why he was there and begged them to lend him their terrible hound.

'You may willingly take Cerberus,' answered Hades, 'if you can overcome him without the use of weapons.'

So Heracles returned to the bank of the Styx, and Cerberus rushed at him, since he was there to prevent the souls of the dead from leaving the Realm of Hades. Cerberus had three mighty heads with lion-like manes bristling with snakes; and in place of a tail a serpent writhed and hissed. Heracles wrapped his lion-skin about himself, seized hold of the brute and squeezed him hard. Cerberus struggled and tried to bite; but the lion-skin was too tough, and Heracles was too strong. Only the serpent-tail managed to hurt him; but even then Heracles would not let go.

At last Cerberus gave way, and Heracles carried him off in triumph, crossing the dark river with the help of Hermes and Athena. They led him up the great cavern near Troezen through which Dionysus had brought his mother Semele, and at last they saw the light of day.

To Heracles this was welcome, but when Cerberus beheld the glorious light of the sun, he struggled, and howled dismally, and the white foam flying from his jaws spattered all the grass. From this foam grew the flower called aconite which gives the deadly poison known as wolf's-bane.

Holding his captive firmly, Heracles set out at once for Tiryns. When he arrived there, he strode straight into the citadel, shouting for Eurystheus. And when the King appeared, Heracles cried:

'My last labour is achieved! Here is Cerberus!'

He dropped the dog on the ground as he spoke, and it rushed at Eurystheus, barking with all three mouths and hissing with every snake on its three manes.

Eurystheus turned with a scream of terror and leapt into his brass pot, where he was still shrieking with fear when Heracles left Tiryns for the last time, carrying Cerberus in his arms.

Straight back to the Styx he went, and placed the terrible Hound of Hell on the gloomy shore. Then he returned to earth rejoicing, his twelve labours ended, free at last.

As before, Heracles came up from the Realm of Hades by the great gorge of Dionysus near Troezen; and he was so weary after his labours that he went to visit his friend Pittheus who was king there.

As he entered the palace he took off his lion-skin and flung it over a chair where it lay in a most life-like fashion. Presently a crowd of children came into the room laughing and talking. But when they saw the lion-skin they turned and fled shrieking that there was a lion in the palace.

All except one. Pittheus had a grandson aged about seven, whose name was Theseus. He did not run away: on the contrary, he snatched an axe from one of the guards and attacked the skin furiously, thinking it was a live lion.

Heracles laughed encouragingly: 'We'll have you following in my footsteps before long!' he cried.

'I could ask for no better fate,' answered young Theseus stoutly.

The Adventures of Theseus

Give me again your empty boon,
  Sweet Sleep – the gentle dream
How Theseus 'neath the fickle moon
  Upon the Ocean stream
Took me and led me by the hand
To be his Queen in Athens land.

He slew the half-bull Minotaur
  In labyrinthine ways.
But, threadless, had he come no more
  From out my father's maze:
Yet I who taught his hands this guile
Am left forlorn on Naxos Isle.

NONNOS: *Dionysiaca* XLVII (Translated by R.L.G.)

14. The Adventures of Theseus

THE boy whom Heracles met at Troezen was the son of Aegeus, King of Athens, who had married Aethra the daughter of King Pittheus. Aegeus never saw his son as a child, for even before the babe was born, he was forced to return to Athens to fight for his throne against his three brothers, who ought really to have been governing with him.

But before he left Troezen he lifted a great rock and placed under it a sword and a pair of sandals.

'If our child is a boy,' he said to Aethra, 'do not tell him who his father is until he can lift this stone. When that time comes, send him to me in Athens for I shall need his help.'

So Theseus was born in Troezen, and grew strong and brave, learning both wisdom and skill at all manly pursuits from his grandfather and his mother. He learnt much from Heracles also during his visit, and determined that when he was old enough he too would spend his life fighting against monsters and savage robbers, of whom there were still plenty in Greece.

It was not until he was eighteen that Theseus was able to lift the stone. When he did, and was told by Aethra that his father was King Aegeus, he buckled on both sword and sandals eagerly and prepared to set out for Athens.

'Go there in a swift ship,' begged Aethra. 'The distance is short, and the dangers few, but overland there are robbers; and your cousins, the fifty sons of Pallas, your father's youngest brother, will try to kill you so as to secure the rule of Athens for themselves.'

Theseus would not listen to such advice. 'If there are robbers on the road,' he said, 'I must go out of my way to fight and slay them. For that is what Heracles would have done if he were still in Greece.'

For at this time Heracles, having killed his friend Iphitus in a moment of fury had, as a punishment, been sold as a slave to Omphale, a queen in Asia, where he was forced to wear women's clothes and work at the loom – which was a far worse fate for him and much harder to endure than performing the twelve labours for Eurystheus.

So Theseus set out on the road to Athens, determined to clear the way of all evildoers: and he had not far to go before he met the first. A few miles from Troezen, at Epidaurus, where the most beautiful of ancient Greek theatres stands today, lived Periphetes the Clubman. He was lame, but what he lacked in his legs he made up for in the strength of his arms. His only weapon was a mighty club shod with iron, which was death to all passers-by – until Theseus wrested it from his hands and paid him out in his own cruel coin.

This was always the method adopted by Theseus, for when he reached the isthmus of Corinth he dealt with Sinis the Pinebender in a similar way. This ruffian accosted Theseus as he approached.

'Sir stranger!' he cried. 'Come and test your strength by helping me bend down this pine tree!'

But Theseus knew what to expect, and when the tree was bent down in a great curve it was he and not Sinis who let go suddenly and sent his partner flying through the air. Then he bent down two trees himself, tied Sinis between them, and allowed them to tear him in half; for he saw the sad remains of former travellers dangling from the treetops on either side.

As he went on, Theseus stopped to kill a wild sow which was ravaging the lands just beyond the isthmus, and then on a rocky cliff where the path was narrow, with a sheer drop into the sea, he met Sciron.

'All who pass this way must pay a toll!' cried this brute rudely. 'So down on your knees, like your betters before you, and wash my feet!'

Now Theseus had been warned about Sciron; so he knelt down warily as far from the cliff edge as he could.

Then Sciron shouted: 'My turtle is hungry today – go down and feed it!' And as he spoke he kicked Theseus, meaning to push him over the edge into the sea. But Theseus was ready for him, and caught Sciron by the foot and flung him over his shoulder shouting:

'Go and feed your turtle yourself!' And Sciron went head first down the cliff into the deep water – and never had that turtle eaten a viler man.

Continuing along the coast road, Theseus came to Eleusis where mighty Cercyon wrestled with all comers and crushed their bones in his bear-like hug. But this time he met with a stronger than himself, and presently he lay on his back upon the ground with all his ribs broken.

Whistling merrily at his success so far, Theseus strode on his way towards Athens, and came in the evening to a dark tower standing by the high road.

'Good evening to you, stranger!' cried the master of this place who was called Procrustes. 'You must be weary after a day's travel in the heat of the sun: come in and rest for the night – I insist upon it! All travellers come to partake of my hospitality, and to try my

140

wonderful bed. . . . What, you've never heard of the Bed of Procrustes? Ah, you've much to learn! It is a magic bed, and it fits all comers, great or small, long or short!'

Some say that an old servant, the only man who had really fitted that bed, warned Theseus of what to expect: but certain it is that when bed-time came Theseus turned suddenly upon his host and cried:

'Come, let me fit you to the bed first!' and flinging him down upon it, in spite of his cries and entreaties, he cut off first his feet and then his head which protruded over the ends – for even so had Procrustes done to all his unfortunate guests, lopping them if they were too long, and beating them out if they were too short as if they had been lumps of lead: and no man ever lived after a night on that terrible bed.

And so, having cleared the road of all these miscreants, Theseus came to Athens and strode into the palace of his father, King Aegeus. He did not say at first who he was, nor show the sword and the sandals and only the Witch-wife who now ruled the old king knew him. Aegeus had taken her because she promised to make him the father of many sons who would grow up to defend him against his fifty nephews, the children of Pallas: but once his wife, she kept him in such fear that he did whatever she commanded.

Now she warned him against this young stranger who professed to have done such mighty deeds for the glory of Athens, so that at last he said:

'Young man, I will believe what you say only if you bring me the Cretan Bull which wastes my land at Marathon, and kills my subjects.'

This was the Bull which Heracles had brought from Crete, and which Eurystheus had allowed to escape into Attica some years before.

Off went Theseus, full of confidence, and in spite of its terrible strength and fury, took the Bull by the horns and dragged it back to Athens where he sacrificed it to Athena on the acropolis.

This was more than the Witch-wife could endure, and she mixed a cup of deadly poison for the feast that night, having warned Aegeus that the stranger came to murder him.

Theseus was determined to show the king who he was that very evening, and as he prepared to feast on the best sirloin from the Cretan Bull, he drew the sword to carve it, and laid it on the table in full view while he paused to drink, taking up the poisoned cup.

Aegeus saw the sword and recognized it. With a cry he dashed the cup from his son's hand, so that the poison was spilt on the floor where it bubbled and hissed, eating its way into the solid stone.

Then the Witch-wife fled swiftly from Athens, and Aegeus welcomed Theseus, and declared him to be the heir to his throne.

This did not please the sons of Pallas, and they gathered together their followers, meaning to attack Athens and kill him. But Theseus armed the Athenians, marched out of the city, ambushed his enemies and defeated them utterly.

When he returned to Athens, he was surprised to find the city in mourning.

'What does this mean?' he cried. 'Have I not just returned from a victory?'

Then Aegeus told him, with tears in his eyes, that the envoys from Crete had just arrived to carry off the tribute of seven youths and seven maidens to be fed to the Minotaur, as agreed when King Minos came to take vengeance for the death of his son whom the Bull had killed at Marathon.

When Theseus heard this he exclaimed:

'I will go myself as one of the young men and meet with this Minotaur!'

In vain Aegeus begged him not to be so foolhardy.

'If I slay the Minotaur,' said Theseus, 'it will surely save our country from further tribute – so go I will.'

'Then promise me,' said Aegeus sadly, 'that if you return victorious you will hoist white sails on your ship; but if you do not, the black sails which waft the Athenian youths and maidens to their doom will tell me that you have perished with them.'

Promising this, Theseus set out for Crete, and in due time arrived at Knossus where mighty Minos ruled. Here the victims were kindly entertained, and took part in racing and boxing contests before the king and his court. As he stood panting at the winning post, Minos' daughter, the Princess Ariadne, saw Theseus and straightway loved him.

In great misery at the thought of the fate which awaited him, Ariadne at length thought of a scheme. That night she visited Theseus.

'Ask to go first into the Labyrinth tomorrow,' she instructed him. 'No one has ever found his way out again, but if you can take with you this clue of thread, without it being discovered, and fasten one end to the door when it is closed after you, unrolling it as you go, you may find your way back by means of it. I will be at the door at midnight to let you out if you are successful: but you must take me with you in your flight, for I will not be safe here when it is known that I helped you.'

Theseus and the Minotaur

Theseus did exactly as he was told, and next day entered the Labyrinth with the clue of thread concealed in his hand. When alone, he attached one end to the lintel of the door, and unwound the thread behind him as he traced his way through the winding passages, leading up and down, hither and thither, until he came to the great chamber or cavern in the centre where the dim light from above showed the monster waiting for him.

The Minotaur was a fearsome creature with a great human body and the head and neck of a bull. Its skin was as tough as the toughest leather and a dull yellow colour like brass.

When it saw Theseus, it rushed upon him, bellowing with rage and hunger. Theseus, of course, had no weapon: but as the creature came he smote it over the heart with his fist, and then leapt aside. Bellowing more fiercely than ever, the Minotaur came at him again; and again he smote, and sprang aside. Again and again he did this, until at last the creature began to weaken. Finally, Theseus seized it by the horns and forced back its head, back and back until with a mighty crack the neck broke, and the Minotaur lay dead.

After resting a little, Theseus picked up the end of the thread, and began to follow it back, winding it up as he went. In this way he at length reached the door, where Ariadne was waiting for him.

Swiftly she led him and the other intended victims to their ship; and while it was still dark they crept on board, cut the cables, and stole silently away.

They sailed over the sea towards Athens, and on the way stopped to rest on the lovely island of Naxos. This, as it happened, was specially dear to Dionysus; and there he and the satyrs were feasting and making merry at this time. Dionysus saw Ariadne as she wandered through the leafy woods, and fell in love with her dark, wild beauty. So he cast her into a magic sleep, as he so easily could by turning a spring or a stream into wine; and when she woke, she remembered nothing about Theseus, nor how she came to Naxos, but willingly became the bride of Dionysus.

Theseus, meanwhile, searched the island for her in vain, and at last sailed sadly away, mourning the princess who had saved him. And he was still so lost in melancholy that as he sailed up the Gulf of Aegina and drew near to Athens, he forgot to hang white sails from his mast in place of black, and Aegeus watching for him believed that his son was dead, and cast himself down from the rock of the acropolis, and so died.

In his memory the sea between Greece and Asia Minor is called the Aegean to this very day.

Minos did not pursue Theseus and Ariadne: instead, he set out in search of Daedalus, the clever craftsman who had made the Labyrinth and sworn that no man could ever find his way out of it.

For Daedalus, as soon as he learnt that Theseus had escaped, fled from Crete, knowing that Minos would seek to punish him. No ship would take him, but Daedalus made wings out of feathers fastened together with wax for himself and his son, Icarus.

'Do not go too high,' cautioned Daedalus as they set out. But Icarus, overbold when he found how well he could fly, went too near to the sun. Then the wax melted from his wings and he fell into the sea, which was ever afterwards called the Icarian, and was drowned.

But Daedalus reached land in safety, and no one knew where he had gone. Minos, however, was cunning and the way he set about his quest was this: he carried with him a spiral shell, and gave out that whoever could thread a piece of silk through it should have a vast reward. He felt certain that no one but Daedalus was clever enough to perform this seemingly impossible feat.

His guess proved correct, for when he came to Sicily, King Cocalus took the shell and brought it back next morning with the thread drawn through it.

'Daedalus is here!' exclaimed Minos, and threatened a terrible vengeance unless he was given up to him.

'You are right,' confessed Cocalus. 'He indeed threaded the shell. He fastened the silk to the hind leg of an ant and allowed it to crawl through the spiral drawing the thread after it. I will certainly give him up to you, tomorrow. But tonight come and feast with us.'

Suspecting nothing, Minos agreed readily. But that night as he lay in his bath, the Princess of Sicily, who had fallen in love with Daedalus, poured boiling water down a pipe which the master craftsman had prepared, and Minos was scalded to death.

Meanwhile Theseus had become King of Athens, and when he heard that Minos was dead, he made peace with the new king of Crete, who sent him his sister Phaedra in marriage, so that, in spite of his loss of Ariadne, he still married a daughter of Minos.

Then he ruled in Athens for some time, bringing peace and order to the country; though he was careful to kill any of his cousins whom he could catch, in case they should try to seize the throne.

In time he grew weary of his peaceful life, and longed for further adventures. So he was overjoyed when a message reached him from a young prince called Jason urging him to join an expedition in search of the Golden Fleece from the ram which carried Phrixus and Helle over the sea from Greece many years before.

Eagerly Theseus set out for Iolcus, where Jason was gathering a band of heroes for his quest, among whom the most famous was Heracles himself – free from his servitude at last and longing for a real adventure after the years as a slave to Queen Omphale.

CHAPTER 15

The Quest of the Golden Fleece

Then Jason said: 'A happy lot is mine!
Surely the gods must love me, since that thou
Art come, with me the rough green plain to plough
That no man reaps; yet certes, thou alone
In after days shall be the glorious one
Whom men shall sing of when they name the Fleece,
That bore the son of Athamas from Greece!'

WILLIAM MORRIS : *The Life and Death of Jason*

15. The Quest of the Golden Fleece

JASON'S father was the rightful king of Iolcus, but he was deposed by his brother Pelias, the father of Alcestis, who tried to murder the true heir. Jason, however, was smuggled away to the centaur Chiron who tended him carefully in his mountain cave and trained him in all things suiting a prince.

Pelias, meanwhile, reigned in Iolcus – though not very happily, since an oracle had told him to 'beware of the man with a single sandal,' who would cause his death.

When Jason was grown up, he set out for Iolcus to seek his fortune there, and also to find his father and see if he could come to some agreement with his wicked uncle. On the way he came to a ford through the river Anaurus, where the flood-water was running swiftly. An old woman sitting on the bank, cried out when she saw Jason:

'Good sir, will you carry me across; for you are young and strong, with mighty things before you: but I am too old and feeble to battle with the waters of this river.'

'Certainly I will, good mother!' said Jason kindly, and he lifted the old woman on to his shoulders and entered the stream. It was a difficult crossing, and Jason was almost exhausted when he struggled up the further bank, and he had lost one sandal in the mud of the river's bed.

He set down his ancient burden – and then fell on his knees with amazement and awe. For instead of the old woman, the tall and stately form of a shining Immortal stood before him.

'Do not be afraid, Jason,' she said. 'I am Hera, Queen of Heaven, and your friend. Go forward as you are, and speak the words that I shall put into your mouth, and you will become one of the most famous heroes in all Greece!'

Then she vanished, and Jason went on his way rejoicing, and came to Iolcus in the evening, when Pelias was holding a great feast.

'*The man with one sandal!*' Pelias turned pale and trembled. And when he learnt that this was his nephew, the rightful heir to the throne, he grew even more afraid. But he hid his fear and his hatred, and welcomed Jason warmly.

'I need just such a man to be my counsellor,' he said heartily. 'And to test your wisdom, let me ask you what, supposing you had the power, you would do if you received an oracle that you were to be deposed by a certain one of your subjects?'

'Do?' exclaimed Jason. 'I would command him to bring home the Golden Fleece from Colchis!'

'Excellent advice!' cried Pelias gleefully. 'You are yourself the man, and you must perform this quest!'

'I will indeed,' said Jason quietly. 'And on my return, I shall fulfil the oracle!'

'I shall yield up the throne to you willingly,' said Pelias, '*when* you return with the Golden Fleece!'

Jason sought the help of Argus, a skilled shipbuilder who, with the aid of Athena, made a ship of fifty oars named *Argo* after its maker; and Athena fastened to its prow a magic branch from the oak-tree of Dodona which on occasion could speak, prophesying the future or offering advice.

Next Jason sent heralds throughout Greece calling on the bravest of the young kings and princes to join him on the quest and win immortal fame. From all parts they came trooping to Iolcus – and their names were the names of heroes still remembered, and their children were the heroes who fought at Troy.

First came Heracles, with Hylas his esquire; and then Theseus from Athens, and young Castor and Polydeuces from Sparta, with their wild cousins Idas and Lynceus. Telamon came, and Peleus, who had been the companions of Heracles on his expedition against the Amazons; and the wondrous sons of the North Wind, Zetes and Calais, who had wings growing from their shoulders. Admetus came, and Oileus; Laertes the father of Odysseus; Meleager whose strange tale is yet to be told, and Atalanta the maiden huntress, the follower of Artemis; Nestor, the only Argonaut to fight at Troy, and many another whose names are recorded in the old books.

There came also the divine singer, Orpheus the son of Apollo. When he played upon his lyre and sang sweetly the wild beasts followed him in friendship, and the very trees and flowers bowed to the power of his music. But his heart was filled with sadness, for his wife Eurydice had been bitten by a snake and died. Orpheus followed her to the Land of the Dead, and at the wonder of his music, Charon ferried him across the black River Styx and Cerberus let him pass: even Hades was overcome and gave him back his lost Eurydice – but on condition that he did not look behind to see if she was following, until they stood again in the sunlight. But Orpheus, fearing lest Charon had refused to take her across the Styx, looked back once – and Eurydice was lost to him for ever.

When the heroes were gathered at Iolcus, they hung their shields upon the rails of the *Argo*, and set sail over the dancing waves, while Orpheus played to them, and Tiphys the skilled helmsman guided the ship.

Northwards they sailed, and came to the land of King Cyzicus, who entertained them kindly. When they put to sea again, a great storm took the ship and whirled it around in the darkness till they came to a shore that they did not know, and the inhabitants took them for pirates and attacked them in the night.

Fiercely the battle raged, and the Argonauts (as those who sailed in the *Argo* were called) proved victorious. But what was their grief and horror to find when the day dawned that it was the land of kind King Cyzicus to which they had returned without knowing, and that he and many of his warriors lay dead at their hands.

Sorrowing deeply, they sailed north again, and came to Mysia, not far from Troy, and here Heracles was left behind. For young Hylas went to draw water from a deep pool, and the water nymphs who dwelt in it fell in love with him and drew him down into the depths to live there with them for ever. Heracles searched for him far and wide, and a great wind drove the *Argo* out to sea, so that he was forced to make his way to Colchis over land.

Next the Argonauts visited King Amycus who challenged any guests he had to a boxing match, and killed each in turn. This time he was met in the ring by Polydeuces, who smote him so hard that he fell to the ground and died.

Sailing onwards they landed in Thrace where the blind King Phineus dwelt, a seer nevertheless, who could look through distance.

'Help us,' they begged, 'and tell us what things to do and what to avoid on our way to Colchis.'

'Help you I will,' said Phineus, 'if you first free me from the Harpies!' Then he set a feast before them: but scarcely had they tasted it when down came the two Harpies – terrible winged women with great claws – who carried off the best of the food, and made the rest uneatable.

Then Zetes and Calais, the winged sons of the North Wind, drew their swords and leapt into the air in pursuit of them, and neither was seen again, though the Harpies never more visited King Phineus.

Now fully instructed as to their way, the Argonauts sailed up the Hellespont and came to the Clashing Rocks which guarded the entrance to the Black Sea. These were great floating masses of blue rock which crashed together and crushed any ship which tried to pass them.

Following King Phineus's advice, Jason let loose a heron, and

The Argo

followed it until they drew near to the Rocks, which were half veiled in mist and spray. The bird sped between them: the Rocks crashed together, just touching her tail, and then rebounded on either side.

Immediately Tiphys guided the *Argo* through the gap, while every hero strained at his oar. The ship shot between the Rocks, which clashed together only in time to nip the ornament from the end of the stern. From this time on the Clashing Rocks stood still, for it was fated that once a ship had passed them in safety, they could move no more.

The Argonauts sailed on, into the Black Sea, and along its southern coast, until they came to the River Phasis at its eastern end – the river that still runs red down from the Caucasus in memory of the blood which Prometheus shed there for mankind.

Up the river they went, and came to the city of Colchis where Aeetes was king, the fierce son of Helios, whose sister Circe and daughter Medea were skilled in the black art of witchcraft.

'I will give you the Golden Fleece,' said King Aeetes when Jason told him of their quest, 'if you can yoke my brazen-footed bulls which breathe fire from their nostrils, plough a field with them, and sow it with dragons' teeth!'

That night Jason sat wondering sadly how he was to accomplish this task; for not even Heracles, who had rejoined the Argonauts, could have performed it. Then Medea the witch-maiden came to him, and said:

'I will tell you how to do this thing, and how to take the Fleece, if you will promise to let me sail back to Greece with you and become your wife.'

This Jason swore to do, though he had little liking for witches and witchcraft: and Medea instructed him, and gave him a magic ointment which would make him invulnerable and unburnable for a single day.

In the morning, Jason anointed himself with the ointment and to the amazement of King Aeetes harnessed the bulls without taking any harm. He ploughed the field, and afterwards sowed it with dragons' teeth. But the moment they were sown, the teeth began to grow: and the crop was not corn, but armed men, all eager for war and ready to slay Jason.

But Jason remembered what Medea had told him, and flung the helmet which had held the dragons' teeth into the midst of the armed men. At once they began to fight fiercely among themselves, and before long they all lay dead.

'Tomorrow you shall have the Golden Fleece,' promised Aeetes: but before then he plotted to burn the *Argo* and murder the Argonauts.

Medea again came to Jason, and warned him, and in the night she led him and Orpheus to the magic garden where the Golden Fleece hung on the tree at the world's end, guarded by a dragon – just as the apples of the Hesperides hung in their garden at the world's opposite end.

It was a dim, mysterious place, high-walled and pillared with the dark boles of mighty trees. Through the dappling moonlight Medea the witch-maiden led the way, until they came to the centre where the Golden Fleece shone in the darkness as it hung from a tree round which coiled a dragon larger and more terrible than any in the world.

'Play and sing!' whispered Medea to Orpheus, and she began to murmur a spell while he touched gently on the strings of his lyre and sang in a sweet low voice his Hymn to Sleep:

> *'Sleep, king of gods and men,*
> *Master of all;*
> *Come to mine eyes again,*
> *Come as I call!*
> *Sleep, who may loose and bind*
> *Each as his thrall,*

> *Come to the weary mind,*
>   *Come at my call!*
> *Tamer of toil and woes,*
>   *Healer of all;*
> *Sleep, whence our solace flows,*
>   *Come as I call!*
> *Brother of all mankind,*
>   *Softly you fall*
> *Leaving the world behind;*
>   *Come at my call!*
> *Sleep, lord of all things made,*
>   *Sleep, over all*
> *Let your warm wings be laid,*
>   *Come as I call!'*

As Orpheus sang it seemed that the very garden slept: the wind grew still; the flowers drooped their heads, and not a leaf stirred. The great gleaming dragon slid slowly from the tree, coil within coil, and, resting its terrible head on a bank of sleeping red poppies, slept for the first and last time in its life.

Only by the charms of Medea did Jason himself remain awake, and when he saw that the dragon slept, he drew near and looked up at the shining Fleece.

Then Medea sprinkled the dragon with her magic brew, and whispered to Jason:

'Climb! Climb swiftly up the coils of its back and take down the Fleece, for my charms will not hold it long!'

So Jason, not without dread, mounted that terrible ladder into the great ilex tree and unhooked the Golden Fleece which had hung there ever since Phrixus stripped it from the magic ram; and by its light he found his way through the garden.

For Medea, by her charms, called for Hecate, the Immortal Queen of the Witches, and by her help the moon was darkened, and night closed over Colchis like a black cloak.

Going swiftly by secret paths, they came to the river's edge where the *Argo* lay ready, and they stepped on board, Medea taking with her the young Prince Absyrtus, her brother. Then the Argonauts bent to their oars, and rowed so mightily that the stout pine, hewn on Mount Pelion, bent like withies of hazel in their hands as they sped towards the sea.

But suddenly in the darkness behind them the dragon woke from its charmed sleep, and found that the Golden Fleece had gone. Then it uttered its terrible voice, a hissing and a groaning cry so fearful that all the people of Colchis woke at the sound and the women clutched their children to them and shivered with fear.

King Aeetes, however, guessed what had happened and, dark though it was, launched a swift ship and set off in pursuit of the Argonauts.

'Row! Row!' cried Medea, when she heard the dragon's cry. 'My father's ships are very swift, and there will be no mercy for any of us if we are taken!'

So they bent to their oars again, and the water was churned into foam as they sped down the Phasis and came with the dawning out into the Black Sea and away to the west.

Before noon they saw the tall ship of King Aeetes drawing up behind them, and in the dim distance others of the Colchian fleet coming in pursuit.

In vain Orpheus played on his lyre to cheer them as they laboured at the oars; and in vain did the winds fill the *Argo's* sail. The great ships of Colchis drew nearer, ever nearer.

Then Medea the Witch did a dreadful thing, while the Argonauts looked on in horror, but dared do nothing because it was she who had saved them, and Jason had sworn to marry her and bring her unhurt to Greece.

She took her brother, the boy prince Absyrtus, and killed him with a sharp sword in plain view of his father, King Aeetes. Then she cut him in pieces and cast the pieces into the sea, for she knew that Aeetes would stop to gather them up so as to give his son due and honourable burial – without which, so the Greeks believed, his ghost could find no rest in the Realm of Hades or in the Fields of Elysium.

All happened as she expected. King Aeetes, standing weeping at the prow of his ship, uttered a terrible curse upon Medea and upon all who sailed in the *Argo*; then he halted his fleet to gather up the remains of his son, and the Argonauts sailed on and were lost to view in the wide sea; nor did Aeetes and his fleet find them again.

But Jason bowed his head with shame and misery: for what Medea had done was terrible and not to be forgiven; but now he was bound to her, and had sworn to marry a witch who would bring him no good fortune in the end.

CHAPTER 16

The Return of the Argonauts

Forth from thy father's home
   Thou camest, O heart of fire,
To the Dark Blue Rocks, to the clashing foam,
   To the seas of thy desire:

Till the Dark Blue Bar was crossed;
   And, lo, by an alien river
Standing, thy lover lost,
   Void-armed for ever.

EURIPIDES : *Medea* (Translated by Gilbert Murray)

16. The Return of the Argonauts

UNDER the dark shadow of Medea's crime, the Argonauts sailed away into the mysterious distance to the north and west of the Black Sea, and presently a storm overtook the ship, spun it round, and carried it through the darkness, no one knew whither. But, as they were driven between islands and the high cliffs of what might be a great river's mouth, the magic branch of Dodona set at the prow spoke to them:

'You who have sinned so deeply cannot escape the wrath of Zeus, nor come to your native land again, until you have visited the Island of Aeaea: for Circe the Enchantress alone can purify you. But the way thither is long and terrible such as no man has sailed before.'

The Argonauts cried out with fear at that eerie voice; then the wind took them again, and darkness closed about them, and they sailed on and on, they knew not where nor whither.

On and ever on they went, sometimes rowing and sometimes blown by the wind; and Orpheus played upon his lyre. Up the river, up and up into the cold north they went; and at length, rowing against the stream until it grew too shallow for them, they landed and carried the *Argo* on their shoulders.

Of that terrible journey little has been told, nor could any of the Argonauts say for certain where they went. But when they were ready to die with weariness, they came to another river flowing north-west and floated down it to a sea where the sun was dimmed by mists, and icicles gathered and hung from the mast and the spars of the *Argo*, and when they landed they saw great white bears.

There were also wild men in those parts; the Laestrygonians, who wore skins and fought with battle-axes, singing wild songs of Odin and the halls of Valhalla, and they foamed at the mouth with berserk rage while they fought.

Shivering with cold, the Argonauts rowed quickly past these frozen coasts where the sun shone at midnight, but did not warm them even at midday. They came then into the Northern Sea and past the land beyond the North Wind, the Ultimate Islands, which in later days were called Britain. Still on they sailed into the Western Ocean where it was said that the Land of Atlantis had sunk beneath the waters not long before; and then south across a stormy bay until at last the sun grew warmer, and one day Heracles cried:

'My friends, we have come back to the known world again! Over yonder stand the two pillars which I set up to mark the entrance to our sea, and to the southward Titan Atlas holds up the heavens upon his mountain peak while below is the Garden of the Hesperides!'

He told them of his quest for the golden apples, and they marvelled at all he had seen and done. They marvelled still more when he led them to the Garden itself: for there lay the serpent Ladon, the tip of its tail still moving, though it was fifteen years since Heracles had slain it with his poisoned arrow.

The Argonauts rested in that fragrant land until their strength and health came back to them; and they raised altars and sacrificed to the Immortals in gratitude for bringing them safely through such dangers.

Then they sailed on once more, over the blue Mediterranean Sea, passing between Corsica and Sardinia, and came to Aeaea, the little island where dwelt Medea's aunt, the enchantress Circe.

Now if they had come along, Circe would have worked some evil enchantment upon the Argonauts, but when she saw Medea she hastened to make them welcome. And when Medea told of her crime and the command of Zeus, spoken by the magic bough, she purified them all of the blood of Absyrtus, and sent them on their way with a load lifted from their hearts.

But their adventures were not yet ended. Near to Aeaea was another island, which is now called Capri, and on it lived the Sirens. These were once maidens who had played with Persephone the Divine Maiden in that fair field of Enna in Sicily from which Hades carried her away to be Queen of the Dead. They had prayed to have wings so as to go through the world in search of her, and Demeter granted their wish. But in some strange way they turned to evil, and so were doomed to live on their beautiful island and lure sailors to their death. They still had wings, but they had the claws and tails of birds also, and they sang so sweetly that no man who heard could resist their singing. For whoever heard that wonderful song forgot all else, plunged into the waves, and swam to shore: and there the Sirens would catch him with their sharp claws, and tear him to pieces. But it was fated that if any one could resist their singing and sail away unhurt, then the Sirens would meet their end.

When the Argonauts drew near and heard the wondrous song of the Sirens, they bent eagerly to their oars, longing only to land on that island and listen to the enchantment of their singing. But

A Siren

Medea knew what fate lay in store for any who set foot on the isle of the Sirens, and she cried to Orpheus:

'Divine musician, play on your lyre and sing for our lives! Surely you, the son of Apollo, can sing even more sweetly than these creatures of beauty and evil!'

Orpheus played as never before, and sang such a strain as that which had ravished the ears of Hades and drawn his lost Eurydice from the dead. And the Argonauts listened to his singing, and forgot the Sirens, and were able to turn the ship from that fatal island and sail for the south. All, that is, except Butes, who sprang into the sea and swam towards the Sirens: but Aphrodite took pity on him, and carried him away in time, to become a priest at her shrine in the south of Sicily.

As for the Sirens, as mortal men had withstood their song, Fate came upon them and, like the Sphinx when Oedipus solved her riddle, they flung themselves down from their rock and died. All except two, who had not joined in the song that day, and so lived to sing still, to lure sailors to their doom until Odysseus passed that way on his return from Troy.

On sailed the Argonauts, seeing many other wonders. They passed the cave where lurked Scylla the many-headed monster; though on that day she slept. They passed the whirlpool of Charybdis in safety, and the Floating Islands which flung out burning rocks, and the island where Helios, the Sun Titan, kept his milk-white kine with horns of gold, and the happy land of the Phaeacians.

Here they tarried awhile, and the wedding feast of Jason and

Medea was celebrated. For while they rested in Phaeacia the ships of King Aeetes arrived, and the Phaeacian king said that while he was ready to give up the daughter of Aeetes, he would defend the wife of Jason! So the Colchians failed of their design, and as Aeetes had sworn to slay them all if they returned without Medea, they settled down and formed a new kingdom of their own next door to Phaeacia.

The *Argo* sailed again soon after the wedding, and a storm took it as it rounded Cape Malea at the south of Greece, and drove it across the sea to Crete.

Now in the early days the smith of the Immortals, Hephaestus, had fashioned for the first King Minos a man of brass called Talos, a giant who ran round the island three times in every day and sank any ship which drew near, by hurling great stones on it.

Minos knew how to control this monster, as did all the kings of Crete until the last Minos had sailed away in pursuit of Daedalus after Theseus killed the Minotaur and escaped from the Labyrinth. But Deucalion, the new king, did not know how to deal with Talos, and he himself had escaped with difficulty from Crete to join the Argonauts and sail with Jason.

The monster Talos was now quite out of control, and Crete was cut off by him from the outer world, for he still ran round the island three times a day, pelting any ship which drew near. At other times he made himself red hot by lying in a bath of fire, and then burned up all that he touched.

Deucalion now begged the other Argonauts to help him to destroy Talos, but not even Heracles could think how to do it.

Then Medea said: 'Only with the help of magic, and by great guile can we overcome Talos. But do just as I say, and all will be well.'

So when she had instructed them, they drew near to the island, and presently Talos appeared, glowing red with heat, a great rock ready in his hands.

Then first of all Orpheus played his sweetest strains, so that Talos paused uncertain, while Medea spoke to him:

'Noble Talos,' said she, 'I am Medea the Witch, and I can make you king of the world, and ruler even over the Immortals, if you will make me your queen.'

'How can you do that?' rumbled the giant.

'Is it not true,' asked Medea, 'that you have but one vein in your body, running from neck to heel, and that instead of blood it contains ichor, the liquid which flows in the veins of the Immortals?'

Talos nodded doubtfully, and Medea went on: 'Although ichor flows in your vein, you are not immortal: but I, by my magic arts, can make you so, if you will let me land safely with one follower.'

Talos agreed to this, and Medea landed, with Poeas, who was the smallest man among the Argonauts. If Heracles or Theseus had tried to step ashore, Talos might have suspected some plot, but little Poeas could arouse nobody's suspicion and Talos did not know that he was one of the most skilful archers living – nor that Heracles had lent him his bow and arrows.

Once on the shore, Poeas wandered away and settled himself quietly out of sight among the rocks. But Medea took a sickle with a blade of brass and began to gather herbs with which to make a magic brew. She mixed them in a cauldron, squeezing the milk-white juices from them, and singing an incantation. Next she stripped off her clothes, bound up her jet-black hair with wreaths of ivy, and bent over the cauldron, chopping the herbs and roots and singing wildly.

Talos was fascinated by the lovely witch and her magic brew; he drew nearer and nearer, but still mistrustfully. For in his heel was set a brass nail, like a stopper, which prevented the ichor from escaping, and he feared greatly lest anyone should touch it.

Medea had soon brewed her magic draught, and now she held it out to Talos in a cup: 'Drink!' she said. 'It is the wine of Immortality!'

And Talos was so bewitched that he took the cup and drained it. But it brought to him only a great drowsiness so that presently he was reeling about as if drunken, but still determined not to fall asleep lest any one should draw out the nail.

Then Poeas rose, fitted an arrow to the bow, and shot with such skill that the arrow struck the nail in Talos's heel and loosened it so that it fell to the ground and the ichor gushed out.

At this Talos cried aloud and groped for the nail: but the magic brew was too strong for him, and he could not find it, and presently he lay cold and still – an image of brass, nothing more.

After this the Argonauts landed in Crete and were entertained lavishly by Deucalion before setting sail for Iolcus which they reached without further adventures.

There they parted, though very soon a number of them met again for the adventure of the Calydonian Boar which, at his home-coming, Meleager found was ravaging his land.

Jason did not live to enjoy the old age of honour which was his due. He died childless and alone, with the curse of Aeetes upon him, for there was no purification which could free him wholly from the guilt of Absyrtus's murder.

When he returned to Iolcus he found his old father was dead, and Pelias still ruling there. Jason was content to let him remain as king for the rest of his life, but Medea the Witch wished to be queen. So while Jason was away at Calydon she said to the daughters of Pelias: 'You know my magic powers: would you like to learn from me how to make your father young again?'

At first they mistrusted her. So Medea mixed a magic brew in a great cauldron; and she took an old ram, so old it could hardly walk. She killed it, cut it into small pieces, and threw them into the cauldron. And at once there leapt out of it a young lamb, strong and bold and frisky.

Then the daughters of Pelias doubted her no longer. They took their old father, killed him and cut him up. But when they placed the pieces in the cauldron, Pelias remained as dead as ever – for Medea had not taught them her evil spell.

But when the people of Iolcus discovered what Medea had done, they banished her and Jason, who wandered away to Corinth. There Jason had a chance of a new kingdom: for the king had only one child, the maiden Glauce.

'You shall marry her and rule this land,' said the king, 'if you will send away that evil witch, Medea.'

Jason, who had never loved Medea, and by now hated her for her cruelty and wickedness, consented to this, and Medea appeared to agree, but she gave Glauce a magic wedding dress which burned her to death the moment she put it on, and burned her father also who tried to save her.

Then Medea killed her own and Jason's two sons, and fled away in a chariot drawn by flying dragons.

But Jason became an outcast, and in his wanderings he returned to where the old ship *Argo* was drawn up on the beach.

'You are my only friend,' he said sadly as he sat down to rest in the shade of the ship. There he fell asleep, and while he slept the front of the ship, grown rotten with age, fell suddenly on his head and killed him.

CHAPTER 17

Meleager and Atalanta

The maid has vowed e'en such a man to wed
As in the course her swift feet can outrun,
But whoso fails herein, his days are done . . .
    Behold, such mercy Atalanta gives
To those that long to win her loveliness.

WILLIAM MORRIS : *The Earthly Paradise*

17. Meleager and Atalanta

MELEAGER the Argonaut bore a charmed life. For when he was but seven days old the Three Fates appeared to his mother, Queen Althaea of Calydon, as she lay in the big shadowy room of the palace lit only by the flickering firelight.

The Fates were the three daughters of Zeus and Themis who presided over the fate of man: and when Althaea saw them, they were busy with the life-thread of her son Meleager.

One Fate spun the thread of life, and that was Clotho, and she was spinning busily, while Lachesis stood by with her rod to measure it. The third Fate, Atropos, held the shears, and she said to her sisters:

'Why trouble you to spin and measure? As soon as that brand on the hearth yonder is consumed to ashes, I must cut the thread with my shears, and Meleager's life will be ended!'

When Althaea heard this, she leapt out of bed, snatched the burning brand from the hearth and put out the flames. Then she hid it away in a secret chest of which she alone possessed the key.

'Now I defy you, Fates!' she cried. 'I have but to preserve that brand, and my son will live for ever!'

Then the three sisters smiled at Althaea, and there was a secret knowledge in their eyes which made her afraid. After that, they vanished, and only the charred brand in her secret chest remained to prove that she had not dreamed it all.

Years passed and Meleager grew into a brave young prince and went with Jason and the other Argonauts in quest of the Golden Fleece. On his return to Calydon he found a savage wild boar ravaging the land, destroying all the crops and killing any who tried to withstand it.

This great boar, with its wonderful tusks and hide was not to be slain by one man, and Meleager sent for his friends among the Argonauts, Heracles and Theseus, Peleus and Telamon, Admetus, and Nestor, Jason himself, and several others – but in particular he sent for the maiden huntress Atalanta. For Meleager had fallen in love with her during their voyage on the *Argo*, and still hoped to persuade her to be his wife, though she had sworn never to marry.

Atalanta was a princess of Arcadia, but when she was born her father, King Iasus of Tegea, disappointed that she was not a boy, had cast her out onto the wild mountain side. Here a she-bear found the baby and brought her up among her own cubs; and Artemis, the Immortal Huntress, trained her in all matters of the chase and allowed her to join with the nymphs who were her followers.

Now she came eagerly to Calydon, and was welcomed by Meleager and the other Argonauts. But Phexippus and Toxeus, Meleager's uncles, the beloved brothers of Queen Althaea, protested when they saw Atalanta.

'It is an insult,' they cried, 'to expect us to go hunting in company with a woman! She should be weaving at her loom, not mixing with men and pretending to skill in the chase!'

Meleager angrily bade them be silent, and the hunt began, with Atalanta walking at his side – a lovely maiden, simple and boyish with hair falling to her shoulders, a tunic of skins, and a long bow in her hand.

'How happy will the man be who can call himself your husband!' sighed Meleager.

Atalanta blushed and frowned, saying: 'Never by my free will shall any man do so. . . . But let us give all our thoughts to this fierce boar which we seek.'

They had not far to go, for in a wooded dell overhung by willows and dense with smooth sedge and marshy rushes, the Boar was roused. Out he came in a fury, levelling the young trees and bushes as he went, and scattering the dogs to right and left.

Echion flung a spear, but in his eagerness pinned only the trunk of a maple tree. Jason hurled his weapon, but it too passed over the Boar's back. Squealing with rage, while its eyes flashed fire, it rushed upon young Nestor – who would never have lived to fight at Troy if he had not swung himself quickly into a tree out of harm's way.

Then Telamon rushed at the Boar with his spear ready, but he tripped over an unseen root, and was barely rescued by Peleus. As he staggered to his feet, the Boar charged: and it would have gone hard with them both if Atalanta had not, with quiet skill and courage, drawn her bow-string and sent an arrow into the Boar's head close to its ear. Yet even her skill could not send an arrow right to the brain, so hard was the creature's skin.

There was no one so delighted as Meleager. 'See!' he cried, 'the Princess Atalanta has taught us men how to hunt boars, and has smitten the creature with a mortal wound!'

Ancaeus, who had also objected to a woman joining in the hunt, was furious at this. 'Watch!' he cried, 'I'll show you how a man settles wild boars! No pin-pricks from a woman will do it.

A battle axe is the weapon, and Artemis herself could not defend this Boar against me!'

So saying, he rushed at the maddened creature and struck – but struck short. The next moment he was on his back, and the Boar had killed him. In an effort to save him, Peleus flung his spear; but Eurytion sprang forward at the same moment with his weapon raised, and the spear meant for the Boar passed through his body.

Theseus also launched a spear, but aimed high in his excitement and transfixed only the bough of an oak tree. But Meleager's aim was true, and the Boar fell to the ground, and he dispatched it with a blow of his second spear.

Then the hunters shouted with joy, and stood around gazing in awe at the great creature covering so large a patch of ground. Meleager knelt down and set to work skinning the Boar, and when he had done so, he turned to Atalanta and presented her with the head and hide.

'Lady,' he said, 'take the spoils and share my glory with me. You were the first to wound the Boar and more honour belongs to you than to me or any other one of us.'

Then the rest envied Atalanta her prize, and Phexippus, Meleager's uncle, could not contain his fury:

'This is the worst insult of all!' he shouted. 'My nephew won the skin, and if he did not want it, he should have given it to me, as the most noble person present! As for you, you shameless girl, do not think that we will suffer this dishonour. You may have bewitched Meleager with your beauty, but it has no power on us!'

At that he and his brother Toxeus seized hold of Atalanta and tore the spoils from her as roughly and insultingly as they could.

Then Meleager lost his temper completely. With a yell of rage he drew his sword and stabbed Phexippus to the heart. Next he turned upon Toxeus, who tried to defend himself, but soon lay dead beside his brother. Then the party set out sadly for the city, carrying the dead bodies with them, while Atalanta held the head and hide of the Calydonian Boar.

When Queen Althaea saw that her two brothers were dead, her grief knew no bounds. But when she learnt that Meleager had killed them, her grief turned to a wild frenzy of fury and revenge.

Suddenly she remembered the charred brand which she had snatched from the hearth when Meleager was a baby. Rushing to her room, she drew it from the chest and cast it upon the fire, where it caught quickly, flamed up, and was soon reduced to ashes.

Now Meleager was feasting his friends in the hall and drinking the health of Atalanta. All at once the cup fell from his hand, and with a cry he sank to the ground, writhing there in agony. He cried out that he was burning from within, and that he wished the Boar had killed him instead of Ancaeus; and in a few minutes he lay dead.

Then there was mourning throughout Calydon, and the great Boar Hunt which had begun so happily ended in sadness and tragedy. Queen Althaea, when she came to herself after her frenzy of grief and rage, was so horrified at what she had done that she hanged herself.

But one happy result came of the Calydonian Boar Hunt, for Heracles fell in love with Meleager's sister, the Princess Deianira. Now King Oeneus had promised her, against her will, to the River Achelous, who came to him in the shape of a fierce man and threatened to destroy his land if he refused his suit.

When Heracles heard this, he went to the river bank and cried: 'Noble River Achelous, we both love the same maiden! Come forth, then, in whatever form you choose, and fight with me for her!'

Achelous accepted this daring challenge, took the form of a great, savage bull, and charged at Heracles. But that mighty hero was experienced by now in such contests, and seizing Achelous by one horn he snapped it off at the root. Then Achelous submitted, and Deianira became the wife of Heracles, and they lived happily for a while at Calydon, helping Oeneus until his young son Tydeus should be old enough to rule.

The other hunters had, meanwhile, returned to their homes; but the beautiful Atalanta, famous now for her part in the battle with the Boar, was claimed by her father, King Iasus.

She settled at his home, at Tegea in Arcadia, but still refused to marry. .

'But I have no son to succeed me!' lamented Iasus. 'Choose whom you will as husband, and you shall rule here jointly, and your children after you.'

'I will obey you, as a daughter should,' said Atalanta at length. 'But on one condition. Every prince who comes as my suitor must race with me. Only he that is swifter of foot than I shall be my husband. But, those whom I beat in the race shall forfeit their lives.'

Iasus was forced to agree, and sent heralds throughout Greece proclaiming that whoever could outrun his daughter Atalanta, should marry her and be king of Tegea; but that those who lost the race would lose their heads also.

*'Heracles drew his bow and shot Nessus with
one of his poisoned arrows'*

Several princes felt confident that they could run faster than
any girl, and came to try their fortune. But each of them in turn
left his head to decorate the finishing-post on King Iasus's racecourse.

Soon no one else dared to try, and Atalanta smiled happily, for
she was determined never to marry.

At length her cousin Prince Melanion fell in love with her and
knowing that he could not surpass her in running, he prayed to
Aphrodite, the Immortal Queen of Love and Beauty, to assist him.

Aphrodite was angry with Atalanta for scorning love and refusing
to marry, and she granted Melanion her help. She lent him the
three golden apples which Heracles had brought from the Garden
of the Hesperides, and which Athena had passed on to her for this
very purpose.

Then Melanion presented himself in Tegea, and in spite of all
King Iasus's warnings, insisted on racing for Atalanta.

The course was set, and the race began. At first Atalanta let
Melanion gain on her, for she knew that she was twice as fast
a runner as he was. When he saw her shadow drawing close to

him, he dropped a golden apple which rolled in front of her.

Atalanta saw the apple, and was filled with the desire to possess this wonderful thing. So she stopped quickly, picked it up and then sped after Melanion, certain of overtaking him easily. And so she did, but as she drew level, he dropped a second apple, and again she could not resist the temptation, but stopped and picked it up.

Once more she sped after Melanion, and once more she overtook him. But a third apple rolled across in front of her, and at the sight of its beauty and wonder, Atalanta forgot all else, and stopped to gather it.

'I can still overtake him!' she thought, and sped on like the wind. But Melanion touched the winning-post a moment before she reached him, and so he won her for his wife. And in a little while they were living happily together as king and queen of Tegea, with a small son to be king after them.

Heracles and Deianira were happy too, living quietly at Calydon, though in time they were forced to move again, as Heracles in a quarrel struck a cousin of the king's so hard that he died. So they bade farewell to Oeneus and set out on their travels towards the north of Greece.

Now on their way, they came to the river Evenus where lived the centaur called Nessus who hated Heracles. This centaur was accustomed to carry travellers across the river on his back; and when he had taken Deianira nearly to the other side, he suddenly turned down stream, and began to carry her away. She screamed for help, and Heracles drew his bow and shot Nessus with one of his poisoned arrows.

As he lay dying on the river bank, Nessus gasped:

'Lady Deianira, I will tell you a secret. When I am dead keep a little of the blood from my wound, and if ever you find that Heracles has ceased to love you, soak a robe in it and give it him to wear: that will make him love you more than ever before.'

Then he died, and Deianira did as she was instructed, believing that Nessus had told her this to show how sorry he was for what he had tried to do. But she did not tell Heracles.

After this they came safely to Trachis, a hundred miles north of Thebes, and were welcomed by King Ceyx. And there they settled down safely and happily.

But for Heracles there was never to be any real peace or rest, and indeed he did not wish it, for very soon he set out on a new and dangerous expedition.

CHAPTER 18

The First Fall of Troy

Where Heracles wandered, the lonely
  Bow-bearer, he lent him his hands
For the wrecking of one land only,
Of Ilion, Ilion only,
  Most hated of lands!

EURIPIDES: *Trojan Women* (Translated by Gilbert Murray)

18. The First Fall of Troy

WHEN Heracles rescued Hesione, daughter of the King of Troy, from the sea monster, he was not able to take the reward with him, as he was still labouring for Eurystheus of Tiryns. But when his labours were ended, he sent to King Laomedon for the two magic horses which he had won.

Laomedon, however, had never been known to keep his word; and this time he did not depart from his usual habits. He sent two horses, it is true, but instead of those which Zeus had given to King Tros in return for Ganymede, which were magic horses who could run like the wind over the sea or the standing corn, he sent two chargers of ordinary, mortal breed.

Heracles vowed vengeance against Laomedon; but it was only when he came to settle at Trachis that he was able to set about gathering followers for this expedition of his own.

Leaving his young wife Deianira safely at Trachis, Heracles set out, accompanied by his nephew Iolaus, to seek for companions; and he turned first of all to his old friends Telamon and Peleus who had been his companions on his expedition against the Amazons, as well as during the Quest of the Golden Fleece and at the Calydonian Boar Hunt.

Telamon lived at Salamis near Athens, and had married not long before. While Heracles was his guest a baby son was born to Telamon's queen, and was named Ajax.

Telamon and Peleus sat feasting with their guest when the baby boy was brought in for his father to see, and Heracles cried:

'By the will of Zeus this son of yours shall be a strong and mighty hero. See, I wrap about him the skin of the lion, the first of my many labours: may Ajax prove as bold as a lion and as strong and fearless!'

When the rejoicings were ended, Telamon gathered a fleet of six ships, and with Heracles in command they set sail for Troy. Now with Heracles were Telamon himself, Peleus, Oicles, Iolaus and Deimachus, each in command of a ship.

They sailed quickly across the Aegean Sea and came unexpectedly to the land of Troy, where they anchored the ships, and leaving Oicles and his company to guard them, marched for the city itself.

King Laomedon was not prepared for this sudden invasion, but he armed as many men as he could, and made a forced march by secret ways to the place where the ships were moored.

He took old Oicles by surprise, and in the desperate battle which followed, Oicles was killed, and his men only saved the ships by entering them and putting out to sea.

Well pleased with this beginning, Laomedon marched back to Troy by his secret route, and after a brisk fight with some of Heracles' men, got into the city and barred the gates.

Heracles surrounded Troy and settled down to besiege it. But on this occasion the siege did not last long, for the walls, although built by the Immortals Poseidon and Apollo, were not themselves immortal since they had been helped in their work by a mortal, Aeacus, the father of Peleus and Telamon.

The first breach in the wall was made by Telamon, who knew from his father where the weakest place was to be found; and through the gap he rushed with his followers, while Heracles was still trying to storm the citadel. Very soon Heracles was in also, and the battle raged fiercely until King Laomedon lay dead, shot by the deadly arrows, and by him all his sons except the youngest. His name was Podarces, and he was spared because he had tried to persuade Laomedon to behave honestly and give up the magic horses.

When the walls were levelled with the ground, Heracles summoned before him all the captives. Among them was the Princess Hesione whom he had rescued from the sea monster, and who should have become his wife.

'But she is now a prize of conquest,' said Heracles, 'and I will give this princess as a slave to my friend King Telamon; and in memory of what might have been, I will give her a bride-gift. Princess Hesione, you may choose one of these captives to go free.'

Then Hesione, weeping for the death of her father and brothers, knelt before Heracles and said:

'Great hero of Greece, spare my brother Podarces and let him go free to rebuild Troy and reign there over my father's people.'

Heracles replied: 'Podarces has been spared, but he is my slave, the spoil of war. Yet I will grant your request, but you must buy him from me: you must pay something in ransom, if it be no more than your veil!'

Then Hesione plucked the veil from her head and with it bought the freedom of Podarces; and ever afterwards his name was changed to Priam, which means 'ransomed'.

When Heracles and his followers had sailed away, Priam gathered all the Trojans together and built the new city of Troy, a great, strong place with mighty walls and gates. And he married a wife called Hecuba, and they had many sons, the most famous of whom were Hector and Paris.

Meanwhile as Heracles and his little fleet of ships were sailing back towards Greece, his old enemy Hera could contain her hatred no longer. She knew that the Giants were stirring in their caves in the wild north and might make war on the Immortals at any moment; and she knew as well as Zeus himself that only with the help of Heracles could they be conquered, yet in her jealousy she made one last effort to destroy the son of Alcmena.

She called to her Hypnos, the spirit of Sleep, own brother to Death, and child of Night:

'Sleep, master of mortals and Immortals,' said Hera, 'go swiftly now to the couch of great Zeus, and lull his shining eyes to rest – for he has great need of you!'

Hypnos went to where Zeus lay, and spread his gentle wings over him, so that presently the great King of the Immortals slumbered peacefully.

Hera thereupon let loose the storm-winds from the north, and a great tempest descended upon the sea, and drove the ships before it, scudding over the waves and among the rocky islands, in deadly peril every moment.

Then indeed Heracles might have met his fate if Zeus had not awoken in time. When he saw what had happened, his wrath was very terrible. He took Hera and hung her by the wrists from heaven, with an iron anvil hanging from each foot: and when Hephaestus tried to set her free, Zeus took him by the leg and flung him out of Olympus, down on to the island of Lemnos, where he was found by the sea-nymph Thetis.

Zeus ordered the storm-winds back to the island where Aeolus kept them in a cave until they were needed, and a great calm fell upon the Aegean Sea, just in time to save Heracles from being wrecked upon the rocky island of Cos.

But scarcely had Heracles and his companions landed, tired and exhausted, when King Eurypylus who ruled the island attacked him with a large force: for Hera had already sent him word that a band of pirates were about to land on the island.

The weary Greeks were defeated and scattered in the darkness, including Heracles himself. He was hotly pursued, since Eurypylus was particularly anxious to kill the captain of the pirates, and only escaped by hiding in a cottage. Here lived a large, fat woman who fled away into the darkness when she saw Heracles; and he had just time to dress himself in her clothes and bend over the cradle, when the men arrived at the door.

Seeing only the old woman, they went on towards the centre of the island, and Heracles was able to rest and eat until his strength came back to him.

In the morning he gathered his scattered followers, attacked the Coans, and defeated them, killing King Eurypylus. They remained on the island of Cos for some time, refitting their ships before setting sail for Greece and resting after the battle.

Then one day the Immortal Queen of Wisdom and Strategy, Pallas Athena, came suddenly to Heracles.

'Up, most mighty of mortals!' she cried. 'The day has come for which you were born! For the Giants are loose upon the earth, and without the aid of the mortal hero appointed, even the Immortals cannot withstand them!'

Then Athena took him up and carried him across the sea to the dread plain of fiery Phlegra, where the ground smokes and trembles like the crater of a volcano.

CHAPTER 19

The Battle of the Giants

When on the smoky Phlegran field
  Immortals fight the Giant clan,
Know that their lives shall only yield
  To arrows of a mortal man;

And he, his Labours done, shall bide
  For ever in Olympian ease;
And Hebe waits to be the bride
  Of the Immortal, Heracles!

PINDAR: *First Nemean Ode* (Translated by R.L.G.)

19. The Battle of the Giants

THE invasion so long dreaded and expected came suddenly. For Earth had made the Giants and hidden them away in great caves far to the north of Greece until the moment came when they were strong and fierce enough to assail heaven.

Then, as soon as Zeus seemed very much engaged in quarrelling with Hera and tossing Hephaestus out of heaven, the Giants came down into Greece and got ready to attack the Immortals.

They camped on the volcanic plain of Phlegra, and the first thing they did was to capture the golden-horned cattle of the Sun-Titan, Helios, and carry them off for food.

The leader of the Giants was called Alcyoneus, and he was immortal so long as he stayed in the land of Phlegra. And at first they did so, attacking Olympus by hurling huge rocks and burning oak-trees.

'We cannot slay the Giants unaided!' cried Zeus. 'So much the Titan Prometheus told me. A mortal must kill them, when we have overcome them – the greatest hero in all Greece, if he be brave and strong enough. And that man is Heracles! For this he was born, my son and the son of a mortal woman. For this he has been trained all these years, and has accomplished such labours as no mortal did before, nor shall do again!'

Then he sent Athena to fetch Heracles. But meanwhile the words of Zeus had reached Earth, and she, fearing lest all her plots should come to nought, bade the Giants seek for a magic herb which would render them proof even against the mortal hero.

Zeus learnt of this, and knowing that there was only a single plant of the magic herb, he instructed Athena to help Heracles in his search for it; and to prevent the Giants from finding it first, he ordered Helios to keep the Sun-chariot at home, and Selene the Moon-chariot also, that there might be no light on the earth save the feeble glimmer of the stars.

In this strange, unnatural twilight Heracles found the herb; and when the sun rose again the great battle began.

Earth sent out a breath of fire from the subterranean caves of Phlegra, and the Giant King spoke in a terrible voice, crying:

'Giants, now is the hour! Tear up the mountains and hurl them at Olympus! Pull down the Immortals from their high thrones and bind them with our kinsmen the Titans in Tartarus! And one of you shall have Aphrodite to be his wife, and another shall have Artemis – while I, your king, claim Hera as my prize!'

The rocks hurtled through the air, and whole hill tops were torn away in the struggle.

First of all, by Athena's direction, Heracles shot Alcyoneus with a poisoned arrow. But as soon as he fell to the ground he began to recover.

'Quick!' cried Athena. 'He cannot die so long as he remains in Phlegra! Drag him away into another country!'

So Heracles hoisted the still-breathing Giant on to his back and staggered with him over the border. There he flung him down and killed him with repeated blows of his club.

Returning to the battle, Heracles found that the Giant Porphyrion had assumed the lead and tried to carry off Hera. They had now piled up great rocks, and were fighting on the slopes of Olympus. Eros, the Lord of Love, wounded this Giant with his arrow, but the only result was to make him fall most desperately in love with Hera. This, at least, drew him from the battle, and when he saw his chance, Zeus felled him with a thunderbolt; and Heracles, returning just in time, settled him with an arrow.

The battle grew fast and furious now, and Heracles stood by to send in the shaft of death whenever an Immortal had laid a Giant low. When, for example, Apollo had smitten one in the eye with his bright shaft, or Hecate had burnt another with her torches; when Hephaestus had laid low a Giant with missiles of red-hot metal, or Dionysus brought down an enemy with his magic thyrsus, or Ares the War Lord smote home with his terrible spear.

Finally the remnants of the Giants fled in terror towards the south of Greece, all except the two greatest ones, Ephialtes and Otus. These made a last, desperate assault; and first of all they captured Ares himself and shut him up in a brass jar.

Then they piled Mount Ossa on top of Mount Pelion, and started climbing up towards Heaven, Ephialtes vowing that Hera should be his prize, and Otus that he would marry the maiden Artemis.

In this emergency even Heracles was powerless to help, for these two Giants could only be killed by their own kind – neither man nor Immortal could do anything against them.

They were easily tricked, however, being stupid as Giants usually were; and when Zeus sent a message that he would give up Artemis to the most deserving of the two, they began to quarrel violently. While they were arguing Artemis turned herself into a white doe and ran suddenly between them. Each, eager to prove that *he* was

The Battle with the Giants

at least the better marksman, hurled a spear at it. Both missed their mark, but each spear pierced the other Giant to the heart. Thus each was struck by his own kind, and so they died, and were chained to a pillar in Tartarus with fetters made of living vipers.

Meanwhile the other Giants fled, pursued closely by the Immortals and Heracles. One was caught by Poseidon, who broke off a piece of the island of Cos and buried him under it, making the Rock of Nisyros which still sticks up out of the sea nearby.

The rest came to Arcadia, and at a place called Bathos the Immortals surrounded them and the final battle took place. There Hermes, wearing the Helmet of Invisibility which he had borrowed from Hades, struck down a Giant; and Ares, whom Hermes had just rescued from the brazen pot, wielded his spear to good effect, while Artemis sped home her arrows and Zeus whirled down his thunderbolts upon the doomed race of Giants. And Heracles, with his fatal shafts and his mighty club, made certain that there could be no recovery from the blows of the Immortals.

The last Giant left alive was Enceladus. Heracles had wounded him and when he saw all his companions, whom he had thought immortal, lying dead around him, he fled before the sword of the drunken satyr, Silenus, who had accompanied Dionysus into the battle.

He rushed across Greece, waded the Adriatic Sea, and was at last overtaken by Athena at Cumae in Italy – where he still lies, breathing fire, under the volcano of Vesuvius. But some Roman writers believed that it was Enceladus, and not Typhon the Terrible, who lay imprisoned under Mount Etna in Sicily.

The battle was ended, the Giants destroyed and the Immortals were saved. Heracles, the great hero, had done his work on earth, and Zeus was preparing to raise him to Olympus and make him an Immortal.

But, a mortal still and a very weary one at that, Heracles went to visit his friend Nestor at Pylos to rest after the battle. This was the same Nestor whom he had known on the *Argo* and at the Calydonian Boar Hunt; and earlier still, he had fought against Nestor's father in a battle where both Hera and Hades tried in vain to overcome him, and though Immortals, both felt the sting of his arrows. After that battle, Heracles had set Nestor on the throne, and he found the young king always a staunch friend and ally.

Now at Pylos Heracles met his friend Tyndareus, father of Castor and Polydeuces, the rightful king of Sparta, who had been driven out by his wicked brother. Heracles already had a grievance against the usurper, who had killed a friend of his for merely striking a Spartan dog which attacked him. As soon therefore as Heracles was recovered from his weariness, he led an army to invade Sparta.

The army came mostly from Tegea, whose king feared to leave his little city unguarded, and would only march out with his men after Athena had given a lock of the Gorgon's hair to Heracles. This was concealed in a bronze jar and entrusted to the Princess Sterope: when, just as the king had expected, a troop of Spartans appeared suddenly in front of Tegea, she waved the lock of hair three times from the city wall – and the Spartans were seized with panic and fled back to Sparta.

There Heracles had already captured the city and killed the wicked king, with all his sons, and Tyndareus succeeded to the throne.

Heracles then set out for his home in Trachis, where Deianira was waiting eagerly for him. Not far from Trachis, on a headland overlooking the sea, he paused to raise an altar and offer a sacrifice to Zeus; and he sent his herald, Lichas, to Trachis for the robe which he usually wore on such occasions.

Now Deianira was intensely jealous, and from some chance remark made by Lichas she jumped to the conclusion that Heracles had grown tired of her and was bringing back a new wife called Iole. In actual fact this captive princess was destined to be the bride of their son, Hyllus.

Suddenly Deianira remembered the love-charm which the dying centaur, Nessus, had given her, and now she determined to use it. So she unsealed the jar, and quickly soaked the robe in it before sending it to Heracles in a casket. Then she tossed a bit of rag which had fallen into the jar out into the courtyard to dry.

Presently, as she sat happily weaving by her window, she glanced out and a sudden chill of terror struck to her heart. For the piece of rag was twisting and burning in the sunlight till it turned into fine white powder like saw-dust; and under it were seething clots of foam like dark bubbles in fomenting wine.

In a panic Deianira jumped to her feet, screaming for Hyllus, and when he came she told him what had happened and begged him to go as swiftly as he could to where his father was performing the sacrifice.

Off went Hyllus in his fastest chariot: but when he reached the place, he realized that he was too late. Heracles had put on the robe; and as soon as the sun melted the Hydra's poison in the blood of Nessus with which the robe was anointed, it spread all over him and began to burn like liquid fire.

In vain Heracles tried to tear off the robe; when he did, it was only to tear the very flesh from his bones with it, while his blood hissed and bubbled like water when a red-hot iron is dropped into it.

Yelling with pain, Heracles flung himself into the nearest stream; but the poison burned ever more fiercely, and that stream has been hot ever since, and is still called 'Thermopylae', or the 'hot ways'. Out of the boiling water sprang Heracles, mad with pain, and catching the unfortunate herald Lichas, who had brought him the robe, he swung him round his head and hurled him far out to sea. Then he went rushing through the woods, tearing boughs off the trees, until he came to Mount Oeta; where his strength forsook him and he sank to the ground.

Here Hyllus found him, and told him what had caused his terrible plight.

'I thought that Deianira had done this to slay me!' groaned Heracles. 'If she had, I would have killed her before I died.'

'She is dead already,' said Hyllus sadly. 'When she knew what she had done, she stabbed herself. But you may rest assured that she never dreamt the blood of Nessus was anything but a charm to retain your love.'

'Then my death is upon me,' said Heracles, 'for Athena warned me that the dead should slay me, though no living creature could. Now swear to do what I bid you: swear by the head of Zeus.'

Hyllus swore this most solemn of oaths, and then Heracles bade him heap a mighty pyre of wood on the mountain top. When this was done, Heracles dragged his tortured body on to it, lay down upon the skin of the lion, with the club under his head, and spoke to Hyllus.

'All is finished,' he said, 'and in a little while I shall be with the Immortals, as Zeus, my father, promised. Go now, wed Iole, and live happily. But first, set a light to this pyre!'

But Hyllus drew away, weeping sorely, and no one dared obey the dying hero. At last Heracles saw a young man driving a flock of sheep, and called to him:

'Young man, come here and I will give you a great reward if you do what I command you!'

The youth came and stood beside the pyre, and when he saw who lay upon it, he began to tremble and said:

'My lord Heracles, I know you well: for my father Poeas the Argonaut has often spoken of you, and of how he alone of mortals once held your bow and loosed an arrow from it, to lay low Talos the Brass Man of Crete.'

'Then, by the friendship that was between your father and me,' gasped Heracles, 'I charge you to set a light to this pyre. Take my bow and arrows as your reward – for you must be Philoctetes, the only son of Poeas. Take them, and remember that without those arrows the city of Troy can never fall to mortal invaders.'

Weeping as he did so, Philoctetes took the bow and arrows. And he kindled fire and set a light to the great heap of wood. Then he drew back, while the flames roared upwards.

Suddenly there was a loud peal of thunder, and a cloud seemed to pass across the pyre, putting out the flames. And when Philoctetes drew near to the blackened wood, there was no trace of Heracles.

But on Olympus, with his earthly, mortal part burned away, Zeus was welcoming Heracles – henceforth an Immortal. And now at last Hera forgot her jealousy and made him welcome also; and to show that she too honoured the hero who had saved the Immortals, she gave him her daughter Hebe to be his wife on Olympus.

Meanwhile on earth Alcmena died of grief when she heard that her son Heracles was dead: and her grandsons put her body in a coffin to carry her to her grave. But Hermes, the Immortal thief, came by the will of Zeus, and stole her away so cunningly that no one knew what had happened, and brought her to live for ever in the Elysian Fields beyond the world's end.

As the sons of Heracles were carrying her coffin they felt it suddenly grow heavier and heavier, and at length in their bewilderment they put it down and opened it – to find inside nothing but a tall block of stone which Hermes had substituted for the body. So they took this for a sign from Zeus, and set it up near Thebes as a monument to Alcmena, although like Heracles himself, she had no true grave anywhere on earth.

CHAPTER 20

Helen of Sparta

'Even such (for sailing hither I saw far hence,
And where Eurotas hollows his moist rock
Nigh Sparta with a strenuous-hearted stream)
Even such I saw their sisters; one swan-white,
The little Helen, and less fair than she
Fair Clytemnestra, grave as pasturing fawns
Who feed and fear some arrow. . . .'

A. C. SWINBURNE: *Atalanta in Calydon*

20. Helen of Sparta

As soon as they heard that Heracles was dead, the Amazons invaded Greece, landing in Attica and marching to attack Athens. But Theseus, the friend of Heracles who was still king there, defeated them on the Hill of Ares, the Areopagus, and drove them away.

Thinking that Theseus would be wearied and weakened after so fierce a battle, King Pirithoüs the wild Lapith, son of the wicked Ixion who was bound to the fiery wheel in Tartarus, chose this moment to attack Athens with his lawless followers.

But Theseus marched to meet him, and there would have been a fierce battle if the two kings had not decided suddenly to make peace instead. For when they met, each loved the other at sight, and they swore a firm friendship.

Theseus then visited the land of the Lapiths to attend the wedding of Pirithoüs, and at the feast a strange battle broke out. For among the guests were many centaurs, and these wild half-men grew drunk with wine and carried off the bride and all the other women present.

A great battle followed this attempt in which the centaurs were driven far away; and after that, King Pirithoüs was even more devoted to Theseus than ever – though he lost his bride in the battle.

Now Theseus was one of the great heroes of Greece, second only to Heracles himself, and his deeds had won him great fame – for he had cleared the land of many pests and monsters, had slain the Minotaur and saved Athens from its tribute to King Minos, besides sailing to Colchis with Jason and the Argonauts, helping to hunt the Calydonian Boar, and defeating the fierce invasion of Amazons.

But after his friendship with Pirithoüs began, he seemed to lose his heroic virtues. He became cruel and despotic, was banished for a year from Athens for a murder, and while away caused the death of his own son Hippolytus in a moment of rage and jealousy.

He had done much good to Athens, and stood as an example of a just and pious king: but now the Athenians began to murmur against him and wish that his cousin Menestheus, the rightful heir, whose father had been driven out by Aegeus, sat on the throne in his place

Theseus was middle-aged by now, but he and Pirithoüs decided suddenly that they must both marry again.

'But *we* cannot stoop to ordinary maidens!' cried Pirithoüs, 'let *our* wives be daughters of Zeus, no less!'

Theseus agreed to anything Pirithoüs suggested, and even swore the most solemn oath possible that he would help him to capture and carry away whoever his chosen bride might be. And Pirithoüs vowed to do the same for Theseus.

Then they cast about for daughters of Zeus. Now this was difficult, since Alcmena had been Zeus's last mortal wife, and Heracles his last human child. But about this time it began to be rumoured that King Tyndareus of Sparta had a daughter who was likely to grow into the most beautiful woman in the world. It was also said that, having been father of the strongest man who ever lived, Zeus had determined that, for purposes of his own, he must have a daughter who would be the most beautiful woman of all. It was further added that he had visited Queen Leda in the form of a swan, and that her daughter, Helen, had been hatched out of an egg.

However this might be, Helen of Sparta, even at the age of twelve, was 'beauty's very self', far outshining even her sister Clytemnestra. Theseus heard of her, and decided that here was his destined bride.

So he and Pirithoüs set off for Sparta, seized Helen while she was worshipping in the Temple of Artemis, and carried her off to Athens. But the Athenians were so disgusted at what Theseus had done that he took her to the castle of Aphidna not far away, and left her there, attended by his mother Aethra and guarded by a band of faithful followers.

It was now the turn of Pirithoüs to choose a wife: for according to their agreement, neither was to marry until both their brides had been captured. Now Pirithoüs, in his mad pride and irreverence, declared that only Persephone herself, the daughter of Zeus and Demeter and wife of Hades, would satisfy him. Theseus tried to persuade him to aim a little lower, but in vain.

So the two set off for the Realm of the Dead, and Theseus, profiting by all that he had heard from Heracles who had entered and returned from that dread land when performing the last of his labours for King Eurystheus, led the way to the Cave of Taenarum.

Down by the steep, dangerous paths they went, and came in time to the gloomy kingdom where Hades reigned. The Lord of Many Guests knew quite well on what impious errand they came, but he hid his knowledge and made them welcome.

'None of the sons of men have ever visited me here while still

alive,' he said grimly. 'For Orpheus was the son of Apollo, while
Dionysus and Heracles had Zeus for their father. And, being still
mortal, only those three have ever returned living to the world
above. . . . Therefore, daring humans, come now and feast with me!'

But Theseus, knowing that those who eat the food of the dead
can never return to the land of the living, refused the invitation
politely, appealing to Persephone who had eaten six seeds of the
pomegranate when Hades carried her off, and so could only return
to earth for six months of the year.

'Then at least come sit with me,' said Hades, and he led them to
a royal throne by the side of softly moving Lethe, the River of
Forgetfulness. All unsuspecting, Theseus and Pirithoüs seated
themselves on the carven stone – and at once the stone held them
and they grew to be part of it, so that there was no way of rising
without tearing away their own flesh.

Then Hades laughed grimly: 'Here is my Queen Persephone,
daughter of Zeus!' he said. 'Come, take her if you can, you rash
and impious men!' But there they sat, while coils of serpents
hissed about them, and the Furies, servants of Hades, tormented
them; nor did Cerberus, the triple Hound of Hell, fail to fasten
his teeth in them from time to time.

It is said that some years later Heracles, while on a visit to
Hades and Persephone, begged for the release of his friend and
managed to tear him from his terrible seat. However Theseus did
not return to be king of Athens, but perished miserably in exile;
and certainly Pirithoüs never again saw the light of day, and Hades
moved his terrible seat near to the wheel on which his father Ixion
suffered.

Meanwhile, Helen was a prisoner at Aphidna, and her brothers
Castor and Polydeuces collected an army and set out to rescue her.
They laid siege to Aphidna, captured it, and razed it to the ground,
regaining Helen and taking away Aethra, the mother of Theseus, to
be her slave.

Then they marched to Athens to punish Theseus himself; but
not finding him and being welcomed as deliverers by the citizens,
they made peace and set Menestheus, the rightful king, firmly on
the throne.

Helen, safe again in Sparta, grew up into the loveliest girl ever
seen, just as Zeus had intended, and King Tyndareus became
anxious about her. For just as Theseus had carried her off, so he
feared that some other king or prince of Greece might steal her
also. He became even more anxious when his brave sons Castor and
Polydeuces were no longer there to protect her.

For on a time a bitter quarrel broke out between them and their cousins Idas and Lynceus, the sons of Aphareus the brother of King Tyndareus, who reigned at Messene near Sparta. The third brother, Leucippus, had promised his daughters in marriage to Castor and Polydeuces, but Lynceus and Idas obtained possession of them, either by bribery or by force, and carried them away into Arcadia.

Then Castor and Polydeuces set out with a band of followers to punish their cousins and retrieve their brides. When the two armies met, a truce was called and Lynceus said:

'Let us not shed blood unnecessarily. We both want these two girls, so cannot we decide the question by single combat? I will fight with Castor, and whoever slays the other shall lead away both maidens without let or hindrance.'

The Spartan twins agreed to this, and all men gathered round to watch the battle as Castor and Lynceus made ready for their deadly combat. With the crests nodding above their helmets, they drew near to one another, great shields held ready and spear-points quivering.

Then they tilted at each other, trying vainly to get past the protective shields, but their spears stuck at last in the tough bronze and leather, and snapped off at the points. So then they flung away the useless shafts, snatched out their glittering swords, and lashed at one another.

Many a time did Castor smite on his enemy's broad shield and horse-hair crest; and many a time keen-eyed Lynceus smote back, and once even shore away the scarlet plume. Then, as he aimed the sharp sword at the left knee, Castor drew back his left foot, and hacked the fingers off from the hand of Lynceus, who cast away his sword and fled towards the tomb of his father Aphareus, behind which Idas had concealed himself.

But as he reached it, Castor's sword pierced his body, and he fell dead to the ground.

Joyfully Castor turned to claim the victory and clasp his bride. But as he did so, Idas rose up from behind the tomb, tore away a great stone from it, and dashed it down upon Castor's head.

Brave Castor fell dying to the ground; but Idas did not live long to rejoice in his treachery, for Zeus hurled down a thunderbolt from Olympus, and blotted him from the face of the earth.

Then in desperate sorrow Polydeuces bent over his dying brother; and when he saw that there was no hope for him, he prayed to Zeus:

'Father Zeus, Immortal son of Cronos, when, oh when will there

*'While dainty Hebe served you with the food and
wine of the Immortals.'*

come a release from this sorrow? Let me die also, King of Life
and Death; let me not survive my beloved brother!'

Zeus, deeply moved, spoke out of the thundercloud in which he
had drawn nigh:

'My son, I had thought to make you an Immortal, to be a guide to
men at sea in times of trouble. Will you then prefer death, and
the dim land of Hades where your brother must dwell, rather than
immortality, with a seat at the heavenly banquet on Olympus?
There you were to sit between Athena and Ares, while dainty Hebe
served you with the food and wine of the Immortals.'

But Polydeuces answered: 'If Castor cannot share it with me,
then I would rather renounce the banquet of the Immortals, and
wander in the shadowy realm where Hades is king.'

Then said Zeus: 'For this great love of yours, I decree that both
of you shall sit on Olympus and go forth to do my bidding on the
deep. But Hades cannot be deprived of his due, so that day and day
about you must be even as the dead in the world of shadows; and
day and day about you may tread the sky with us the Immortals.'

And so it came about that neither Castor nor Polydeuces dwelt any longer among men, but became the 'Dioscuri', the 'Striplings of Zeus', and had their twin stars in heaven, and brought kindly succour and guidance to those in peril on the sea.

King Tyndareus mourned the death of his two brave sons, and troubled more and more as to what should chance on account of his wonderful daughter, Helen.

Then at last he sent heralds throughout Greece and the Islands, proclaiming that the time had come when he would choose her a husband; and that her husband should also rule over Sparta and defend it against all invaders.

The kings and princes of all Hellas, the sons of those who had fared with Jason in quest of the Golden Fleece, and of those who had stood beside Meleager when the Boar of Calydon was slain, came hastening to Sparta.

And there came Odysseus the wise son of Laertes, King of Ithaca; and Diomedes son of Tydeus; Menestheus of Athens came, and Aias the son of Oileus. From rich Mycenae and Tiryns came Agamemnon and Menelaus, whose father was a cousin of Eurystheus and had succeeded to his throne; Eumelus was there also, the son of Admetus and Alcestis, and Philoctetes who now owned the bow and arrows of Heracles. There was Ajax the son of Telamon, the old friend of Heracles who had helped him to sack Troy; and there was Ajax's half-brother, young Teucer, whose mother was that Hesione whom Heracles had saved from the sea-monster; and many others whose names were soon to become famous.

Seeing the numbers of them, Tyndareus grew afraid lest if he chose one, some of the others might try to steal the bride and start a disastrous war. Not knowing what to do, he consulted Odysseus the Prince of Ithaca who, though only a young man, was already famous for his wisdom and cunning.

'Why,' said Odysseus, 'the obvious thing is to make all the suitors swear a most solemn oath before you announce your choice. Make them swear to abide by your verdict; that they will defend whoever you choose and come to his aid with a good array of men and ships if anyone whatever should steal away Helen and carry her off.'

Tyndareus thought this an excellent scheme, and the suitors all agreed to it, swearing most solemnly an oath that none of them would dare to break.

Tyndareus chose as the husband of Helen Menelaus, the brave young prince of Mycenae, whose elder brother, Agamemnon, would soon be king there. To make still more certain the alliance with Mycenae, Tyndareus gave his other daughter Clytemnestra to be Agamemnon's wife. And in gratitude to Odysseus he persuaded his brother Icarius to give him his daughter, Penelope, in marriage.

When all these things were settled, and Helen was married to Menelaus, the kings and princes departed to their own homes, and peace descended upon the lovely land of Lacedaemon, of which Sparta was the chief city. Very soon Tyndareus gave up the throne and retired to enjoy his old age in peace and quiet, so that Menelaus and Helen became King and Queen. And there they lived in great happiness for some years, and had a lovely daughter called Hermione, and then a son called Nicostratus.

CHAPTER 21

The Marriage of Peleus and Thetis

'For late between them rose a bitter strife
  In Peleus' halls upon his wedding day
When Peleus took him an immortal wife,
    And there was bidden all the gods' array,
    Save Discord only; yet she brought dismay,
And cast an apple on the bridal board.'

ANDREW LANG: *Helen of Troy*

21. The Marriage of Peleus and Thetis

JUST before the war with the Giants, when Hera made her attempt to kill Heracles, Zeus flung Hephaestus out of heaven for trying to defend her conduct and he fell upon the island of Lemnos.

As he lay there, bruised and shaken, Immortal though he was, after so terrible a fall, the sea nymph Thetis came to his aid. Of all nymphs of the sea Thetis was the most beautiful, and she had the power of turning herself into any shape that she pleased, like her brother Proteus, the 'Old Man of the Sea'.

Thetis led Hephaestus to her coral caves beneath the ocean and there nursed him back to health. When Hephaestus returned to Olympus, and after the War of the Giants was ended, he spoke of lovely Thetis, and Zeus was interested.

'I will marry no more mortal women,' he said, 'but a sea nymph is a different matter. If Thetis really is so lovely and so clever, she shall be my bride! We are safe from the Giants and the threat of overthrow, and now I can cease to trouble and make merry with the Immortals.'

So Zeus visited the caves of Ocean, and found that Thetis was everything that Hephaestus had reported. Then he arranged for a great wedding feast, and announced his intention to the other immortals. Hera, of course, was furious: but she feared to make any objections lest Zeus should cast her out of heaven altogether. He had threatened to do this when she so nearly caused the downfall of all the Immortals of Olympus by her attack on Heracles.

Then suddenly the good Titan, Prometheus, came to Zeus and said:

'Great Zeus, though you treated me cruelly in the beginning, I know that what you did was due to fear. I would not tell you how to avoid the certain danger which threatened you: the danger of the son who would cast you out as you cast out Cronos, and rule in your place as you ruled in his. No, though you sent your eagle to prey on my liver, I would not speak. But you know well that the future, hidden even from you, is sometimes clear to me. For did I not warn you of the coming of the Giants, and that you would only defeat them if there was a human hero strong and brave enough to fight on your side? Well, that man was Heracles, and the battle fell out even as I prophesied.'

Then Zeus bowed his head and answered:

'Titan Prometheus, it is even as you say. In the beginning I had no love for mankind, and hated you for stealing fire to give to them. As you say, I was cruel and merciless: but I have learnt through suffering, and I no longer hate you, nor wish you ill, even though you know of the danger which threatens me. And to prove this, I sent my son the hero Heracles to shoot the eagle and free you from your bonds, leaving only the ring on your finger in token of your sufferings for mankind. I asked nothing of you in return for your freedom; and indeed I am glad and contented to see you working again upon the earth for the noble race of men.'

'Although I can see much of the future,' said Prometheus, 'I cannot see how the hearts of men and of Immortals may change. Yours has changed, great Zeus – and now I can speak to the merciful Father of Gods and Men and tell you of your danger and how to avert it. Listen to the prophecy which I have known from the beginning: *The son of Thetis shall be greater than his father.* So small a matter, and so easy a danger to escape – and yet it might have proved the overthrow of great Zeus himself!'

Then Zeus smiled and uttered a great laugh of joy and relief; and the thunder rumbled, while the summer lightning flashed out of a clear sky.

'I thank you, Titan Prometheus!' he cried. 'Yet once again you are my friend and my helper. . . . Now we will marry Thetis to a mortal husband, and their son shall be the last of the heroes. For it is in my mind to cause the great and glorious War of Troy that shall be famous to the end of time. And famous too shall be the names of the heroes who fight at Troy; but with them the Age of Heroes shall end, and the Iron Age of ordinary men shall follow.'

The hero chosen to be the husband of Thetis was Peleus the Argonaut, who had assisted Heracles and Telamon to sack Troy when King Laomedon refused to keep his word by giving up his magic horses in return for rescuing Hesione and killing the sea monster.

In the Calydonian Boar Hunt, Peleus killed his friend Eurytion by mistake, and in consequence had to leave that country. He went next to live at Iolcus where Acastus the son of Pelias was king; and there he dwelt happily for some time.

But now Zeus brought it about that Queen Astydamia fell in love with him, and begged him to run away with her. But Peleus refused, for he would not do anything so wicked and dishonourable as to steal the wife of his friend. Astydamia was furious, and in time her love turned to hatred so that at length she wished only to see Peleus dead. So she went to her husband with a lying tale that Peleus had tried to persuade her to run away with him, and had threatened to carry her off by force if she refused.

Naturally King Acastus was furious: he did not wish to kill Peleus, who was his guest, but he decided to cause his death.

So he and his lords took Peleus out hunting on Mount Pelion, and they proposed a contest to see who could kill the most game that day. Peleus was a skilful hunter; moreover he possessed a magic sword, given to him by the Immortals in reward for his virtue, which made him always successful in the chase and always victorious in battle. And on this occasion, as he suspected trickery, whenever he killed an animal he cut out its tongue and put it away in his pouch.

At the end of the hunt, Acastus and his followers claimed all the spoils as their own, and jeered at Peleus for having killed nothing.

'You have indeed hunted well,' said Peleus quietly, 'but I have hunted better: for I slew just as many animals as I have tongues here in my pouch!' And with that he produced his spoils, and made Acastus and his friends look thoroughly silly.

But a little later in the day, Peleus fell asleep, lying on the lonely mountainside, and Acastus stole his sword and hid it in a pile of dirt. That done, he and his friends went softly away, leaving Peleus alone.

Evening came, and Peleus woke to find himself deserted, unarmed, and surrounded by the wild centaurs who drew near to kill him. But one of them, Chiron the wise, who had trained Jason as a boy, came to his rescue, found the sword, and brought him in safety to his cave.

There he taught Peleus many things, and finally instructed him how he should catch and hold the sea nymph Thetis, his destined bride.

Peleus did as he was instructed, lying in wait for her on the lonely sea-shore at the foot of Pelion, and catching her unawares. Then she changed herself into fire, water, wind, a tree, a bird, a tiger, a lion, a serpent, and a cuttle-fish in which form Peleus seized her so tightly and held her so fast that she gave up the struggle and returned to her own shape.

Then Peleus led her unwillingly up Pelion to Chiron's cave. But soon she grew happy again and consented to become his wife: for Zeus promised her that she should have a son who would be the most famous hero to fight at Troy; and that, meanwhile, all the Immortals would attend her wedding.

On the slope of Pelion, in the cave of wise Chiron the good old centaur, such a wedding-feast was prepared as had never been seen on earth. For Hebe and Ganymede brought from Olympus the divine food of the Immortals, sweet nectar and the scented food ambrosia, in golden jugs and dishes; they set these upon silver tables laid by Themis herself, and all the Immortals gathered to the feast and sat down at the banquet board. The Muses sang sweetly to the company, and the nymphs danced for them, while Hephaestus filled the cave with cunningly wrought flame that harmed nobody, but shed a heavenly radiance over all.

Then the Immortals gave wondrous gifts to the honoured bridegroom; there was a matchless spear of ash-wood hewn by Chiron, polished by Athena and pointed by Hephaestus; and the two deathless horses Balius and Xanthus, the gift of Poseidon.

But one Immortal was forgotten that day, and her name was Eris. She was hated by all the other dwellers on Olympus, for she was mean and cross, and her other names were 'Strife' and 'Discord'. Suddenly she arrived, quite uninvited, at the banquet.

'I have come!' she cried harshly, 'and I bring with me a present!' Then she cast down on the table a golden apple, and went laughing away; and on the apple were written these words: *For the Fairest.*

Just as Eris intended, discord broke out immediately where all had been peace and happiness before, and there was strife as to who could claim the golden apple.

'It is mine!' cried Hera. 'I am the Queen of Olympus, and it belongs to me by right.'

'I claim it, rather,' said Athena, 'I, the eldest daughter of Zeus. And I will prove my right to it. . . . Not for nothing am I the Immortal Lady of Wisdom!'

'You are both mistaken,' murmured Aphrodite gently. 'It is mine, and no one else has any right to take it. For am not I the Immortal Lady of Beauty and of Love?'

Zeus stilled the wrangling of the three Immortals for the moment, and the wedding ended without many of the guests feeling that its brightness had been marred.

Peleus and his lovely bride thanked their Immortal guests, bade farewell to kindly Chiron, and came down from Pelion to dwell in their kingdom by the sea. And before long Peleus ruled Iolcus also, having deposed Acastus and his wicked queen. The people of the land were delighted to welcome King Peleus, the most virtuous of men, who had been honoured so uniquely by the Immortals:

'Thrice and four-times blessed are you, happy Peleus, son of our old king Aeacus!' they cried. 'And blessed be also the lovely Queen

Achilles

Thetis whom Zeus has given you as wife, honouring your marriage with his presence, and bestowing on you such wondrous gifts. Truly Zeus has set you apart among men, the hero more honoured than any other of the heroes!'

The new King and Queen dwelt happily for a while; but as year followed on year Peleus grew troubled. For six sons were born to him and Thetis, and all six of them disappeared mysteriously, nor could he learn what became of them. But Thetis grew more and more silent and sad, and her eyes turned with longing to the bright sea-waves under which she had lived before her wedding to Peleus.

Then a seventh son was born, and they called him Achilles.

'See now,' said Thetis. 'I will make our child invulnerable, so that he may be the greatest of heroes!'

And she carried him away by night to the River Styx, the black River of the Underworld, and dipped him in the swift-flowing stream. But, fearful lest he should be drowned or washed away, she held him by the heel; and the heel and instep alone were un-touched by the magic water.

When she carried him home, Peleus breathed a sigh of relief that the child was still alive and well. But he determined to watch carefully, and that night he remained awake, though pretending to be asleep.

Presently he saw his wife slip quietly out of bed, take the baby from the cradle, and, having anointed him with ambrosia, advance towards the fire. Peleus watched anxiously, and saw Thetis place the child in the heart of the flames.

At that he leapt out of bed with a cry, snatched Achilles from the fire and turned in fury upon Thetis.

But she exclaimed: 'Oh, fool, fool! Had you left him, he would have become immortal, and never known old age! For all I had to do was to burn the mortal part of him away, after anointing him with the food of the gods. . . . True, our other sons perished in the flames – but this time I would have been successful, for he was dipped in Styx and so was invulnerable.'

Then she cried aloud: 'Farewell now, Peleus the foolish. Nevermore shall you call me wife, for I go back to the sea, never to return to you again.'

So saying she fled away like a breath of wind, passed from the palace as swiftly as a dream, and leapt into the sea.

Peleus sorrowed deeply at the loss of his lovely wife, and he never married again, though he lived to sad old age.

Meanwhile he took the baby Achilles to Mount Pelion and entrusted him to the wise centaur, Chiron. And there the boy dwelt, feeding on the marrow of lions, wild honey and flesh of fawns; and Chiron taught him the arts of riding and hunting, and how to play the lyre.

Thetis, although she had deserted Peleus, still watched over Achilles; and when he was nine she set about hiding him from a danger which she saw was drawing nearer and nearer to him. She dressed him as a girl and sent him to the island of Scyros where Lycomedes was king. There Achilles was hidden among the other maidens who attended on the little princess Deidamia, and indeed he himself almost believed after a time that he was really a girl called Pyrrha.

Thetis did this when the great war between Greece and Troy seemed about to begin; for she knew that if Achilles went to Troy he would never return.

And the beginning of that war went back to the day of her marriage to Peleus. For the golden apple of Discord kept the three Immortals. Hera, Athena and Aphrodite wrangling and quarrelling until Zeus bade Hermes take them to Mount Ida near Troy and let a shepherd called Paris judge between them.

CHAPTER 22

The Judgement of Paris

'Was this the face that launched a thousand ships
And burnt the topless towers of Ilion?
Sweet Helen, make me immortal with a kiss!'

MARLOWE: *Dr Faustus*

22. The Judgement of Paris

AFTER Heracles, Peleus and Telamon killed King Laomedon and destroyed the town of Troy, his youngest son Priam became king. He called together the Trojans from near and far, and at his direction they built a new city, larger, stronger, with great gates and walls and towers.

For long he ruled there in peace and the land grew rich. His Queen, Hecuba, bore him many handsome sons, the eldest of whom was called Hector. But just before the second son, Paris, was born, Queen Hecuba dreamt a terrible dream.

She dreamt that the child was born, but instead of an ordinary baby it turned out to be a Fury (such as those daughters of Hades whom the grim Lord of Death sends out to work vengeance on the wicked), a Fury with a hundred hands and every hand holding a lighted torch. And in her dream the Fury rushed through Troy, setting all on fire and pushing down the newly-built towers.

When she awoke, Hecuba told Priam of her dream, and he sent for all the wise men of Troy to see if any of them could say what the dream meant. They told him that Paris, if he lived, would bring about the ruin of his country and the destruction of Troy itself; and they advised Priam to kill the child quickly.

Priam was very sad at this, but when the baby boy was born he gave him to a faithful servant and bade him carry the child far away onto the wild slopes of Mount Ida, and leave him there to be eaten by wild beasts. The servant did as he was told, leaving the child near the den of a fierce bear. But five days later, when hunting on Ida, he visited the place and to his amazement found the baby Paris alive and well in the bear's very lair, lying among the cubs.

'The child is fated to live,' thought the servant, 'since even the wild beasts feed and tend it,' and he picked up Paris and took him to his own cottage.

Here he brought up the boy as his own son, teaching him to hunt, and to tend the flocks and herds on the mountain slopes.

Paris grew up strong and brave, and from the beginning he was one of the handsomest boys to be seen, so fine indeed that the nymph Oenone fell in love with him, and they were married and lived in a beautiful cave on Mount Ida; and there a son was born to them called Corythus.

Paris took particular interest in the herd of cattle which was his charge, and when he was still quite a boy he drove away a band

of robbers who tried to steal them. He was particularly proud of
the herd bull, a beautiful milk-white animal stronger and finer than
any other bull on Ida. He was so confident in the superior merits of
his bull that he offered to crown with gold any finer than his own.

One day, as a jest, the Immortal Ares turned himself into a bull
and got Hermes to drive him up Ida to compete with Paris's animal.
The stranger was even more beautiful and stronger than the champion, and Paris without hesitation awarded it the promised crown.

It was on account of this scrupulous fairness that Zeus, who
refused to judge them himself, sent the three lovely Immortals,
Hera, Athena and Aphrodite, to have their contest for the owner-
ship of the golden apple of Discord decided by Paris.

Hermes, the Immortal Guide, led the way to Mount Ida, and there
he found Paris, young, strong and handsome in his goat-skin cloak,
seated on the hillside playing sweet tunes on his pipe, with his
herdsman's crook laid beside him.

Looking up, Paris beheld the Immortal drawing near to him, and
knew him by the winged sandals and the herald's wand. Then he
would have leapt up and hidden in the woods, but Hermes called to
him:

'Do not fear, herdsman Paris – you who are greater than you yet
know. I come to you from Zeus, who knows of your fairness in
judgement, and I bring with me three Immortal Queens. You must
choose which of them is the fairest – for such is the will of Zeus.'

Then Paris answered: 'Lord Hermes, I am but a mortal, how can
I judge of immortal loveliness? And if judge I do, how can I escape
the vengeance of those who are not chosen?'

'They will abide by your decision,' answered Hermes, 'and it is
a mortal choice that Zeus requires. As for what will come of it,
that Zeus alone knows, for all this happens by his will.'

Then the three Immortals drew near, and Paris stood for a little,
dazzled by their shining loveliness.

Presently Hera came to him, tall and stately, a queen of queens
with a shimmering diadem on her beautiful forehead and her large
eyes shining with majesty.

'Choose me,' she said in her rich voice, 'and I will make you lord
of all Asia. You shall have power greater than any king: if you will
it, Greece shall be yours also. . . .'

Paris looked upon her, and the beauty he saw was the beauty of
power, of sway and dominion: he saw all his dreams of such am-
bition given shape and form in this lovely Immortal Queen.

He gasped and hid his eyes; and when he looked again Athena
stood before him in quiet dignity. From her eyes shone wisdom and

thought, and the helmet shimmered on her head in token of deeds done and not merely planned.

'I will give you wisdom,' she said. 'You shall be the wisest of all men, and the kings of the earth shall come to you for counsel. With this wisdom you may conquer in war and rule if so you choose.'

Then Paris forgot his dreams of kingship and majesty: instead he saw knowledge and skill in all arts and in all learning – and they took the form of the wise-eyed, dignified Immortal whose cool hand rested for a moment on his shoulder.

Paris bowed his head, and when he raised it again he saw Aphrodite, lovelier than a dream of beauty, standing before him. Her garments were spun by the Graces and dyed in the flowers of spring – in crocus and hyacinth, in flourishing violet and the rose's lovely bloom and heavenly buds, in narcissus and lily. Her face and form were beautiful beyond imagining, and her voice was soft and thrilling.

'Take me,' she murmured, 'and forget harsh wars and cares of state. Take my beauty and leave the sceptre and the torch of wisdom. I know nothing of battles or of learning: what has Aphrodite to do with the sword or the pen? In place of wisdom, in place of sovereignty, I will give you the most beautiful woman upon earth to be your bride. Helen of Sparta is her name, and she shall be called the World's Desire and beauty's very self.'

Then Paris did not hesitate, but gave the golden apple to Aphrodite, and she laughed sweetly and triumphantly.

'Now Paris,' she said, 'I will be ever at your side and I will lead you to the golden Helen!'

But Hera and Athena turned away with anger in their eyes, and from that moment began their hatred of Troy and of all the Trojans.

Paris slept on the flowery slope of Mount Ida, and when he awoke he could not tell whether he had given judgement in a dream or in reality. But now he could no longer be happy with Oenone, nor as a herdsman in the woods and on the mountain slopes. For, waking and asleep, he saw the fair form of Aphrodite and heard her voice; and the form and the voice changed and took the shape and tones of a mortal woman, more lovely than any dream, who was destined to be his bride. He did not have to wait long to see what Aphrodite would do to fulfil her promise.

King Priam, believing his son Paris to be dead, held funeral games each year in memory of him, and this year he sent his servants up on to Ida for a bull to be the chief prize.

They chose the magnificent white bull which was Paris's pride, and drove it away, in spite of all he could say to persuade them

The judgement of Paris

to leave it. So, half in anger and half in curiosity, Paris followed them down to Troy, and found a great crowd gathered to watch the chariot race.

When this was ended, Priam declared that the boxing match would be open to all comers – and Paris at once entered for it. He boxed so well that he won the laurel crown; and, competing in the foot-race, won that also. The other sons of Priam were so furious that a strange herdsman should win, that they challenged him themselves; but once again he outran them all, and having won three events was declared victor of the day and winner of the prize bull.

Then Hector and his brother Deiphobus were so angry that they drew their swords to slay Paris. But the old servant flung himself at Priam's feet, crying, 'My lord king, this is Paris, the son whom you bade me cast out to die on the mountain-side!'

Then Paris was welcomed eagerly by the King and Queen, and by his brothers as well, and was soon re-instated as a prince of Troy.

But his sister Cassandra, who was a prophetess, cried to all the Trojans that if Paris were allowed to live, Troy was doomed. Priam, however, just smiled at her, and answered playfully: 'Well, well, better that Troy should fall than that I should lose this wonderful new son of mine!'

Cassandra suffered this fate: that she should speak the truth and not be believed. For she had offended Apollo and, since he could not take from her the gift of prophecy which he had bestowed, he took this means of rendering the gift useless.

After a while, Aphrodite instructed Paris to build ships and sail to Greece, and she sent her son Aeneas with him. For Zeus, angered with Aphrodite when she boasted that she had made all the Immortals fall in love with mortals, except the Three Heavenly Maidens, Hestia, Athena and Artemis, had made Aphrodite herself wed a human. And he chose Anchises, a prince of Troy, the grandson of King Ilus and cousin of Laomedon, who was at the time a herdsman on Mount Ida. There Aeneas was born, and Aphrodite warned Anchises that he would be punished if ever he boasted of his Immortal bride: but boast he did, one day when he had feasted over-merrily, and a flash of fire struck him to the ground. Yet, for the sake of Aeneas, and for his own virtues, Aphrodite spared his life: but he went lame from that day.

So the ships were built, and Paris sailed joyously forth over the dancing waves, though Cassandra prophesied of ills to come, and Oenone wept, lonely and deserted, in her mountain cave.

At Sparta, Paris said that he had come to Greece on an embassy from King Priam to enquire after Hesione who was now the wife of King Telamon of Salamis. Menelaus greeted his guest kindly, and he and Helen entertained the Trojan strangers for nine days.

On the tenth a message came for Menelaus that his mother's father, Catreus, had died in Crete, and he was wanted at the funeral. Suspecting no evil, he sailed away, leaving Helen to entertain the guests until they were ready to leave for Salamis.

Next day Paris said farewell to Helen and embarked with Aeneas and all his followers. But that night he returned to Sparta, and next morning he was on the high seas with Helen aboard his ship.

For once Paris had seen the beauty of Helen, he cared for nothing else in the world but to win her – by fair means or foul. And Aphrodite, having promised, was ready to help him with her magic arts.

Some say that he carried off Helen by main force, robbing the palace of all its treasures at the same time; but others say that by the spells of Aphrodite Paris was able to assume the form of Menelaus, and that Helen followed him at once, accompanying him as in a dream, and leaving Hermione, her beloved daughter, behind in Sparta, though she took the baby Nicostratus with her.

Away they sailed, and Hera called up a storm-wind to blow them out of their course. But they landed on Aphrodite's island of Cyprus; and afterwards visited Sidon (where Paris treacherously slew the king and stole his treasure), Phoenicia and Egypt.

Some even say that in Egypt Helen remained and was worshipped as a goddess, the Strange Hathor, until Menelaus came many years later to fetch her, and that Hermes beguiled Paris by sending with him a phantom Helen fashioned out of clouds.

But most of the Greeks believed that Paris reached Troy at last, bringing the beautiful Helen with him, and there they were married amid the rejoicing of the Trojans. For when Cassandra stood on the citadel, tearing her hair and crying: 'Woe, woe to Troy! Helen has come, who will bring ruin and death to us all,' Priam replied that death and ruin were worth risking merely to look upon the beauty of Helen and to have her at Troy. And all the Trojans agreed with him, and vowed never to give her up.

But she dwelt amongst them in sadness and shame, once the magic of Aphrodite had faded. And from that day forth Helen wore on her breast the shining Star-stone which she found waiting for her in the citadel of Troy. Moment by moment the red drops from the ruby heart of the star fell on her snowy raiment, fell and vanished – fell and vanished – and left no stain; even as if the drops were the drops of blood shed for her, the innocent cause of so much war and sorrow.

CHAPTER 23

The Gathering of the Heroes

In Troy, there lies the scene. From isles of Greece
The princes orgulous . . . their vow is made
To ransack Troy; within whose strong immures
The ravisht Helen, Menelaus' queen,
With wanton Paris sleeps; and that's the quarrel.

SHAKESPEARE: *Troilus and Cressida*

23. The Gathering of the Heroes

No sooner had Paris the Trojan sailed away carrying Helen with him, than Hera, Queen of the Immortals and his sworn enemy, sent her messenger Iris to tell Menelaus of his loss. Iris was the bright sister of the evil Harpies, the servant of the Immortals, and of Hera in particular; and when she went on a message, Zeus spread his rainbow as a bridge for her from heaven to earth.

Full of sorrow at the loss of Helen, and anger against the daring Trojan thief, Menelaus hastened back to Greece. First of all he went to his brother Agamemnon, lord of rich Mycenae, who was the husband of Helen's sister, Clytemnestra.

'The beautiful Helen has been stolen away by Trojan Paris!' he cried. 'Now is the time to gather all the kings and princes of Greece, according to their oath when all were her suitors at Sparta, and set sail for Troy to exact vengeance!'

Agamemnon was not quite as eager to go to war as his brother was, and first of all sent a swift ship to Troy, demanding Helen's instant return. But the ship, making the crossing in three days, reached Troy long before Paris, and Priam sent back an insolent answer:

'How can you Greeks make so much fuss about one missing woman? First of all return the women of Asia whom you have stolen – Medea of Colchis, and my own sister Hesione!'

This reply angered Agamemnon: for Medea had come to Greece of her own wish, and brought much evil to Jason by so doing. As for Hesione, Laomedon had promised her to Heracles if he could save her from the sea monster. But the theft of Helen was a crime committed by a guest against his host – one of the worst of sins in Greek eyes.

So Agamemnon sent out heralds through all Greece bidding the kings and princes gather men and ships, and meet at the port of Aulis, on the coast not very far from Thebes.

Presently the heralds began to return, bringing news of the eagerness with which the heroes were answering the summons. But one startling piece of news brought back by them was that Odysseus of Ithaca, son of Laertes the Argonaut, the very man who had suggested the oath which bound the suitors of Helen, could not come – for he had gone mad.

Anxious to investigate this extraordinary rumour, Agamemnon and Menelaus set out for Ithaca, accompanied by Palamedes, the young prince of Nauplia. Sure enough, when they landed it was to find Odysseus ploughing the sand on the sea-shore, with an ox and a horse harnessed to his plough, and sowing salt instead of seed.

He seemed to be very mad indeed: but Palamedes had a suspicious mind, and thought he would test this madness. So he seized Telemachus, the infant son of Odysseus and Penelope, and placed him in front of the plough. Sure enough, when Odysseus saw his beloved son in such danger, he reined in his strange team and made haste to pick up the baby.

After that, his pretence of madness was at an end, and he explained that he had only assumed it because of an oracle which warned him that if he went to Troy he would not return home for twenty years.

Odysseus loved his island home, and adored his wife and child, so he could never forgive Palamedes for having ruined his clever scheme for avoiding the summons to Troy. Nevertheless he went now with a smile and a shrug, and not one of the heroes did better service in the war than he.

On their voyage to Aulis, Odysseus and Palamedes went out of their way to visit Cyprus, to persuade King Cinyras to join the Greek Allies against Troy. In the end Cinyras promised solemnly to send fifty ships, and Menelaus sailed on to Aulis with the good news. But when the contingent from Cyprus arrived, it consisted of one ship only – which carried forty-nine others, modelled in clay. It was believed by many of the Greeks that Cinyras had in fact bribed Palamedes to relieve him from his promise.

Odysseus also visited Delos, accompanied this time by Menelaus, to beg the aid of the three daughters of King Anius, the son of Apollo. These three wonderful maidens were called 'The Wine-growers', for Dionysus, whose daughter Rhoio was their mother, had given them the magic touch. One of the maidens could turn what she would into wine: the second could produce corn in the same fashion, and the third olives.

King Anius, who had a gift of prophecy from his father, would not at first allow his daughters to go.

'But,' said he, 'why not come and live here – all of you – for nine years? Then I'll see what I can do; for it has been revealed to me that Troy will not fall until the tenth year! And my daughters can feed you here just as well as at Troy!'

Menelaus would not believe this: however he returned with the message. But Agamemnon was already beginning to feel the corrupting joys of absolute power, and he sent Palamedes to fetch the Wine-growers by force – and the maidens fed the Greek army for nine years. In the end they escaped, but were pursued by Agamemnon's orders. When they were overtaken, they prayed to Dionysus for aid, and he turned them into doves – which were ever afterwards held sacred on the lovely little island of Delos.

It was some time before the kings and princes of Greece were all assembled at Aulis with their fleets and armies; but in the end there were one thousand and thirteen ships, with forty-three leaders. And when they were all assembled, there was no wind to waft them across the sea.

Then Calchas, a priest of Apollo, began to prophesy. He was a Trojan traitor who had come to Agamemnon saying that he had left Troy because his foresight told him that Troy must fall: moreover, he said, he could not remain in a city guilty of such a crime as the theft of Helen.

Agamemnon believed everything that Calchas told him, for he was very superstitious, and Calchas began by prophesying that Troy would never fall unless Achilles, the young son of the hero Peleus who was too old to come in person, led his people, the Myrmidons, to the war. It was rumoured that young Achilles, aged eighteen by this time, was concealed at the court of King Lycomedes on the island of Scyros, and Odysseus set out at once to find him, accompanied by Diomedes.

On the way Odysseus laid his plans, and Diomedes made ready to play his part. They arrived at Scyros dressed as merchants, though Odysseus drew King Lycomedes aside and gave him a message from Agamemnon demanding that Achilles should be given up to them.

'He is not here,' answered Lycomedes boldly. 'You may look anywhere you like in my palace.'

As search proved of no avail, Odysseus put his scheme into action. Still disguised as a merchant, he visited Princess Deidamia and her maidens carrying a goodly roll of merchandise, which he spread out before them.

'Now then, fair ladies!' he cried. 'Come and take your choice! There are gifts for all of you – a poor return for all King Lycomedes's kindness to us merchants.'

The maidens gathered round, and began fingering and trying on the brooches and jewelled belts, snoods, and other trifles. But the maiden Pyrrha lighted upon a sword which was somehow mixed up with all the feminine gewgaws and trumperies, and fingered it longingly. Suddenly a martial trumpet sounded just outside the door, and there was a cry from Diomedes and a clash of weapons.

The maidens screamed and turned to fly, but Pyrrha snatched up the sword, flung off cloak and robe, and stood forth to do battle – Achilles revealed in all his young strength and daring.

'Ah-ha!' cried Odysseus. 'Up, son of mighty Peleus and come with us to Troy. No more can guileful Thetis conceal you here; come, and show your metal, and bring honour to your father who in olden days stood beside Heracles, the greatest of heroes!'

So Achilles made haste to collect his troops, and left behind him Princess Deidamia whom he had married in secret, and their young son Neoptolemus. Soon he and his Myrmidons arrived at Aulis; and with him came his cousin Patroclus, some years older than he was, but already his dearest friend.

Now everything seemed ready for the expedition to set out, and Calchas offered up a great sacrifice to the Immortals. While all the chiefs were gathered together round the altar, a blue snake with red markings darted suddenly from beneath the stone, climbed to the topmost branch of a plane-tree which stood close by, and there devoured eight baby sparrows in their nest, finishing off by eating the mother sparrow also. Having done this, the snake was turned immediately into stone.

'An omen!' cried Calchas. 'An omen from Zeus! He has shown us this sign, late come, of late fulfilment, the fame of which shall never perish. For even as the snake swallowed the eight baby sparrows and then the parent bird, so shall we war against Troy for nine years: but in the tenth year we shall take that wide-wayed city.'

Then the great fleet set sail, with Agamemnon in command of the whole army, and Odysseus, Diomedes, and Palamedes as seconds in command, while Achilles was admiral of the fleet. Nestor, the old hero of Pylos, was Agamemnon's chief adviser; and he took heed of his words even more readily than those of the wise Odysseus.

Achilles did not prove a very satisfactory admiral, for he led the fleet so badly that they landed in Mysia, several hundred miles south of Troy. Then, thinking that they had reached their journey's end, they set to work to ravage the country and burn down the villages, at which Telephus, King of Mysia, who was a son of Heracles, gathered his army together and chased the Greeks back to their ships. Unfortunately for himself, he tripped over a vine and was wounded in the thigh by Achilles.

The Greeks, realizing their mistake, set sail again: but a fearful storm broke upon them, and drove them back towards Greece, scattering the fleet far and wide.

When at length he came to land, Agamemnon found that he and

a large portion of the fleet had been driven to his own homeland of Argolis: so he returned to Mycenae while his ships were repaired, and sent messengers bidding the other heroes assemble once more at Aulis the following spring.

Meanwhile King Telephus was suffering so sorely from his wound, which showed no sign of healing, that he consulted an oracle, and was told 'Only the wounder can heal!' Accordingly he set out for Greece, disguised as a beggar, and came to Mycenae where many of the leaders were assembled. Clytemnestra hospitably offered him a place by the fireside, and there he suddenly seized Orestes, the baby son of the King and Queen of Mycenae, from his cradle, and cried:

'I am Telephus, King of Mysia, whom you wronged! If you will cure me of my wound, and swear that no harm shall befall me, I will guide your fleet to Troy. But if you attempt to kill me, I will slay this young prince.'

Then Agamemnon swore the required oath, and Achilles cured Telephus of his wound with the aid of the magic spear which had inflicted it.

Now, with a trustworthy pilot assured, the Greeks assembled once more at Aulis and made ready for the invasion of Troy. But a dead calm lay over all the sea for day after day, and sail they could not. At last the prophet Calchas arose and said:

'King Agamemnon, the Immortal Artemis has caused this calm, to punish you for boasting that you were a better shot than she is. And you will never sail to Troy until you sacrifice to her your daughter Iphigenia.'

Agamemnon was filled with grief, and at first wished to abandon the whole expedition. But presently he changed his mind and sent Odysseus to fetch Iphigenia.

'Tell my wife, Queen Clytemnestra,' he said, 'that Iphigenia is to come here as a bride. Say that Achilles wishes to marry her, and will not set sail for Troy until after the wedding.'

Believing this, Clytemnestra set out herself with her daughter and arrived at the Greek camp. Here she met Achilles, and greeted him as her future son-in-law; but he was amazed, for not only had he heard nothing of the matter, but was already married to Deidamia.

Very soon Clytemnestra discovered Agamemnon's shameful trick and failing to turn him from his purpose, she begged Achilles to save Iphigenia. Full of indignation against Agamemnon, Achilles agreed to do so; but what was his consternation when he discovered that Calchas had spread abroad his prophecy, and all the army,

Artemis

including the Myrmidons themselves, were clamouring for the sacrifice to be carried out.

To the reproaches of Clytemnestra and the terrified prayers of Iphigenia, Agamemnon answered sadly and bitterly:

'I am no madman, nor have I ceased to love my children. This is a fearful thing, yet I must do it. Unless this sacrifice is made, Calchas swears we can never reach Troy: and all the Greeks are burning to smite the foe. If Paris goes unpunished for the theft of Helen, they believe that the Trojans will come to Greece and steal more women – steal their wives – steal you and our daughters. I do not bow to the will of Menelaus: it is not merely to bring back Helen that we go. But I do bow to the will of all Greece, and bow I must whether I will it or not – for Greece is greater far than any personal sorrow. We live for her, to guard her freedom.'

Clytemnestra would still have struggled against it, and Achilles offered to fight in her defence single-handed, but Iphigenia rose to the sacrifice.

'I have chosen death,' she said, 'I choose honour. With me rests the freedom of our beloved land, the honour of our women through many years to come. My death will save them – and my name will be blessed as the name of one who freed Greece from fear and slavery.'

So Iphigenia, hailed by the army as the true conqueror of Troy, went steadfastly to her death. But Immortal Artemis took pity on her youth and on her great courage. As the knife was actually falling and the fire was already kindled, she snatched her away and set a doe in her place.

After that the wind rose strongly from the west, and the great armada set out joyfully in the direction of Troy.

CHAPTER 24

The Siege of Troy

Paint with threads of gold and scarlet, paint the battles fought
  for me,
All the wars for Argive Helen; storm and sack by land and sea;
All the tales of loves and sorrows that have been and are to be.

Paint the storms of ships and chariots, rain of arrows flying far,
Paint the waves of warfare leaping up at beauty like a star,
Like a star that pale and trembling hangs above the waves of war.

ANDREW LANG: *The World's Desire*

24. The Siege of Troy

THE Greek fleet did not come to Troy without adventures on the way, even this time when the winds were favourable and the sea was calm. Before landing at Troy they put in to the little island of Tenedos a few miles from the coast, to wait while ambassadors were sent to King Priam, and as they came ashore there they had a brush with the inhabitants, and Achilles killed their chief, Tenes, who was the son of Apollo. Achilles knew then that he must expect the anger of that Immortal Archer, for Thetis had warned him what might happen: but the only person to suffer at the time was Philoctetes, the man who had lit the funeral pyre of Heracles on Mount Oeta, and who still carried the bow and deadly arrows, dipped in the blood of the Hydra, which the dying hero had given to him. Philoctetes was bitten in the ankle by a snake which crept out from under the altar when the kings were sacrificing to Apollo; and the sore did not heal, but grew so noisome that the other men could not endure the stench of it, nor the cries of the wretched sufferer. So Agamemnon ordered Odysseus to take Philoctetes to the desert island of Lemnos and maroon him there. And there Philoctetes remained for nearly ten years, living on the birds and beasts which he managed to shoot with his bow and arrows.

Menelaus and Odysseus then landed near Troy itself as ambassadors, and marched inland to the city which stood several miles from the shore.

The Trojans received them coldly, but Prince Antenor, cousin of King Priam, made them welcome in his house. Next day, in the assembly of all the Trojan lords and princes, Menelaus and Odysseus asked for Helen to be restored, suitable fines to be paid, and hostages given; and they said that if this were done, the Greeks would sail away in peace.

The Trojans admired the broad shoulders and kingly aspect of Menelaus, and still more the wonderful voice and the persuasive words of Odysseus, though he was below medium height and made no flourishes with his hands when he spoke. But Antimachus, who had been bribed by Paris, urged the Trojans to keep Helen, and to kill both the envoys; and murdered they would have been, had not Antenor saved them, and got them quickly out of the city.

When they returned to the fleet with their news, the Greeks were filled with rage at the insolence of the Trojans, and decided to land at once and teach them a sharp lesson.

So the fleet drew in towards the beach, and the Trojans came rushing down in thousands to oppose their landing. Achilles was about to leap ashore to deal the first blow in the war, but Calchas held him back.

'There is an oracle,' he cried, 'which says that the first to land is the first to be slain – and we cannot afford to lose you, son of Thetis!'

Then, while the Greeks hesitated, brave Protesilaus, son of Iphiclus the Argonaut, cried:

'Heroes of Hellas, follow me! To die in glory is to live for ever on the lips of men!'

So saying, he leapt ashore, and after slaying many Trojans, fell at the hands of mighty Hector, bravest of the sons of Priam. Over the sides of their ships poured the rest of the Greeks, and a tremendous battle was fought that day in which many fell.

For a time the Greeks were held at bay by Cycnus, the invulnerable son of Poseidon, who killed numbers of them. Achilles rushed to meet him, but found that even the spear which Chiron had cut for him could not pierce the unwoundable Cycnus. Then he slashed at him with his sword, but once more in vain.

'No weapon can pierce me!' laughed Cycnus. But even as he spoke Achilles dashed him in the face with his shield, made him give ground, and tripped him dexterously. Then he seized his fallen foe and exerting his great strength he strangled him with the straps of his own helmet. But Poseidon saw the fate of his son, and bearing his body swiftly away he turned him into a snow-white swan.

When the Trojans knew that Cycnus was slain, they fled back into Troy Town and barred the gates; nor would they venture out again for many a long day.

So the Greeks made their great encampment all round the city, and laid siege to it. But Troy was so large and the Trojans, both within its walls and in the country round about, were so strong, that the Greeks could not blockade it completely, and the Trojans never suffered the full hardships of a long siege. They had plenty of water: they could always get food, and from time to time reinforcements won their way into the city.

Failing to take Troy by storm or siege, the Greeks enlivened their ten-year campaign by overrunning the country round and sacking the other cities under Trojan rule or in league with them.

The years dragged by in this way; city after city was besieged, attacked and finally destroyed, but few notable deeds were done of which any record survives.

One event which has grown with the telling concerned one of Priam's sons called Troilus. It is said that he loved the daughter of the traitor-prophet Calchas who was still in Troy, and that their love prospered, thanks to the encouragement of the girl's uncle, Pandarus. But Calchas, being certain that Troy would fall, persuaded Agamemnon to exchange the girl for an important prisoner. Troilus was heart-broken, but consoled himself with the vows of eternal love and faith which he and his beloved had exchanged – until he discovered that, the moment she arrived in the Greek camp, the faithless girl had transferred her affections to Diomedes.

When Calchas announced that Troy would never fall if Troilus reached the age of twenty, determined efforts were made to kill him. Finally Achilles surprised him in the sanctuary of Apollo on Mount Ida, and slew him mercilessly.

Not long after this Achilles marched against Aeneas who, although he had been with Paris when Helen was carried off, had taken no part in the war. Achilles attacked his stronghold on Mount Ida, after driving away all his cattle, and Aeneas only escaped by the help of Aphrodite, and so made his way into Troy.

In the ninth year of the war, Palamedes met his end mysteriously. Though not much of a warrior, he had earned the gratitude of the Greek soldiers by inventing games for them to play during the long, weary siege – both draughts and dice were credited to his ingenious mind.

One day the dead body of a Trojan spy was discovered and on it was a letter from Priam to Palamedes saying, 'The gold which I have sent to you is the reward for betraying the Greeks to me.'

Palamedes was brought before Agamemnon, and denied having received gold from Priam, or from anyone else. But when a search was made of his tent, treasure was discovered buried under it.

That was the end of Palamedes, who was condemned as a traitor, and stoned to death. When sentence was passed on him, he cried: 'Truth, I mourn for you: I am about to die, but you have perished before me!'

His brother Oeax believed that he was really innocent, and that Odysseus and Diomedes had forged the letter and hidden the gold, with the help of Agamemnon himself. So he sent a message to his father King Nauplius, accusing the Greek leaders of murdering Palamedes; and Nauplius, though unable to take vengeance while they were still at Troy, prepared for them an unpleasant welcome on their return to Greece.

But meanwhile, in the beginning of the tenth year of the war, a great quarrel broke out among the Greek leaders themselves, due to the pride and insolence of King Agamemnon.

Not long before, Achilles had captured two maidens named Chryseis and Briseis, the first of whom was the daughter of a priest of Apollo, and sacred to that Immortal. Agamemnon, as lord over the lesser kings of the Greek host, divided up all spoils of conquest – and usually kept the best for himself. On this occasion he gave Briseis to Achilles as a handmaiden, but kept Chryseis, and when her father came to beg him to give back the girl, drove him away with harsh and impious words.

Apollo's priest prayed to Apollo for aid, and that immortal Lord of the Silver Bow came down in anger from Olympus and discharged several of his deadly arrows of pestilence into the Greek camp.

As usual when anything occurred which was obviously the work of some angered Immortal, Agamemnon and the other kings consulted Calchas, and he, having secured the protection of Achilles, turned on the 'King of Men', and declared:

'Apollo has smitten us because you, King Agamemnon, did not harken to the prayer of his priest; and he will not remove this loathsome pestilence from the Greeks until you return Chryseis to her father – with a great gift as compensation.'

Agamemnon was furiously angry: 'You vile seer!' he cried. 'Never yet have you told me anything pleasant: all your prophecies are of evil, and I am the one who has to suffer for them!'

Nevertheless he was forced to give up Chryseis; but because Achilles had promised to protect Calchas from his rage, Agamemnon turned on him and took away Briseis to replace his own lost handmaiden.

Then it was Achilles who lost his temper.

'You shameless, crafty, grasping wretch!' he began. 'You dog-faced cheat! Was it for this that we followed you from Greece and have obeyed you all these years? Well, I for one have had enough of it, and I am minded to sail away with all my men and ships before you rob me of the few spoils that are still mine.'

'Flee if you like!' shouted Agamemnon. 'I will make no attempt to hinder you, nor to beg you to remain! There are many to stand by me and treat me with the honour which is my due. Go home, you coward, and lord it over your Myrmidons: I shall be well rid of you!'

Mad with rage, Achilles set his hand to his sword, meaning to draw it and slay Agamemnon there and then. But Athena was watching, and she drew near quickly, invisible to all but Achilles, and caught him by his golden hair.

'Achilles!' she said, and her eyes shone terribly. 'I come to you from the high place of the Immortals to stay your anger. Harken to me, for I am sent by Hera, the white-armed Queen of Olympus, who loves you both equally, and would not have the blood of either of you spilt in civil strife. Therefore fight only with words, if fight you must, and then retire to your tents: for I promise you that honour and good things are reserved for you in threefold measure.'

Achilles bowed to the will of the wise Immortal; but he turned upon Agamemnon and said:

'Listen, you drunken, dog-faced, deer-hearted coward, who has never once dared to lead the Greeks in battle, or to lie in ambush with the other princes of Hellas! I swear, by this staff which shall never more grow in the earth nor bring forth green leaves, that however much you may long for my aid when the Greeks fall before manslaying Hector, I will not raise a finger to help you until my own ships are in danger!'

So Achilles retired to his tents and hung up his armour: and his cousin Patroclus did likewise, and so did all the host of the Myrmidons. But Agamemnon sent Chryseis back to her father, and took Briseis from Achilles with further insulting words.

Then Achilles called to the sea nymph Thetis, his mother, and she came to him out of the waves, and he told her all that had happened and begged her aid.

'I will go at once to Olympus,' said Thetis, 'and pray mighty Zeus to help us. Surely he will bring it to pass that the Trojans may gain such a victory over the Greeks that Agamemnon will be forced to humble himself before you and beg your help on his knees!'

Thetis did even as she had said, and Zeus was gracious to her, and that very night he sent a deceitful dream to Agamemnon. And that dream took the shape of old Nestor, wisest of the Greeks, whose advice Agamemnon was always ready to take.

'Rise, King of Men,' cried the Dream, disguised in the likeness of King Nestor, 'I come as a messenger from Zeus himself. The Immortals have been swayed by the counsel of Queen Hera, and if you lead the Greeks in full force against Troy this day, you will take the city and level its walls with the ground. . . . Keep this in your heart and forget not my words when you awake – for they are words of truth!'

Agamemnon woke rejoicing, called together the leaders of the Greeks, and told them of his dream. They believed it also, and, arming themselves, marched out to do battle with the Trojans.

Menelaus and Paris

Meanwhile the news of Agamemnon's quarrel with Achilles had been brought to Troy, and the Trojans themselves decided to march out and scatter the Greeks while their most mighty warrior was sulking in his tent.

So the two armies met on the level plain outside Troy; and Paris, seized with unexpected boldness, offered to meet Menelaus in single combat.

'If I slay you,' he said, 'then the Greeks must swear to return home without Helen. But if I fall, Helen shall be returned, and a great treasure besides.'

The Greeks, who were heartily sick of the war, agreed eagerly to this, and both sides swore to keep the truce and to abide by the outcome of the battle between Menelaus and Paris.

When she heard of what was about to happen, Helen came hastening to the wall above the scene of the single combat. And Priam, who was there to see it also, exclaimed at the sight of her amazing beauty:

'Small wonder is it that Trojans and Greeks should endure long hardships and battles for such a woman – for indeed she is marvellously like to one of the Immortals in her very loveliness!'

But Helen sighed, and made answer:

'Would that sore death had come to me before ever your son Paris led me away from happy Sparta and my dear daughter Hermione. Alas, my lord Menelaus must think me the most shameful of all women!'

Menelaus, however, was preparing to do battle for Helen as if she had been as perfect a bride as Alcestis was to Admetus; and Paris was doing the same, as if she had been, in fact, his lawfully wedded wife, and as though there were no deserted wood nymph Oenone pining in tears on lonely Ida.

First each of the heroes set the greaves upon his legs, beautifully fashioned and fastened with silver ankle-clasps; next upon his chest each fastened the moulded corselet of beaten bronze; and over his shoulder cast the baldric which held his brazen sword with the silver-studded handle. And on his mighty head each set a cunningly wrought helmet with a great crest of horse-hair that nodded terribly, and took in his hand a strong ashen spear with a point of bronze.

So, when they had armed themselves, they stood forth between the ranks of Trojans and Greeks, who sat in their long lines to watch the battle.

First Paris hurled his spear and smote Menelaus on the shield, but the point was turned and did not pierce it. Then Menelaus, uttering a prayer to Zeus, threw his weapon. It smote the round shield of Paris, and passed through it – so mightily did he cast in his anger. It pierced the wrought breast-plate also, and Paris would have died then and there had he not managed to twist away so that the blade did but graze his side.

Menelaus flung down his shield with a cry of triumph, and leaping forward seized Paris by his horse-hair crest, and swinging him round, dragged him by the head towards the Grecian lines. And Paris would have been strangled like Cycnus by the straps of his own helmet, if Aphrodite had not come to his aid. She snapped the straps suddenly, so that Menelaus rolled over backwards, holding the empty helmet in his hands, and when he leapt to his feet – Paris was gone. For Paris was no longer the brave young herdsman of Ida: rather than feats of strength and daring, he preferred to dally away the hours with his unwilling bride. Now, shielded by Aphrodite in a magic mist, he fled swiftly back to Troy, and hid himself in Helen's bower.

But Menelaus, failing to find him, marched proudly up and down between the armies, shouting:

'Harken to me, Trojans and Greeks! Paris has fled, and the

233

victory is mine! Therefore Helen is mine! Give her back to me, and we will sail away and trouble Troy no more!'

All the Greeks and Trojans agreed with this, and a cry of joy went up from either side, for the war was over, and they could go home in peace!

CHAPTER 25

The Horses of Rhesus

What eyes, what ears hath sweet Andromache,
  Save for her Hector's form and step; as tear
    On tear made salt the warm last kiss he gave?
He goes. Cassandra's words beat heavily
  Like crows above his crest, and at his ear
    Ring hollow in the shield that shall not save.

D. G. ROSSETTI : *Cassandra*

25. The Horses of Rhesus

THIS would indeed have been the end of the war, had it not been for the treachery of the Trojan Pandarus. For when he saw Menelaus striding boastfully up and down and taunting Paris for running away, he fitted a sharp arrow to his polished bow of ibex horn, and loosed a shaft which wounded Menelaus in the side, just where he had wounded Paris with his spear.

At this cries of rage and scorn rose from the Greeks. 'Now we will smite the Trojans!' they cried. 'For they have broken the truce, and Zeus will surely be on our side!'

They armed in haste, and the Trojans did the same, and both sides rushed together and engaged in the hottest battle there had been since the very beginning when the Greeks first landed on Trojan soil and brave Protesilaus was slain. The noise of shield meeting shield was like the roar of a mountain torrent at midwinter; and when a man fell he was stripped of his armour and trodden underfoot.

Many deeds were done in that battle of which the minstrels sang in after days. They told how Menelaus slew fierce Scamandrius, the mighty hunter; how Diomedes fought with Aeneas and would have slain him had not Aphrodite come to her son's aid, and suffered a wound herself, Immortal though she was. They told also of the mighty doings of Odysseus who ranged through the cowering Trojans like a wolf in a sheep-fold.

While this great battle was raging, and the Trojans were getting the worst of it, their great champion Hector was in Troy, searching angrily for Paris. He found him at last in Helen's room where she was weeping and calling him a coward.

'Would that the winds had wafted me away, and that the waves had drowned me before ever I came to Troy with such a one as you!' she cried.

Paris hung his head, and made excuses, and at last consented to re-arm and go down into the battle.

Then, leaving his cowardly brother reluctantly buckling on his armour, Hector strode away to his own house; and there he found his beloved wife Andromache, nursing their little golden-haired son Astyanax, beautiful as a star.

'My dear lord,' said Andromache, weeping softly, 'do not go out to battle this day, for I fear greatly lest you should be slain. My father was killed by Achilles in the beginning of this dreadful war, and if you fall, Troy will fall also. So go not to the battle, but stay here with us; for if Troy falls, I shall be sold into slavery – and our son they will surely slay, child though he be, lest he grow up to avenge your death upon their children.'

But Hector made answer:

'Indeed I think of all these things, dearest wife, but if I held back from the battle I would never again be able to hold up my head before the men and women of Troy. I fear that Troy is indeed doomed, and that it will soon be laid low and its people slain or sold into slavery. But let me fall honourably in battle – for death is better than shame, and how could I endure to see you led away captive.'

So spoke Hector, and stretched out his arms to Astyanax. But the child shrank away crying, afraid of the great nodding crest on his father's helmet. Then Hector laughed, and Andromache also, and he took off his helmet and laid it on the ground, and lifted the child and dandled him in his arms, saying:

'Now I pray to Zeus, and to all the Immortals, that my son may grow up to be as valiant as I am, and a mighty king of Troy. May people say, when they see him return victorious from battle, "Far greater is he than ever his father was!" And may he live long to gladden your heart when I am no more.'

So saying he placed the child in its mother's arms, and kissed and comforted her: 'Dearest, do not sorrow over much,' he said, 'no man may escape his fate, be he coward or hero.'

Then he went swiftly to the battle, while Andromache wept and would not be comforted; for she was certain that they had said their last farewell.

Down on the battlefield Hector rallied the Trojan ranks with such good effect that presently it was the Greeks who were retreating. Then he cried aloud a challenge:

'Come forth and do battle with me, man to man, whoever is bravest and most daring among the Greeks! I am not Paris, but Hector – and Hector will not run away!'

This challenge was meant for Achilles who was still sulking in his tent, but he would not come, even to show his strength against Hector. But many of the Greek leaders sprang forward as volunteers – Agamemnon among them, and Diomedes, Ajax, and Odysseus, and more besides. Then at Nestor's suggestion they cast lots in a helmet, and that of Ajax first fell to the ground.

So Ajax stepped forward in his flashing bronze, the biggest man among all the Greeks, looking as fierce and as mighty as Ares the Immortal Warlord himself.

'Now, Hector!' cried he exultantly. 'Come and fight me if you dare! I'll show you what men there are among the Greeks, even though Achilles is not with us today.'

The two champions attacked each other with spear and sword, and many were the blows dealt and guarded. But neither could win the advantage, and soon darkness began to fall, and the heralds cried a truce. As night came on, the warriors drew apart, and exchanged gifts – one worthy foeman with another.

That night the Greeks laboured without ceasing and made a wall and a ditch to protect themselves and the ships from the Trojans. In the morning the battle was resumed with even greater fury, and the Greeks were driven back behind their new wall.

As for the Trojans, they camped out in the plain and did not bother to return for safety to their city, but sat about their campfires singing and rejoicing in their victory, feeling certain that next day they would conquer the Greeks and burn all their ships.

But in the Grecian camp the leaders sat in council together with long faces and troubled hearts.

And first Agamemnon spoke, saying:

'My friends, leaders, and captains of the host, surely Zeus has smitten us this day, and there can be only one meaning in what he has done, that we shall never conquer Troy. Therefore let us flee swiftly while yet the ships remain to us, and return home to our own land.'

'Go if you like, coward king!' cried Diomedes at this. 'But I at least will stay and fight it out!'

The other kings applauded him, and Nestor advised that first of all a good watch should be kept along the wall lest the Trojans planned a night attack. So Diomedes, with five hundred men under Nestor's son, Thrasymedes, went to see to this important task, while Nestor went on:

'Most noble Agamemnon, King of Men, all this woe comes of your folly in robbing Achilles of the girl Briseis. You know well that without him we cannot conquer Hector nor take Troy. Therefore my counsel is that you swallow your pride and send to Achilles offering him back the girl with many fair gifts, if only he will pardon the insult which you did him and return to the war.'

'Wise Nestor,' answered Agamemnon, 'I was indeed a fool, and I readily admit my folly. I will send Odysseus and brave Ajax to Achilles with such a message as you suggest; and they must promise him Briseis, and twenty Trojan maidens, besides a shipload of gold and bronze. If these will not suffice, he shall have his choice of one of my daughters to be his wife, when we return from conquered Troy.'

Off went the two kings on this errand, but even the persuasive speech of Odysseus could not move Achilles, who only smiled grimly and answered:

'My advice is for us all to return speedily to Greece. You cannot conquer Troy without my aid – and I am minded to withhold that aid, and so save the life which otherwise I am fated to lose. I sail home in the morning.'

When Agamemnon heard this, he wept and tore his hair. But Nestor strove to encourage him, and Menelaus joined him, saying:

'We must prepare for tomorrow's battle. Is there anyone who will dare to go secretly among the Trojans and spy out their camp – and perhaps overhear their counsel.'

'That will I!' cried Odysseus, and Diomedes volunteering to go with him, the two set out, wearing leather caps and no armour, but taking their swords.

Meanwhile the Trojans had hit upon the same idea, and a young man named Dolon had volunteered to spy for them if Priam would promise him the magic horses of Achilles – Poseidon's wedding present to Peleus and Thetis – as a reward.

This was agreed and he went out in the night, wearing a grey wolf skin over his shoulders and carrying his bow in his hand.

When Odysseus and Diomedes saw him coming, they lay down quickly among the dead, and pretended to be corpses also. But as soon as he had passed, they sprang up and seized hold of him from behind.

'Do not kill me!' begged Dolon, green with fear. 'My father is very rich, and will pay a vast ransom for my life. Moreover, I will give you news of the Trojans – anything, if only you will spare me!'

'Speak swiftly!' said Odysseus, and the wretched youth began to tell them about the Trojan plans for the morrow.

'But what you should do,' he babbled, 'is to steal away the horses of King Rhesus. He arrived this evening from Thrace with all his men, and there is a prophecy that Troy will never fall if once his wonderful white horses have entered the city. Now send me, a prisoner to the ships, and if I have spoken truly, set me free and my father will pay ransom.'

'Not so,' answered Diomedes, 'a spy and a traitor is not fit to live!' And with that he smote off the wretched Dolon's head.

Then he and Odysseus stole on through the darkness, and soon

King Rhesus

came to the place where the newly arrived Thracians were camped. Here they slew several men in their sleep, including the unfortunate King Rhesus himself. Then they loosed the horses, tied them together, and Diomedes drove them carefully between the sleeping men, and away towards the Greek camp.

But presently a Thracian woke suddenly, and when he saw dead men lie bleeding on the ground and the white horses gone, he cried aloud, and his comrades leapt to their feet, snatching up their swords.

Then Diomedes leapt upon the back of the nearest horse and galloped away until he came to the tent of Agamemnon. But Odysseus remained among the Thracians, in deadly peril, and indeed he was soon surrounded by them.

'Here's the man who killed our king!' shouted a Thracian captain.

'Fool!' cried Odysseus in a voice of authority. 'You'll suffer for this if you are not careful!'

'Then give the watchword,' persisted the captain, 'or I'll drive my spear into you!'

'The watchword is "Phoebus",' answered Odysseus quietly, having had the foresight to learn it from Dolon.

'Right!' cried the captain, letting go of him. 'Do you know which way the murderer went?'

'Of course I do,' answered Odysseus angrily. 'I was pursuing him when you were fool enough to stop me! Come along with me!'

With that he set off at his best speed and was soon back in the Greek camp, while the Thracians were receiving a warm welcome from Thrasymedes and his five hundred guards on the wall.

CHAPTER 26

The Death of Hector

But one that was my comfort and my joy,
Hector, the very pride and prop of Troy,
One that the bulwark of his brethren was,
Him hast thou slain, and I am left alone!

HOMER: *The Iliad* (Translated by Andrew Lang)

26. The Death of Hector

DAWNING day brought a mass attack from the Trojans, furious at the death of King Rhesus and the theft of his white horses. The Greeks, encouraged by the exploits of Diomedes and Odysseus, met them fiercely, led by Ajax; and one of the greatest battles of the Trojan War began.

At first the Greeks had the better of it, as Hector was not fighting in the Trojan vanguard but marshalling his troops from behind. Agamemnon, putting from him his usual cowardice, led his army to such good effect that the Trojans at last broke and fled back towards their city. But near the gates Hector rallied them, and Agamemnon was wounded by the spear of a Thracian captain, and carried back to the ships in his chariot. Then Hector charged at the head of the Trojans, and the Greeks fled before him. Near the encampment Diomedes and Odysseus turned at bay, and held off the pursuers while the Greeks reformed their ranks.

Then Hector led another charge, but Diomedes took good aim with his mighty spear and struck him on the helmet. The spear did not pierce it, but so heavy was the blow that Hector fell stunned to the earth, and was carried out of the battle in his chariot.

Diomedes was shot through the foot by Paris shortly after, so he was also out of the battle, leaving Odysseus to rally the front ranks. Long he fought there and slew many Trojans, but at last a spear pierced his shield and bit deep into his side. With a cry he plucked it out and with it slew the man who had wounded him: then, as he sank to the ground he called aloud to Ajax and Menelaus, who rushed forward to the rescue. Ajax with his great shield protected Odysseus while he climbed into a chariot, and then Menelaus drove him back to the ships to have his wound dressed.

While Ajax was doing great deeds and keeping back the advancing Trojans, the wounded kings were holding a hurried conference beside the ships.

'The only thing to do is to keep them off until night, and then launch our ships quietly and escape!' urged Agamemnon.

But Odysseus turned on him fiercely:

'You should be leading some band of common cowards,' he cried, 'not the army of the Greeks! We will fight, every one of us, and perish to a man rather than run away. Be silent, if you have no other advice to give, for it would be shameful if the common soldiers heard the King of Men utter such cowardly words.'

Agamemnon, shamed once more into courage, urged the Greeks to make another charge, and Ajax led them as bravely as ever. Meeting Hector, he smote him with a great stone, so that he was carried away bleeding at the mouth. The tide of battle turned then for a while and the Trojans retreated; but when Hector had recovered he led such a charge, with Paris on one side of him and Aeneas on the other, that the Greeks fled in good earnest.

'To the ships! To the ships!' cried Hector. 'Burn the ships so that they cannot get away! Time for spoils when the battle is over! Burn the ships first!'

They were fighting now on the very sea-shore, and Ajax was aboard his own ship wielding a great spear which was kept for repelling boarders in a sea-fight. Twelve men who tried to set fire to his ship were slain by him; but he could not guard all the ships, and presently Hector himself flung a torch on to the one from which brave Protesilaus had leapt to his death at the beginning of the war.

But help came unexpectedly. Patroclus, cousin of Achilles, had been tending a wounded friend, but when he saw that the Trojans were trying to burn the ships, he rushed off to Achilles.

'If you will not fight,' he cried, 'at least let me lead our Myrmidons to battle! The ships are on fire and most of the Greek kings wounded.'

Then Achilles was sorry that, in his anger, he had sworn not to fight until his own ships were in danger. But he bade Patroclus wear his own armour so that the Trojans should think that Achilles himself was leading the Myrmidons, and urged him forth before it was too late.

Meanwhile Ajax fought fiercely on; but he was growing weary and could hardly hold up the great spear any longer. Then Hector attacked him, and cut off the spear's brazen point with a blow of his sword. Ajax drew back, and a moment later his ship was ablaze.

Just at that critical moment there rose a cry of fear from the Trojans, and they fell back hurriedly, shouting:

'Achilles! Achilles the invincible comes against us once more!'

And there was Patroclus, in the shining armour which all knew so well, and drawn in the chariot by the two magic horses which Poseidon had given to Peleus. Straight to the ships he went, and quenched the flames which were destroying the ship of Protesilaus. Then he turned the chariot and led the whole Greek army in a tremendous charge against the Trojans, who fled in disorder across the ditch and over the wide plain towards the city of Troy.

For a while the flight was stayed by King Sarpedon of Lycia,

'Sleep and Death carried away the body'

an ally of the Trojans. He engaged with Patroclus and a fierce
combat ensued. Patroclus struck the first blow, but his dart went
wide and transfixed the charioteer. Sarpedon retaliated with two
darts, one after the other, but in his over-eagerness he missed his
aim with both. Then Patroclus launched a spear with all his strength
and it pierced Sarpedon so that he fell like a tall tree smitten down
on the hillside by the sharp axe of the woodman.

But as he lay dying he cried out:

'Fight on, brave Lycians! Do not fly because I am down! Rescue
my body from the Greeks to give it worthy funeral!'

Fiercely the fight raged over his dead body, but in the end the
Greeks tore the armour from him. Yet Apollo, pitying the fallen
champion, sent out Sleep and Death, and they carried away the

body, over land and sea to Lycia, there to be laid quietly to rest.

But Patroclus pursued the flying Trojans right to the very walls of Troy, and strove even to enter, but was pushed back three times. Then Hector came thundering out of the gateway in his chariot, mowing down all who came in his way, and drove straight at Patroclus – who flung a heavy stone at him, missed his mark, but killed the charioteer. For a few minutes the two heroes struggled over the body of the slain man, and then the surge of battle parted them.

The sun was sinking when they met again, and Patroclus had lost his helmet in the thick of the battle, and was weary and wounded. Nevertheless he charged at Hector, who met him in full career and transfixed his body with a spear. Then Patroclus fell to the ground, and as Hector stood over him with drawn sword, he gasped:

'Do not boast greatly at my slaying, noble Hector – for stern Fate decreed it – Fate that no man may escape. And know that you yourself have not long to live, for already Death is on his way from the realm of Hades: and by the hand of great Achilles shall you fall!'

Then Patroclus died, and his charioteer sped like the wind out of the rush of battle, drawn by the two magic horses, and brought the news to Achilles as he sat alone in his tent.

When Achilles heard that his beloved cousin was dead, he covered his face with his hands and wept. By and by, as he still sat there alone, his mother the sea nymph Thetis came to him, and for a long time she strove in vain to comfort him.

'Let me die, let me die!' groaned Achilles, 'since I might not save my friend from death, and through my foolish anger he is dead. . . . All I ask is to slay Hector who has done this thing!'

Then, unarmed as he was, Achilles rushed out of his tent and on to the wall of the camp. There he stood, tall and godlike, with the red sunset blazing behind him. Down on the plain he saw the battle raging fiercely. He saw that Hector had stripped the armour from dead Patroclus – the golden armour which the Immortals had given to Peleus – and that the Greeks, still led by Ajax, were fighting to bring the poor, maimed, naked body of the dead hero back into their camp.

Achilles saw, and he raised his mighty voice in a cry which rang like a clarion call over the field of battle; and the thunder rolling on Mount Ida seemed to be but the echo of his voice. Thrice Achilles uttered that terrible cry, and the Trojans drew back in fear, while the very horses snorted and shied away.

Then the Greeks took up the body of Patroclus and bore it back to the camp; and as they did so, night fell.

Once more the Trojans camped on the open plain, and Hector would not return to Troy, though his friends warned him that Achilles would never rest now until one or the other lay dead.

'Never will I flee!' he cried. 'What though the great Achilles come against me? One of us must fall – but Ares the Immortal Warlord may guide my spear so that Achilles is the one who dies!'

But Achilles rested in his tent, grieving over the loss of Patroclus; and presently, by the will of the Immortals, sweet Sleep came to him and he was at rest. There was no rest in the forge of Hephaestus the Immortal Smith that night, however: for at the prayer of Thetis he was forging new armour for Achilles.

In the grey morning Thetis, the sea nymph, came down from high Olympus bearing the wonderful armour for her son – a shield of five thicknesses tooled and engraved all over with scenes and devices; a corselet brighter than a flame of fire, a massive helmet with its golden crest, and greaves of pliant tin.

Achilles beheld these wondrous things, and his eyes glittered with delight. Swiftly he put them on and took a great spear in his hand. Then he went down by the shore, shouting his terrible cry, and all the Grecian warriors sprang up from sleep, buckled on their armour, and made ready for battle.

But first Odysseus came to Achilles and persuaded him to visit the wounded Agamemnon, to receive his apologies and the gifts which were to be made him.

Peace restored between the leaders, Achilles went forth to war in his brazen chariot drawn by the two magic horses. And as he was tightening the harness on their backs, one of them spoke to him in a human voice, saying:

'We shall bear you swiftly and speedily: but your day of death is near – death that will come to you in battle.'

'Well do I know it,' answered Achilles, 'but I shall not cease from fighting until that day, unless I may lay proud Troy in the dust.'

All day long the battle raged, and the Trojans fled before the wrath of Achilles, leaving many, many dead upon the field. Across the River Scamander he drove them, and did not stop, though the River rose against him in an angry flood. Over the plain fled the Trojans, with Achilles hot at their heels, and they did not pause from flight until they were safe behind the walls of Troy.

But Hector alone stood at the Scaean Gate of the city, waiting for Achilles who came rushing on, shining like a shooting-star in his golden armour.

'Come within the gate!' cried King Priam. 'This terrible man has slain many of my sons, and if he slays you also, who shall I have to help me in my old age?'

But Hector would not listen, and he went forth to meet Achilles, leaving Priam and Hecuba on the towers over the gate with Andromache and the other Trojan wives. They met near where a spring still bubbles out of the plain by a little grove of trees, and as they fought they moved out of sight round a corner of the city walls.

Achilles hurled his spear and missed Hector, who in his turn hurled his own weapon which failed to pierce the wondrous shield. Then Hector drew his sword, but Achilles had a second spear and caught him on the point of it as he rushed against him.

Hector fell in the dust, and Achilles cried:

'Slayer of Patroclus, dogs and birds shall tear your flesh as you lie unburied!'

'Do not do this great shame!' gasped Hector. 'Take the store of gold my father will offer you, and let my body be burnt in Troy!'

'Hound, even if Priam offered me your weight in gold, I doubt if it would save your corpse from the dogs!' shouted vengeful Achilles.

'Remember me in the day when Paris slays you in the Scaean Gate!' said Hector quietly, and with that he fell back dead.

Then Achilles pierced his feet, and having stripped him, tied him to the back of his chariot and drove in triumph round and round the walls of Troy, while Andromache shrieked and fainted, and Priam and all the Trojans wept.

Next day Achilles burned the body of Patroclus on a great funeral pyre, and sacrificed twelve prisoners of war to his ghost – a deed of shame which caused great Zeus to turn away his eyes. And he caused games to be held in honour of Patroclus, and all the Greek kings took part in them.

And each day he trailed the body of Hector round the walls of Troy, until the Immortals grew angry, and sent Thetis to tell her son that he must render up the body for an honourable funeral. For without the rites of fire, the Greeks and Trojans believed that no spirit could depart into the Kingdom of Hades through which all must pass, even if they were fated to dwell in the Isles of the Blest and the sweet Elysian Fields.

That night King Priam came through the ranks of the Greeks to the very tent of Achilles, and kneeling at his feet he kissed the terrible hands which had slain his son and wept silently.

Then Achilles remembered his old father Peleus, waiting alone in distant Hellas, and he wept also and raised the sorrowing king with gentle words, gave him food and drink and sent him back to Troy with all honour.

In the morning he bade Briseis and the other handmaidens wash the body of Hector and clothe it in fair linen.

Then he set up a great pair of scales under the walls of Troy and placed the body in one pan: for he had sworn only to give up the corpse of Hector in exchange for his weight in gold.

But when Priam had stripped his treasury to make up the weight, the scale still trembled and would not turn, till Hector's lovely sister Polyxena, youngest of Priam's children, leant over the wall and cast her golden bracelets into the scale, then Hector's body rose as the weight of gold sank to the ground.

So they carried Hector into Troy, amidst great lamentations and, bending over him, fair Helen cried:

'Hector, of all my brethren in Troy the dearest, since Paris brought me here – but would that I had died ere ever that day dawned. Hector, in all the years since then I have never heard from you a word that was bitter or unkind. Others spoke cruelly to me, for whom this bitter war is fought: but ever you would restrain them with gentle, courteous words. Ah woe is me! Woe is me! Now there is none like you left in all Troy, and my one true friend is dead.'

CHAPTER 27

Neoptolemus and Philoctetes

Yet is there hope; slow hope yet comfort sure,
I had forgot it in my wrath and pain.
Is there no oracle? Troy cannot fall.
I guard thine arrows, Heracles divine,
And Troy falls not without them.

LORD DE TABLEY: *Philoctetes*

27. Neoptolemus and Philoctetes

THE Trojan War did not end with the death of Hector, but now the Trojans ventured out into the open less and less often, while the Greeks besieged them even more closely than before.

Yet, though all the lesser cities lay waste far and wide, the Trojans still had allies: and the first of these that came to their aid after the death of Hector was the beautiful Penthesilia, Queen of the Amazons.

The Trojans sallied out to battle when they saw her coming, but Achilles drove them back again, and turned against Penthesilia. Their meeting was sharp and brief, for Achilles pierced her with his spear and she fell dying to the ground. As he bent over her to strip off her armour, he realized for the first time that he had slain a lovely girl. Then his heart was stirred with regret at the thought that he might instead have captured her and carried her away to be his slave-wife – or even his queen, if Deidamia were dead; and he mourned his unlucky stroke with tears, for indeed the lovely Amazon was divinely fair and like one of the Immortals, since her father was Ares the Warlord.

Then Thersites, the ugliest and vilest of the Greeks, jeered at Achilles:

'Sorry-souled Achilles! It only needs a pretty face to turn you from a warrior into a womanish traitor worse than Paris himself! As for this dirty Amazon slut, she's only good for dogs' meat!' And with that he began jabbing at the corpse with his spear.

Then Achilles lost his temper completely.

'Take that, shameless wretch!' he shouted. 'No man shall revile Achilles and go unpunished!' and he struck Thersites such a blow on the side of his head that his teeth were scattered on the ground and he fell upon his face and died.

Having slain a Greek of noble birth (for Thersites, for all his vileness, was cousin to Diomedes), Achilles needed to be cleared of blood-guilt, and sailed away to the island of Lesbos for this purpose.

While he was away, Priam's last ally arrived with an army. This was Prince Memnon of Ethiopia, son of Eos the Dawn-Titan and her mortal husband King Tithonus. The story of these two was very sad: for Eos when she fell in love with Tithonus, the most handsome of mortal men, prayed Zeus to grant that he should never die. Zeus granted this prayer without a moment's thought, and all seemed well. But Eos realized too late that, though Tithonus

255

Achilles

could never die, he could still grow old. For in time he grew so
ancient that he was no more than a little shrunken, chirping creature
like a large grasshopper, who could not see nor hear, but merely sit
gibbering and chattering to himself, locked far away from sight in a
room in the golden palace of Immortal Eos.

Strong Memnon, however, came to Troy with his swarthy
followers, and once more the Trojans ventured out of their city,
and together they chased the Greeks for the last time down almost
to their ships. Night fell just as Ajax was preparing to go out against
Memnon; and in the morning Achilles returned from Lesbos and
turned the tide of battle, slaying the Ethiopian King and scattering
his forces. Then he chased the Trojans helter-skelter across the
plain and into Troy, mocking them and boasting that even the
Immortals would not be able to withstand him, if he came in arms
against them.

But as he stood there in the Scaean Gate, Paris took an arrow
from his quiver, set it to his bow, took careful aim and loosed.
Away sped the shaft, guided by Apollo who was angry at Achilles's
words. It struck him in the heel – the one vulnerable part of his
whole body – the heel by which Thetis had held him when she
dipped him as a baby in the River Styx.

The arrow was poisoned, and presently Achilles fell to the ground with a great cry and died.

For a little while friend and foe stood staring and aghast, for neither could believe that so great a hero could really be dead. Then, with a shout of triumph, the Trojans rushed forward to spoil the body: but mighty Ajax seized it, swung it over his shoulders, and raced for the ships with it, never heeding the showers of darts which were sped after him.

Mad with rage and grief the Greeks, headed by Odysseus, drove the Trojans back into Troy, and invested the city more mercilessly than ever. Next day they burnt the body of Achilles on a great pyre, and buried his ashes with those of Patroclus on the sea-coast and heaped a great mound over them which is there to this day. But Thetis snatched away the soul of her son and took him to the Isles of the Blest reserved for the spirits of the heroes.

Once again, the Greeks did honour to a dead hero by holding games; and at the close of them Agamemnon rashly said that he would give the armour of Achilles to the bravest of the Greeks.

At once quarrels arose as to who could claim that honour. Agamemnon favoured his brother Menelaus, but the general vote placed the contest between Ajax and Odysseus. No one dared to decide which of the two had the best claim, and the argument grew more and more heated.

At last wise old Nestor exclaimed:

'Friends, we cannot settle this question ourselves – but why should not the Trojans decide it for us? Send spies quickly to Troy: let them listen under the walls and tell us what the Trojans think of our two great heroes – who to me seem absolutely equal in courage!'

Everyone praised the wisdom of Nestor's suggestion, and the spies were sent accordingly. Presently one returned, and said:

'My lords, as we listened beneath the walls we heard the women of Troy speaking above us. One said: "Ajax is the bravest of the Greeks! Why, he carried the body of Achilles out of the battle, which even Odysseus did not dare to do!" But another answered her: "What nonsense you do talk! Even a woman could have carried him away, if somebody put him on her back: but she could not fight as Odysseus did – she would faint with fear if it came to fighting!"'

Even this was not quite conclusive, but a secret vote among the Greek kings showed that most of them considered Odysseus to be the victor.

Hearing this, Ajax turned without a word and strode blindly to his tent, so dazed with grief and fury that presently his mind gave way and a bout of madness descended upon him. In his frenzy he imagined that Agamemnon and Menelaus had cheated him and given the armour to Odysseus just to insult him; and he rose up in the darkness and set out with drawn sword to slay all three of them in their sleep.

Athena, however, was watchful that night, and knowing what Ajax was minded to do, she led him astray in the darkness so that he stumbled among the flocks of sheep and began slaughtering them, thinking they were his enemies. He even took two rams to his tent, tied them to the pole, and scourged them with a great whip, under the impression that he was beating Agamemnon and Menelaus to death.

In the morning he recovered his senses, and was filled with such shame, both at his childish anger and his murderous madness, that he went away to a lonely part of the sea-shore and there flung himself upon his sword.

When the Greeks found what had happened they mourned him sadly, and none was so filled with grief as Odysseus, who vowed immediately to give up the armour to Neoptolemus the son of Achilles as soon as he was old enough to wear it.

Ajax was buried in a stone coffin, amidst the lamentations of the Greeks: as he had not fallen in battle he could not be burnt on a pyre like the other heroes.

When the funeral was over a fresh council was called and Agamemnon spoke angrily to Calchas.

'The ten years are up!' he cried. 'You said it would be ten years before Troy fell – and Troy still stands. Now we have lost Achilles and Ajax: how can we conquer Troy?'

'You have neglected one of my earliest prophecies,' answered Calchas, who never failed of a ready reply. 'Troy cannot be conquered unless you have the arrows of Heracles to use: for by one of them Paris is fated to die. And the son of Achilles must go up against Troy, which cannot fall until he comes against it.'

Then the Greeks cheered, eager to see these prophecies fulfilled and the war ended at last; and they chose Odysseus and Diomedes, who ten years before had been to Scyros for Achilles, bidding them draw out a swift ship and bring back his son Neoptolemus.

Over the waves went the two heroes and came safely to Scyros. They drew the ship to shore and went striding up to the palace of old King Lycomedes. There in the morning light they saw Neoptolemus, still only a boy, yet tall and strong and wondrously like his father, driving his chariot and practising with spear and dart.

The boy welcomed them eagerly, and his eyes flashed with excitement when they told him the reason for their coming.

'Come to Troy!' urged Odysseus. 'We cannot take the city without you, now that your noble father Achilles is dead. All of us will welcome you with many gifts: for a start you shall have your father's golden armour as a gift from me – armour that the Warlord Ares would be proud to wear, since immortal hands fashioned it. And when the war is won and we return to Greece, Menelaus will give you his lovely daughter Hermione to be your bride.'

Neoptolemus needed no bribes to make him eager to set out for Troy; and set out he did, in spite of the tears and prayers of his mother Deidamia, who feared greatly that she would lose her son as she had lost her husband. But the sea nymph Thetis rejoiced, knowing that her grandson went to win glory, not death at Troy; and she made no attempt to stop him as she had tried to stop Achilles.

Once more the swift ship sped over the blue Aegean: but it did not make straight for Troy. Instead, Odysseus guided it to rugged Lemnos where Philoctetes had been marooned on account of his terrible snake-bite, hid it in a deep bay, and went ashore with only Neoptolemus and a few sailors. On the way Odysseus told his young companion about Philoctetes and how he had been left there ten years before, with only the bow and arrows of Heracles.

'We can only catch him by guile,' ended Odysseus, 'and that is where you can help. If he sees me, he'll shoot: and there is no cure for the Hydra poison. So you must pretend to have quarrelled with the Greek kings and with me in particular: say I refused to give you your father's armour. Anyhow, pretend that you left the war in a fury and, on your way home to Greece, have come to rescue him and take him with you. Once he is on the ship we can easily get the bow and arrows from him.'

Neoptolemus did not much like this kind of trickery, but he consented to do as Odysseus said, and went off by himself towards the rocky hillside where it seemed probable that Philoctetes would have found a cave in which to live. There he found the wretched man, with tangled hair and beard, dwelling in a cave with two entrances to guard against surprise, and living precariously on such game as he could shoot with his bow – which never left his hand, waking or asleep.

It was easy to make friends with the poor castaway, and very soon he was treating Neoptolemus like a son; and Neoptolemus was feeling more and more ashamed of the part which he was playing.

Presently one of the sailors arrived, pretending to be a merchant newly come from Troy, and warned Philoctetes that he was in danger.

'Odysseus and Diomedes are coming,' he cried. 'They have sworn to carry you off by force!'

Then Philoctetes hesitated no longer. 'I will accompany you, son of Achilles!' he exclaimed. 'Take me away quickly before Odysseus comes!'

On the way to the shore Philoctetes was seized with a terrible spasm of pain from his snake-bite. 'Hold the bow and arrows!' he gasped to Neoptolemus, 'and be ready to shoot if Odysseus arrives before my fit has passed. . . . You see how I trust you: no one else has ever held the bow of Heracles except my father Poeas and myself.'

Then Philoctetes rolled on the ground in his agony and at length fainted with the pain.

When he recovered, Odysseus stood above him, and Philoctetes knew that he had been tricked. Sadly and bitterly he limped away to his cave to gather his few possessions, while Odysseus set out for the ship to send back men to bring him.

But when he returned it was to find that Neoptolemus had been overcome by his natural sense of honour and decency.

'Philoctetes,' he said, 'I cannot cheat you like this. Here are the bow and arrows: I beg you not to use them against us, even against Odysseus. What he has done is only for the good of our armies at Troy. . . .'

Odysseus, returning at that moment, frankly confessed the whole scheme and begged Philoctetes to come with them of his own accord – to be received with all honour.

'I did wrong,' he said. 'First, when I marooned you here at the command of Agamemnon, and now when I sought to take you by guile.'

Philoctetes was so far moved that he made no attempt to shoot Odysseus, as he could easily have done: but he still refused to accompany him to Troy. Neoptolemus was ready to abide by his promise and take him back to Greece; and Odysseus said sadly:

'Then I must return to our friends having failed in my task. Troy cannot fall unless you two are with us!'

On a sudden, even as he spoke, Heracles, now an Immortal dwelling in the golden halls of Olympus, came down to Lemnos.

'Philoctetes!' he cried in his great voice. 'Listen, it is I, Heracles, come down from my high seat to tell you the will of Zeus. You must not return yet to Greece, but hasten to Troy with the son of Achilles. There you will be cured of your sickness and win glory as great as that of any hero. For you are now the chosen champion of that great army: seek out Paris, cause of all this evil, and strike him down with these arrows that once were mine. With them I destroyed Troy: and now for a second time Troy must fall before them.'

'It is the voice I have so often longed to hear,' whispered Philoctetes, 'the face even as I once knew it, but now divine. Indeed I shall not disobey.'

'Nor I,' echoed Neoptolemus.

'Then make haste!' cried Heracles. 'The wind is fair, and Troy is ripe to fall!'

Then Heracles went back to Olympus where the Immortals dwell. But Philoctetes, Neoptolemus, and Odysseus clasped hands in token of friendship, and set sail for Troy – where Machaon, son of the Immortal Physician, Asclepius, waited to cure the ten year old snake-bite so that Philoctetes could once more take his place among the warrior kings of Greece.

CHAPTER 28

The Theft of the Luck of Troy

Strong Tydeus' son should with Odysseus scale
The great wall . . . and should bear away
Pallas the Gracious, with her free consent,
Whose image was the sure defence of Troy:
Yea, for not even a god, how wrath so e'er,
Had power to lay the City of Priam waste
While that immortal shape stood warder there.

QUINTUS SMYRNAEUS : *Fall of Troy* (Translated by A. S. Way)

28. The Theft of the Luck of Troy

PARIS was immensely proud of himself for shooting Achilles; and now that Hector was dead he would, of course, be the next King of Troy when Priam died.

Helen smiled wearily and sadly as she sat in her room longing for her home in far-away Sparta; and the blood dripped from the Star-stone, dripped and vanished, dripped and vanished, and left no mark.

One day a handsome youth, little more than a boy, came to see her. Through the quiet palace he was led, and reached the shaded room where Helen sat weaving at her loom.

'Lady,' he said, 'my name is Corythus, and I have a message for you alone, and for your lord, Prince Paris.'

Then Helen sent her maidens from the room, and with a smile took the scroll of bark which Corythus handed to her. Breaking the golden thread with which it was fastened, she opened and read – and her eyes went wide and the colour forsook her face.

'Your mother is called Oenone,' she said in a strangled voice, 'and she is the wife of Paris – and you are their son?'

Corythus nodded. 'My mother sent me,' he answered simply. 'It was time, she said, that I came to Troy and claimed my rightful place as eldest and only son of the heir apparent.'

Then in a flood all that she had lost came to Helen: Menelaus, her home, Hermione, the name of true and faithful wife. And all for what? For Paris, doubly a cheat and traitor, who had deceived both her and Oenone.

She uttered a little choking cry and slipped to the floor in a faint, while Corythus bent over her anxiously, pitying her grief, marvelling at her beauty.

At this moment Paris strode into the room. He gave one glance, and his mad jealousy flared up. Without a moment's pause he snatched the sword from his side and struck Corythus dead with a single blow.

Then, so fierce was his rage and jealousy, he would have slain Helen also, but he saw the scroll and, reading what Oenone had written, he realized what he had done. Then he flung himself upon the ground and wept.

Corythus was burnt on a great pyre as became his rank, and Paris mourned sincerely for him. Helen wept too; but she spoke no more to Paris, and sat alone day after day gazing out towards the Grecian tents, or weaving on her loom all the tales of sorrow that had befallen on account of her, since Paris had come and carried her away from her happy home in Sparta.

Paris suffered too, and grew more reckless, though he had seldom been much of a fighter since he brought Helen to Troy. And soon after this the day came when Philoctetes was healed of his evil wound and came out to battle among the Greeks, bearing the great bow of Heracles in his hand.

Then for the last time the Trojans sallied out on to the plain and fought the Greeks hand to hand, with Paris cheering them on. Seeing him, Philoctetes fought his way fiercely through the thick of his foes until he drew near to Paris who, on his side, kept a sharp look-out. When he thought that Philoctetes was in reasonable range, Paris set an arrow to his bow and loosed at him. But Philoctetes dodged to one side so that another Greek took his death by it.

'Dog! Your day has come!' cried Philoctetes. 'Make haste to the land of shadows, and let there be an end to the destruction which you have caused!'

Then he drew the plaited cord to his breast, the great bow arched, the terrible point peeped out over the hand which held the curving wood. Loud sang the string as the death-hissing shaft sped on its way – and it missed not, though death was not yet, and the point did but graze the white wrist of Paris. Once again the avenger drew the bow and a barbed shaft screamed on its way, and this time buried itself in Paris's side.

Then Paris turned and fled into Troy, and night came down to cover the city and the plain. All through the hours of darkness the most skilful of the Trojan surgeons strove in vain to stop the terrible torment of the Hydra's burning blood, while Paris groaned and writhed sleeplessly. And before dawn he bade men carry him swiftly and silently out of Troy, up into the forests on Mount Ida; for he knew that in all the world only his deserted wife the nymph Oenone could cure him.

They came at last to her cave, where she sat weeping, ever weeping for her lost love and her slaughtered son.

Then Paris begged Oenone to save him. 'My lady,' he ended, 'I have sinned in my folly – but spare me! Save me from death!'

But Oenone answered in cold, dead tones: 'Go back to Helen and bid her to cure you! You slew our son, and you have killed my heart. Go quickly, you who are the cause of many a thousand deaths – not my son alone, but the sons of the women of Troy and of Greece cry out for vengeance.'

Then she turned away and sat silent, gazing into the distance.

They bore Paris away, down the steep slope towards Troy; but he was dead long before they reached the edge of the forest. So there they built a huge pyre and laid him upon it, and kindled it with fire.

But meanwhile Oenone repented of her anger, remembering only the love which had been between them, and the happy years when they dwelt together upon Ida, before the fatal coming of the three Immortals. So she gathered together her drugs and herbs, and hastened down the mountain side towards Troy. But presently she saw a glow ahead of her, and came suddenly to the pyre on which dead Paris lay.

Oenone gazed for a moment, and then with a bitter cry she sprang forward, and flung herself beside Paris, clasping him in her arms. Then the flames roared up, and the pyre fell in, and the ashes of Paris and Oenone were mingled in death.

Helen was free now; but the Trojans did not even think of sending her back to Menelaus. Indeed two brothers of Paris quarrelled as to which of them should now marry her; and when Priam promised her to Deiphobus, Helenus fled from Troy and was captured by the Greeks or gave himself up to them.

Odysseus brought him before the assembled kings, for Helenus was a prophet, and Calchas was at his wits' end to know why Troy had not yet fallen.

'I owe no allegiance now to Troy,' said Helenus, 'and I will tell you of the one thing lacking. You must steal the Luck of Troy: the city can never be taken while that remains within its walls!'

'The Luck of Troy?' asked Agamemnon, puzzled.

'The Palladium,' answered Helenus, 'the stone which fell from Heaven in the days of King Ilus. It is said to be the image of Pallas Athena that Zeus cast down from Olympus at the prayer of King Ilus to show where Troy should be built. Certainly no city can fall in which the Palladium rests. Of old we kept it secretly in a temple on Mount Ida – and Troy fell when Heracles came against it with Peleus and Telamon. But when Paris brought Helen to Troy, my father King Priam, by my advice, brought the Palladium to the Temple of Athena in Troy.'

Helenus would say no more, and at length it was decided that some spy must make his way into Troy and discover how the Palladium could be stolen.

Odysseus, most cunning of the Greeks, volunteered for this service. He dressed himself in rags, got some of the Greeks to beat him until the blood ran down his face and back, and covered himself in filth: there was no beggar in all the Greek camp so foul as he. In this disguise he won admission into Troy, pretending that he had been beaten and driven away by the cruel Greeks.

The Trojans welcomed him, hoping to obtain news of the Greek plans, and Odysseus played his part so well that no one suspected him, and whatever he told them was believed.

Pallas Athena

Beggar though he was, the Trojans decided that this valuable ally must be treated as well as possible. So he was taken to the tower overlooking the plain of Troy where Helen lived to be bathed and clothed in decent clothes, and entertained.

Helen herself tended him, anxious for any news of the Greeks – and in spite of all his cunning she at length recognized him as Odysseus. For a long time he denied it with clever words, but at length Helen swore by the most solemn oaths not to betray him, and he confessed that she was right.

Then Helen wept, and told him how wretched she was. 'When Paris died,' she ended, 'the last touch of the strange magic of Aphrodite faded from me. I scarcely could remember that I had not hated him – and oh, how I hate Deiphobus who wishes to have me now!'

'Could you not escape to us?' asked Odysseus.

'Escape? I have tried again and again,' sighed Helen. 'Only the guards along the Trojan walls could tell you how often I

have tried – how many times they or Deiphobus have caught
me with the rope already round my waist – once I was actually
hanging down outside the wall. . . . But how would I be received
in the Greek camp, I who, alas, am the cause of so much misery?
And my husband, Menelaus, surely he hates me – though it was
not of my own free will that I went with Paris in that night of
evil magic so many weary years ago.'

After this they spoke long together, making plans for the theft
of the Palladium, and for the taking of Troy. But Odysseus the
over-cunning did not tell Helen everything; though in his mind
he was already inventing the device of the Wooden Horse, he
spoke of it to her only in double meanings and half-concealed
hints, and left her doubting and even rather resentful.

But that night she helped him to escape from Troy, allowing
the watchmen to catch her in one of her own attempts and so
distracting their attention while Odysseus climbed down to Diomedes who was waiting for him. But she herself remained in Troy
to do her part on the night of the great attack.

Before this could be launched, however, the Palladium had
still to be stolen, and on a dark night Odysseus and Diomedes
came for it. They entered Troy this time by means of a narrow,
evil-smelling drain arched with great stones – a drain that may
be seen at Troy to this day. This low tunnel led them, through
mire and filth, to the very middle of Troy. It came up near the
temple and here they persuaded Theano the priestess, wife of
Antenor, to give up the image to them (though the Trojans insisted
afterwards that she gave only a copy and kept the real Palladium).
They were able to carry it away – though not to enter the city
again by that path.

Outside in the pale moonlight the evil magic in the misshapen
idol began to exert itself upon the thieves. For as Diomedes walked
ahead with it on his back a madness came upon Odysseus: not
knowing what he was doing, he fell behind his friend, drew his
sword and crept stealthily up, meaning to stab him in the back.
But as luck would have it the moon shone out from behind a cloud
as he was about to strike, and the flash of light on the sword-blade
caught the eye of Diomedes who wheeled round just in time to
avoid the blow. The madness was succeeded by a blank horror:
Odysseus dropped his weapon and allowed Diomedes to drive him
in front of him like a cow while he beat him with the flat of his
sword.

When they came to their senses neither Odysseus nor Diomedes
bore any malice towards each other. But the Greeks decided that

the Luck of Troy would bring only bad luck to them, and carried it hastily to a shrine of Athena on Mount Ida. There it remained until after the fall of Troy, when Aeneas took it with him on his wanderings.

Whether or not the loss of the Palladium made any difference to Troy, it was immediately after its theft that Odysseus suggested the plan of the Wooden Horse. He went off to Mount Ida with Epeius the skilled ship-wright and a band of men to fell trees, and brought back the timber to the Greek camp. Here a high wall was built to hide from the Trojans what was going on, and Epeius set to work, using all his skill to build the Horse according to the plans prepared by Odysseus.

First he made the hollow body of the Horse, in size like a curved ship; and he fitted a neck to the front of it with a purple fringed mane sprinkled with gold. The mane fell below the cunningly fashioned head which had eyes of blood-red amethyst surrounded with gems of sea-green beryl. In the mouth he set rows of jagged white teeth, and a golden bit with a jewelled bridle. And he made secret air-holes in the nostrils and the wide mouth and the high-pricked ears.

Then he fitted legs to the Horse, and a flowing tail twisted with gold and hung with tassels. The hooves were shod with bronze and mounted with polished tortoise-shell, and under them were set wheels so that the Horse might move easily over the ground.

Under the Horse there was a secret trap-door so cunningly hidden that no one, looking at the Horse from outside, could suspect it; and the door fastened from within with a special catch that only Epeius could undo.

So high and so wide was the Horse that it could not pass through any gate of Troy, and the secret hollow inside it was big enough for thirty men to enter and lie concealed with all their armour and weapons.

When all was ready, Odysseus begged Agamemnon to summon all the kings and princes of the Greek force, and he rose up in the assembly and said:

'My friends, now is the secret ambush prepared – thanks be to Athena, my Immortal counsellor and protector. Let us set all upon the hazard of a single exploit – an exploit that will live for ever on the lips of men. Let those of you who dare follow me into the Horse: for my plans are all laid, and my cousin Sinon is instructed how to beguile the Trojans. You, my lord Agamemnon, when we are safely in the Horse, must wait until darkness, then pull down the wall surrounding it and destroy the camp. Afterwards sail away with all our ships – but wait in hiding beyond the island of Tenedos. On the following night, if all is well, Sinon will kindle a fire on the grave of Achilles as a signal. Come all of you then back to land, and in darkness and silence speed to Troy Town and lay it low! For the gates will be open – and Helen will set a lamp in her window to guide you.'

Then all the Greeks cried out in praise of Odysseus and the greatness of his scheme – and all wished to accompany him into the Horse. But besides himself and Epeius he chose out no more than twenty-eight, and these included Menelaus and Teucer the brother of dead Ajax, Aias the son of Oileus, Thrasymedes the son of Nestor, Eumelus the son of Admetus, and two sons of Theseus called Demophon and Acamas who had come to Troy with Menestheus the King of Athens to rescue their grandmother Aethra, who was still Helen's attendant.

The thirty climbed up the ladder into the Horse, drew it after them, and closed the door, which Epeius then sat upon, while Odysseus settled himself in the Horse's neck to look out through the hidden holes.

Then Agamemnon caused the walls to be levelled, the camp to be torn down, and the whole army embarked in the ships.

When day dawned the plain of Troy lay empty and deserted except for the great Horse towering there alone. And on the wide sea not a ship was to be seen.

CHAPTER 29

The Wooden Horse

But Helen stood bright-eyed as glancing day
Nearby the Horse, and with a straying hand
Did stroke it here and there, and listening stand,
Leaning her head towards its gilded flank,
And strain to hear men's breath behind the plank.

MAURICE HEWLETT: *Helen Redeemed*

29. The Wooden Horse

MORNING dawned over the windy plain of Troy, and the Trojans looked out towards the great camp of the Greeks which had stood there so long – looked, and rubbed their eyes and looked again.

The camp was a deserted ruin of tumbled stones, and charred huts and palisades; and there were no ships to be seen drawn up on the shore, nor upon the sea.

While they were wondering at this and hardly able to believe their eyes, scouts came hastening to King Priam.

'The Greeks have indeed gone!' they cried. 'The camp lies in ashes; there is not a man, not a ship to be seen. But there stands in the midst of the ruins a great wooden horse the like of which we have never seen.'

Then the gates of Troy were flung open and out poured young and old, laughing and shouting in their joy that the Greeks were gone at last. Priam led the way with Queen Hecuba, followed by Polites and Deiphobus, the only sons remaining with them, and their daughters Cassandra and Polyxena. They came to the ruins and stood gazing at the great Wooden Horse.

And now they could see letters of gold inscribed on the Horse's side:

ΤΗΣ ΕΙΣ ΟΙΚΟΝ ΑΝΑΚΟΜΙΔΗΣ

ΕΛΛΗΝΕΣ ΑΘΗΝΑ ΧΑΡΙΣΤΗΡΙΟΝ

(*For their return home, the Greeks dedicate this thank-offering to Athena*)

At once a great argument broke out among the Trojans as to what should be done with the Horse.

'It is a gift to Athena,' cried one chief, 'so let us take it into Troy and place it in her temple!'

'No, no!' cried another, 'rather let us fling it into the sea!'

The arguments grew fierce: many wished to destroy it, but more to keep it as a memorial of the war – and Priam favoured this course.

Then Laocoon the priest, a man of violent temper who had already insulted Poseidon the Immortal Lord of the Sea by failing to offer him his due sacrifices, rushed up crying:

'Wretched men, are you mad? Do you not realize that the *Greeks* have made this? May it not be some cunning engine devised by that evil creature Odysseus to break down our walls or spy into our houses. There is something guileful about it, I am certain, and I warn you, Trojans, not to trust this Horse. Whatever it is, I fear the Greeks most when they make us gifts!'

So saying Laocoon hurled his spear at the Horse, and there came from it a strange clash and clang as of metal.

Then indeed the Trojans might have grown suspicious, and broken open the Horse with axes as some suggested; but at that moment several shepherds appeared, leading between them the wretched figure of a man who was caked from head to foot with mud and filth and dried blood; and his hands were fastened together with fetters of bronze.

'Great King of Troy!' he gasped. 'Save me! Pity me! I am a Greek, I confess it, but no man amongst you can hate the Greeks as I do – and it is within my power to make Troy safe for ever.'

'Speak,' said Priam briefly. 'Who are you, and what can you tell us?'

'My name is Sinon,' was the answer, 'and I am a cousin of Odysseus – of that most hateful and fiendish among men. Listen to what chanced. You have all heard of Palamedes? He was a Greek, and your enemy, but his gifts to mankind, and his wondrous inventions benefit you and all men. Odysseus hated him, for he it was who saw through his feigned madness and forced him to come to the war. At length that hatred could be endured no longer, and Odysseus of the many wiles devised a hideous plot whereby Palamedes was accused of betraying the Greek army to you Trojans. On the evidence of a forged letter he was convicted and stoned to death – and I alone knew that Odysseus wrote the letter and arranged the plot. Alas, I reproached my cousin with what he had done, and ever after he sought to have me slain.

'At length the time came when the Greeks despaired of conquering Troy: for it was revealed that never could they do so during this invasion. But our Immortal Lady Athena made it known to us that if we returned to Greece and set out afresh, we should conquer Troy. But first we must make this monstrous Horse as an offering to her – and make it so large that it could never be drawn into Troy: for *whatever city contains this Horse can never be conquered*.

'So the Horse was made. But Odysseus beguiled Calchas the prophet into declaring that, even as the Greek forces could not leave Aulis until the innocent maiden Iphigenia was sacrificed, so they could not leave Troy without the sacrifice of a noble warrior: and, by the evil workings of Odysseus, I was chosen as the victim.

'Last night they would have sacrificed me: but rendered desperate I broke away, and fled to hide myself in the foul mud of a noisome marsh that drains all Troy. Then the wind rose suddenly and the Greeks sailed away; but whether another was sacrificed instead of me, I cannot say. Only this I can tell you, noble Priam: this Horse is sacred to Athena and – since they have treated me so cruelly I can betray their secrets without incurring the anger of the Immortals – if you take it into Troy, the Greeks will never conquer you. Instead, you will be sailing to Greece, to sack rich Mycenae and proud Athens, Argos of the many horses and windy Iolcus, and Sparta in the fertile plain of hollow Lacedaemon.'

Then Priam and the other Trojan lords consulted together, and many of them were minded to believe Sinon; but others still doubted. While fate hung in the balance, there came two serpents out of the sea and made for the altar where Laocoon had retired with his two sons to offer up a sacrifice to the Sea-lord Poseidon. Straight to the place they went, terrible to be seen, and seized upon the two boys, and began to crush them in their deadly coils.

Laocoon strove to save his sons; but the serpents seized him too, and in a little while all three lay dead beside the altar of Poseidon.

Now all the Trojans cried out that Laocoon had been justly rewarded by the angry Immortals for casting his spear at the glorious offering made to Athena. Without further ado they twined the Horse about with garlands of flowers, and dragged it across the plain towards the city.

When they reached the gate, the Horse proved too big to enter by it; but the Trojans gaily pulled down a section of the wall, and brought it through in triumph, right to the courtyard of Athena's temple from which the Palladium, the Luck of Troy, had been stolen.

As evening fell, Cassandra came and stood beside the Horse.

'Cry, Trojans, cry!' she screamed. 'Your doom is upon you! I see warriors come from their hollow abode! I see Troy burning, her sons slaughtered and her daughters carried away to slavery! Cry, Trojans, cry! For madness has come upon you, and your doom is here!'

But no one would believe her, for still the curse was upon her that she must speak the truth and not be believed; and presently she went into the Temple of Athena and knelt in prayer before a statue of the Immortal whom she worshipped.

Night fell, and the Trojans feasted and revelled in their joy that the great war was over and the Greeks had gone. At last, worn out with excitement and celebration, they fell asleep, leaving few guards by the walls and gates – and few indeed that were sober.

But Aphrodite was loath to admit that Paris's people were about to be destroyed on account of the bribe which she had given him for the golden apple; and she made one last attempt to save the Trojans.

She went to Helen as she sat waiting in the palace, and cast her spell over her once more – though it was but faint and very brief. But Helen forgot for an hour that she hated Deiphobus, forgot that she was longing with all her heart for Menelaus and her lost Hermione. She rose like one in a dream and went to seek for the Trojan lover whom she detested.

'Dear my lord,' she said in her sweet voice as she laid her hand on his arm. 'Come with me, I beg you: for I would see this wondrous Horse made by the Greeks who were once my people.'

Intoxicated with joy at this sudden change in Helen's manner towards him, Deiphobus went with her willingly, and they came together into the courtyard of Athena's temple.

'Suppose,' mused Helen in a dreamy voice, 'the Kings of Greece – Menelaus, and Agamemnon, Odysseus and Diomedes and the rest – suppose they were all shut up inside this Horse!'

'If you think that,' exclaimed Deiphobus, 'we must have it broken open at once!'

'No,' murmured Helen, 'I have a better means than that. If they are there, I will lure them out!'

Now all her life Helen had the powers of mimicry: she could assume any voice so perfectly that no one who heard could tell her from the actual person.

So now, walking round and round the Horse, she called softly and sweetly, first in her own voice:

'Menelaus! Menelaus! Come to me, my lord and my love!' And then she called to Agamemnon in the voice of her sister Clytemnestra; and to Odysseus in the voice of her cousin Penelope. To Diomedes she called in the very tones of his wife Aegialia; and to each in the tones of one dearest to him.

Inside the Horse the heroes were sitting trembling and alert: only Neoptolemus showed no fear but gazed fiercely in front of him and gripped his sword. But when they heard their wives calling to them, the voices they had not heard for ten long, wretched years, the tears coursed down their cheeks and they found it hard indeed to stop themselves from answering.

Only Anticlus, the youngest man in the Horse, could not bear it.

278

The Wooden Horse

When he heard his wife Laodamia calling to him, he leapt forward to unfasten the trap-door and he opened his mouth to answer her. But watchful Odysseus caught hold of him in time, gripping him tightly and placing a hand firmly over his mouth.

But Anticlus seemed mad with his desire to cry out and escape from the Horse, and in deadly terror lest he should utter a sound and they should all perish, Odysseus held him tighter and tighter; and, without meaning it, he choked him so that Anticlus died there in the Horse, and his friends wept silently for him and wrapped his body in a cloak.

'There is no one in the Horse,' exclaimed Deiphobus at length. 'Come away, Helen, I am weary and would sleep.'

So he led her to her room in a high tower overlooking the plain of Troy; and Deiphobus slept – for the last time. When she was alone, the spell of Aphrodite passed from Helen, and she was overcome with shame and self-loathing at what she had done. All that night she sat in her window with a bright lamp beside her so that the Greeks could find Troy in the darkness, and she held out her white arms as if to draw Menelaus to her. And ever the Star-stone on her breast dripped its red drops which fell on to her snowy raiment, fell and vanished – fell and vanished – and left no stain.

Behind her a great silence lay upon the doomed city of Troy. Not a sound of song or of revelry broke the stillness of the night, not even the baying of a dog was to be heard, but perfect silence reigned as if Night held her breath, awaiting the sudden outbreak of the noise of war and death.

Through that silence the Greek fleet stole back to the beaches; for on the mound which marked Achilles' tomb a great fire burned, kindled by Sinon. And from Helen's window the light shone out so that the Greeks drew nearer and nearer to Troy, silent and sure, stealing through the early night to be there before the moon rose.

And when the first silvery beams came stealing over the black shape of distant Ida, Odysseus gave the word, and Epeius undid the bolt and opened the door beneath the belly of the Wooden Horse. In his eager haste Echion sprang out before the ladder was ready, and the fall killed him. But the other heroes climbed down in safety, stole through the silent streets, killed what sleepy sentinels there were on watch, and opened the gates of Troy to Agamemnon and the armies of Greece.

CHAPTER 30

The Fall of Troy

Come, Helen, come, give me my soul again:
Here will I dwell, for Heaven is in those lips,
And all is dross that is not Helena . . .
Oh thou art fairer than the evening air
Clad in the beauty of a thousand stars.

MARLOWE: *Dr Faustus*

30. The Fall of Troy

THE storm of war broke without warning over the doomed city of Troy. Suddenly the Greeks were everywhere, killing the Trojans in their sleep, killing them half awake, killing them in little bands – those few who had time to seize their weapons.

Old men, women, children died on that terrible night, for the ten-year-old fury of the Greeks made them merciless during those hours of darkness.

Priam met his end at the threshold of his own palace. When the alarm broke out he would have buckled on his armour and gone out to fight, but Hecuba persuaded him to remain with her by the altar of Zeus in the courtyard of the palace.

But presently their son Polites came staggering into the yard, wounded and pursued by Neoptolemus who was mad with the lust of slaughter. Right in front of his parents' eyes he struck the unfortunate boy through the body with his spear so that he fell dead on the altar steps before them.

Then old Priam sprang to his feet.

'Ah what wickedness!' he cried. 'Thus to kill my son before my face! Achilles would never have done that; he was merciful! He gave me the body of Hector when I went to beg it, and treated me kindly, remembering his own father. Surely you are no true son of his!'

So saying, Priam flung a spear at Neoptolemus; but the arm of the old king had lost its strength, and the weapon clattered harmlessly down on to the stone floor.

'Indeed,' laughed Neoptolemus grimly. 'If you find me so much worse than my father you had better hasten down to the realm of the dead and tell him about me!'

With that he seized Priam by the hair, dragged him to the door of the palace, and cut off his head.

But all kindness was not forgotten that night. Odysseus saw one of the sons of Antenor attacked by two Greeks, and protected him and helped him home to his house. For he remembered how Antenor had entertained him and Menelaus when they came to Troy to demand the surrender of Helen, and how it was Antenor who had saved their lives when treacherous Paris urged the Trojans to murder them.

So now he hung a leopard skin from the window of the house as a sign that no one in it was to be hurt; and in the morning he saw to it that Antenor and his wife Theano, who had handed over the Palladium, were allowed to escape with their children and servants, and an ass laden with the choicest of their possessions.

Another Trojan prince who was allowed to escape was the pious Aeneas. King Agamemnon saw him walking through the streets with his old father Anchises on his shoulders carrying the holy images from his house, and leading by the hand his little son Ascanius, while Creusa his wife followed behind. Pleased to see such family affection, Agamemnon gave orders that they were to be spared, and Aeneas won safely to the slopes of Ida with his precious burden, and his beloved child. But Creusa was lost in the turmoil as they left the city, and he never found her again.

The two sons of Theseus, Acamas and Demophon, struck no blow save when a Trojan attacked them. But they searched through Troy for their grandmother Aethra, who had been a slave attending Helen ever since Castor and Polydeuces took Aphidna and rescued their sister after Theseus had carried her away as a child. When they found Aethra, still beautiful and regal, though very ancient, they led her, with all the honour due to a queen, out of Troy and down to their tall ships; and they claimed no other spoils or rewards for their services in the war.

While these things were happening, Menelaus was seeking through Troy for Helen, and at length Odysseus guided him to her tower. There Menelaus entered sword in hand and a fury of jealousy in his heart; but Odysseus remained at the door and fought his fiercest and most desperate battle of any in the whole war.

Up to Helen's chamber went Menelaus, and there Deiphobus met him, heavy with drink and sleep. They fought, and before long Menelaus struck the sword out of the prince's hand and had him at his mercy.

'Dog!' he hissed. 'Never again shall you see the dawn over Troy Town, for Justice comes at last, however slow her steps, and no man may elude great Themis. Now black death has trapped you, here in my wife's bower – and I would that I could have dealt out the same punishment to Paris!'

Then he plunged his sword into the evil heart of Deiphobus so that he fell to the ground and died, and his wicked spirit fled to the judgement hall of Hades.

But Helen came to Menelaus out of the shadows and knelt to him, love struggling with fear in her wonderful eyes as she looked up at him.

Then Menelaus raised his bloodstained sword, and a terrible

urge went through him as he thought of all that he had suffered for this woman's sake, and all the woes she had brought upon Greece and Troy.

Yet in a moment the sword fell useless from his hand, and as he gazed upon that beauty, which surpassed the beauty of all other women, the rage and jealousy went out of his heart. She knelt there before him, the magic Star-stone rising and falling on her white breast, while the red drips fell and vanished – fell and vanished – and left no stain. And suddenly, he knew that there was no stain on her either, and that their love had been only interrupted by the spells of Aphrodite – but not broken.

'Helen!' he said, and in another moment he held the World's Desire in his arms, and the bitterness of the long years fell away from them and was forgotten.

Cold morning dawned over the stricken city, and still the Greeks slew and slew until the streets and houses were heaped with dead. And without the city the captive women were herded together in weeping droves among the piles of loot. Cruel Neoptolemus took Andromache as his prize, and flung Astyanax, Hector's baby son, to his death from the walls of Troy.

'He is a fool who kills the father and lets the children live,' was his brutal excuse. 'If the boy had grown to be a man he might have sought to slay me, since my father slew his. And we want no more kings of Troy!'

Aias the wild son of Oileus tried to take Cassandra as his share of the more noble captives, but she clung to the statue of Athena and begged him to spare her, since she was sworn to the service of the gods of Olympus. Aias however shouted that he feared neither god nor man, and dragged her roughly away.

Then the whole temple was shaken with an earthquake, and the very statue turned up its eyes in horror. And when Agamemnon heard of this, he had Aias chased out of the Greek camp with threats of execution, since his deed might call down the vengeance of Athena on them all. Agamemnon, however, felt that as the deed had been done, it was a pity to lose so lovely and high-born a captive, and he took Cassandra himself to be his handmaiden.

Aias sailed away in a fury, cursing Agamemnon and defying all the Immortals, and Athena in particular. But Poseidon wrecked his ship in a great storm and he was cast up on a rock in the middle of the sea where he drew himself into safety above the raging waves. This was his last chance, but still his pride was unbroken, and he taunted the Immortals, crying:

'You are not gods, why you cannot even drown the man who has insulted you!'

The lightning flashed ominously through the storm clouds, but in his madness Aias cried again:

'You think to frighten me with your thunder, do you? Lightning, I defy you!' At this Zeus took the matter into his own hands and hurled a thunderbolt which split the rock and sent Aias to his doom on the instant.

When Troy had been thoroughly pillaged, and the captives taken down to the sea-shore, the Greeks set fire to the town. Then the tall towers burned, and the houses were reduced to ashes. The falling buildings brought the walls crashing down with them, and the Greeks completed the destruction so that only the foundations remained over which the weeds grew and the earth was piled up, until three thousand years later the remains were uncovered, and today stand gaunt and mysterious above the plain to bear witness to the basic truth which blind Homer wove into the first and greatest of romantic tales, the *Iliad* and the *Odyssey*.

The Greeks went down to their ships and remained for a while encamped near the tomb of Achilles at the mouth of the River Scamander; some even crossed the Hellespont to the utmost tip of Europe: for the winds blew strongly across the Aegean Sea, and there was no sailing west or south.

When Menelaus led Helen down to the ships, the soldiers cried out that she must be slain, and took up stones to cast at her. But when they beheld her beauty, the stones fell from their hands, and they stood in awe as if she had been an Immortal, nor had they any further wish to do her aught but honour.

Day after day the winds were contrary, until Calchas declared that, just as when they left Aulis, there must be a sacrifice of a royal maiden.

That same night Neoptolemus dreamt that his father Achilles rose from the tomb, shaking his terrible spear and crying:

'Shame on you, Greeks! All have your reward from the spoils of captured Troy, save only I! Give to me the prize which by right is mine, even the fairest of royal maidens – Polyxena, daughter of Priam. If I have her not, never will you come in safety to fair Hellas!'

When Neoptolemus told of his dream, all doubt was at an end. The soldiers cried aloud for the sacrifice: Polyxena, they remembered, was loved by Achilles in his lifetime, for he had seen her, when she leant from the walls of Troy to fling her bracelets into the scale at the ransoming of Hector's body. It was even said

that there had been a secret marriage – and the Trojans added that
Achilles had offered to betray the Greeks if Priam gave him
Polyxena.

Certainly it was believed that Achilles demanded Polyxena to
be his bride in the Elysian Fields, and Neoptolemus slew her on

'Neoptolemus slew her on his father's tomb'

his father's tomb, despite the piteous prayers of her wretched
mother, Queen Hecuba.

The aged queen of Troy was released from captivity after her
daughter's death, and given to her son Helenus, who carried her
away, shrieking curses on the Greeks. The story got about that as
soon as he landed with her beyond the Hellespont, Hecuba turned
into a black hound – just such a hound as howls at night among
the graves, or follows in the train of Hecate the Queen of
Witches.

Besides Helenus, the Greeks allowed Antenor to sail away with
all his family, servants, and possessions. This honest Trojan made
his way to the head of the Adriatic Sea and founded a new Troy,
which in later days was called Venice. A son of his travelled to the

land which was afterwards known as France, and the French royal family could trace their descent from him.

The few other Trojans who escaped from the destruction of Troy fled on to Mount Ida and joined Aeneas who was in hiding there. When the Greeks had sailed – which they were able to do soon after Polyxena had been sacrificed – Aeneas and his companions cut down trees, built great ships, and sailed away to seek for a new home.

Early in their wanderings they came to an island on which grazed some fine fat cattle, and there was no sign of any herdsmen. So they killed several, cooked them, and settled down for a good meal. But no sooner had they begun to eat than the Harpies – the same winged women with sharp claws that the Argonauts had met and Zetes and Calais had driven away from the land of King Phineus – swooped down and snatched their meat away. Three times they tried to eat, and three times the Harpies robbed them: and after the third time one of the Harpies perched on a rock and cried:

'You Trojans who kill our cattle and try to drive us from our own island, listen to me! Sail away quickly, and doubtless you will reach the new home which Aphrodite is planning for you in a land called Italy: but I tell you that before you build the walls of your new city, you will be so hungry that you will be driven to eat the very tables on which you place your food!'

After this the Trojan fleet set sail sorrowfully, and met with several adventures during their wanderings. Old Anchises died, and was buried in Sicily; and then Hera stirred up the winds so that several of the ships were wrecked, and the rest of them were driven to North Africa where they were made welcome in the newly built city of Carthage, where the Phoenician called Elissa by the Greeks and Dido by the Trojans, was Queen.

She and her Phoenicians had sailed away from the coast of Asia far to the south of Troy some years earlier, and landed in North Africa where they demanded a site on which to build a city. The king of that country did not want them, but he said: 'You may have just as much land as the hide of an ox will enclose!'

Dido however took an ox-hide and cut it into such thin strips that it surrounded all the lands she needed – and Carthage was built on that site.

After resting there for some time, Aeneas was anxious to sail on his way, but Dido had fallen in love with him and wished him to marry her and become King of Carthage.

Aeneas, however, stole away by night with all his ships: and when Dido found that he had cheated and deserted her, she killed herself. But Aeneas sailed happily on his way, and at last came to Italy at a place called Cumae where dwelt a famous prophetess called the Sibyl. She told him that he was near the spot where he must build his city, and that this city would in years to come rule the world and be called Rome.

On went Aeneas rejoicing, and came presently to a great river with yellow water, which was called the Tiber. Up this he sailed, and anchored at last in a beautiful wood.

Here they landed and collected fruits to eat. As they had lost all their dishes during the voyage, they mixed flour and water and made plates and tables of dough. When the fruit were done and they were still hungry, they began to eat the dough, and the boy Ascanius exclaimed laughing:

'What, are we so hungry that we even eat our tables!'

Then Aeneas knew that they had reached the place where his new city was to be. He had many adventures before it was built, but all ended well, and he married Lavinia, the only daughter of King Latinus who ruled that country.

Their descendants became Kings of Rome, and in later years Emperors of the Roman Empire. One grandson of Aeneas called Brutus was said to have wandered away to the island of Albion in the north-west, and become king of it: that island was re-named after him and has ever since been known as Britain, and its kings and queens are said to be descended from him.

But Troy itself was never again a great city. Several small towns were built on the spot in after years, but were all soon destroyed and quickly forgotten: its glory departed from it three thousand years ago – to live for ever in song and story, and to stir our imaginations even to this day.

CHAPTER 31

Agamemnon and His Children

Not yet to dark Cassandra lying low
  In rich Mycenae do the fates relent;
The bones of Agamemnon are a show,
  And ruined is his royal monument.

ANDREW LANG: *Sonnet on the Iliad*

31. Agamemnon and His Children

AFTER the sacrifice of Polyxena the wind fell and the Greeks were able to sail away; but their adventures were by no means ended: Diomedes, Nestor, and Agamemnon were the only leaders who came straight home – and of these only Nestor found all well with his kingdom and was able to settle down comfortably to enjoy his old age in peace.

Diomedes suffered ship-wreck on the way, but it did not delay him for long. However, when he reached Argos he found that his wife had married someone else, and that the people were quite content with their new ruler and not in the least pleased to see him and his companions back again. In disgust he sailed off once more; and finally he came to Italy, settled there and lived to a ripe old age, much honoured by his new countrymen.

Agamemnon was not so fortunate. Ever since the sacrifice of Iphigenia at Aulis, Clytemnestra's hatred of him had grown more and more bitter. Finally she decided that he had forfeited all right to be her husband, and she married his cousin Aegisthus instead.

She did not let Agamemnon know this, however, and she kept a watchman on the roof of the palace of Mycenae to watch for the signal that Troy had fallen, which was to be brought by a series of beacon fires on the tops of lofty mountains.

When the news came of the sack of Troy, she made haste to send young Orestes away to his uncle King Strophius, and she kept Agamemnon's two daughters Electra and Chrysothemis well out of the way. As for Aegisthus, he remained hidden in the palace while Clytemnestra went out to welcome Agamemnon as if really delighted to have him home again.

Agamemnon came up to the palace in great pride and triumph, and entered over a purple carpet as became the conqueror of Troy. With him he brought much treasure and many Trojan captives of whom the chief was Cassandra, the dark, mysterious daughter of King Priam who could foresee the future but whose prophecies were never believed.

Now she stood on the wide terrace, high above the great plain of Argos, and cried aloud that death waited in the palace – death for Agamemnon and death for herself. Then, with head held high, she went in to her doom, noble and fearless as befitted a Princess of Troy.

But first the Queen of Mycenae, still pretending to welcome Agamemnon, led him to the marble-floored bathroom, and bathed him with her own hands, bidding him make haste to the feast which waited them.

Still swelling with pride at this royal welcome after his mighty deeds, Agamemnon rose from his bath, and took the finely embroidered shirt which Clytemnestra had made for him. She slipped it over his head, and the folds of it fell about him, and he was caught in it: for she had sewn up the neck and sleeves.

While he struggled in this silken web, she struck him down with an axe; and Aegisthus came out of his hiding place and helped in the slaying of the King of Men. And when Agamemnon lay dead, Clytemnestra took up her axe once more and went to meet and slay Cassandra: for in spite of her hatred of Agamemnon, she was still jealous.

After Agamemnon was dead and buried, Clytemnestra and Aegisthus ruled Mycenae. He wished to have Orestes killed, but Clytemnestra was not quite so wicked as that, and she refused to say where the young prince was hidden. Her younger daughter, Chrysothemis, did not seem to mind what had happened; but the elder, Electra, hated Aegisthus and could not forgive her mother. Clytemnestra would not consent to her death either, but fearing lest she should marry a prince and persuade him to punish her and Aegisthus she gave Electra to a poor peasant who lived in a cottage not far from the city of Mycenae.

This good man, however, felt that marriage with him would be an insult to the daughter of so great a king.

'Princess,' he said to Electra. 'Let us pretend to have obeyed the wicked commands of Queen Clytemnestra: but it need only be a pretence marriage – then when some brave prince comes along to help you, you will be able to marry him.'

So matters stood for seven years. Aegisthus reigned in Mycenae, though very much under the powerful thumb of Clytemnestra, and boasted often that he feared no vengeance; but in fact he was in constant terror lest Orestes should return and slay him. Electra desired above all things that this should happen; and whenever she could do so in safety sent messages to her brother reminding him that vengeance was still to be accomplished.

Orestes grew up at his uncle's court, and his dearest friend Pylades, the son of King Strophius, swore to stand by him in whatever he might do.

At last Aegisthus grew so angry with Electra for her constant threats and taunts that he declared he would send her to a distant city and shut her up in a deep dungeon. Then she sent in haste to Orestes, and he knew that the time had come to act.

First of all he visited Delphi to consult the oracle of Apollo: for he was in a great dilemma. According to Greek beliefs it was his duty to avenge his father's murder by killing the murderers; this was all right so far as Aegisthus was concerned – but to kill his mother was the worst of all crimes, and he knew that if he committed it, the Furies would pursue him and drive him mad.

Nevertheless Apollo, speaking through the mouth of his priestess at Delphi, commanded him to proceed and fear nothing, for though suffering would follow, all should be well in the end.

Consequently Orestes set off in disguise, accompanied by Pylades, and arrived at Mycenae where Electra was overjoyed to see them.

'Let Pylades go to the palace with the news that Orestes is dead,' suggested Electra, 'then Aegisthus will be off his guard and you will soon find a chance to kill him. As for our mother, I will send word that I am ill, and she will certainly come and visit me: all you have to do then is to lie in wait here at the cottage.'

All worked out just as they had planned. Both Orestes and Pylades went to tell the false news to Aegisthus, who was so pleased that he invited them to help him offer a great sacrifice of gratitude to the Immortals. And at the sacrifice Orestes slew him, and revealing who he was, won instant forgiveness from the people of Mycenae, who were thankful to be rid of the tyrant and have the son of Agamemnon as their king.

But when Orestes, urged on to the deed by Electra, killed Clytemnestra also, the Mycenaeans were not so anxious to have him. Indeed they were prepared to stone him to death: but before they could do so, madness fell upon him and the Furies came up from the realm of Hades to haunt him, and to pursue him wherever he might go until at length he should die.

While matters were still in doubt, old King Tyndareus of Sparta, Clytemnestra's father, arrived at Mycenae, bringing with him his grand-daughter Hermione, who had been promised in marriage to Orestes. Tyndareus came because news had reached him that Menelaus and Helen, after long wanderings, had been sighted off Cape Malea. But when he learned what Orestes had done, he urged the people of Mycenae to stone him and Electra without further delay.

In desperation Electra captured Hermione, brought her on to the roof of the palace, and when the people arrived with Tyndareus at their head she cried:

'I have the Princess of Sparta here, and I will kill her before your eyes unless you let Orestes go free!'

The Eumenides

At this crucial moment Immortal Apollo appeared to them, and told the people of Mycenae that Orestes had done the deed by his command.

'He must wander as an exile for one year,' Apollo concluded, 'and then come to Athens for judgement. But when all is ended, he will return here to be your king, and he shall marry Hermione.'

All happened as Apollo directed. Orestes set out on his wanderings, pursued by the Furies and accompanied by his faithful friend Pylades. He visited many places during his year of exile, but could never stay anywhere for long, since always the Furies would overtake him and drive him onward, ever onward.

When the year was over, Orestes came to Athens, and there the great court of the Areopagus met on the Hill of Ares to try his case. Erigone, daughter of Aegisthus and Clytemnestra, hastened from Mycenae to plead for the punishment of Orestes, but nevertheless the twelve judges were equally divided. Then Athena, the Immortal Lady of Athens, appeared on the Hill of Ares and spoke to the Areopagus:

'You just and mighty men of Athens, hear my decree! Long may this Court remain, and ever shall it be famous for the justice and righteousness of its judgements. And when, as now, the judge-

296

ment falls equally on two sides, the casting vote shall rest with me: and my vote shall be the vote of mercy. Orestes goes free, pardoned and acquitted: and so shall all after him who stand before this Court and find equal judgement!'

So Orestes went forth, cleared of the blood-guilt and free of the Furies. But they, filled with anger, demanded of Athena whether they were to be dishonoured and deprived of their rights.

'On the contrary,' answered the wise Immortal, 'your honour shall be made all the greater by this day's judgement. Beneath the rock of Ares' Hill shall be your shrine, and there all honour shall be done to the three of you, Alecto, Megaera, and Tisiphone. You will preside over Justice, seeing that evil is punished: but no longer will you be called the Furies – I change your name to the Eumenides, the "Kindly Powers", for it is more noble to cherish the right than to punish the wrong.'

All was at peace now; but Orestes could not yet return to Mycenae. He had still one quest to perform before the madness and the stain could quite be washed from him. By the command of Apollo he must journey to the land of Tauris and fetch back the image of Artemis.

Tauris was at the north of the Black Sea, being the land which we now call the Crimea: and its inhabitants sacrificed all strangers who came there to their cruel idol, and flung their bodies into a fiery pit through which the flames came up from Tartarus.

Orestes and Pylades set out on their voyage in a swift ship with fifty oarsmen. They reached Tauris by night, left the ship ready in a secret cove, and started inland by themselves, hoping to find the image unguarded and to carry it off before morning. But a band of shepherds surprised them on their way, captured them and led them before Thoas, the savage king of the Taurians. He was delighted at having two Greek victims, and handed them straight over to the priestess of Artemis with instructions to prepare them for sacrifice.

The priestess looked at the two victims pityingly, and when they were alone asked them if they were Greeks. When she learnt that they were, she spoke to them in their own language, saying that she was held there by force, being a Greek herself, and loathed the rites of human sacrifice.

'I will save one of you,' she said, 'if he will promise on his return to Greece to carry a message for me.'

'What is it?' asked Pylades. 'I will surely carry it!'

'The message,' answered the priestess, 'is to Orestes, the son of King Agamemnon. Say that his sister whom men thought was slain at Aulis, lives in this terrible place and begs of him to come with a great fleet and save her. Say that I am indeed Iphigenia!'

As seriously as possible Pylades repeated this message to Orestes himself, and then turning with a smile, said:

'Lady I have performed your request. Let Orestes himself answer it!'

Then there was great rejoicing and delight as Iphigenia told Orestes how she had been carried away in a cloud from Aulis while Artemis placed a doe on the altar in her place just as Agamemnon's sword was falling.

Orestes told why he had come to Tauris, and Iphigenia nodded.

'I knew,' she said, 'that someone would come. Artemis does not like her sacred image to be drenched in blood by these barbarians: it must be brought to Greece and set in a safe place.'

Reaching up, she lifted down the image which, like the Palladium, had fallen from the sky as a meteor falls. Even as she did so, King Thoas strode into the shrine.

'Why are you so long?' he demanded. 'And why do you lift down the holy image of Artemis?'

'Alas,' exclaimed Iphigenia readily, 'as I strove to make the victims ready for the sacrifice, the image averted its eyes. Then Artemis spoke to me and said that already her shrine was polluted, since one of these men has murdered his mother, and the other is his helper. So now I must take them and the image to the shore and wash them in the salt sea. And you must bring fire and water to cleanse the evil from this shrine.'

Thoas suspected nothing, and readily believed what she said. So while he remained to purify the shrine, Iphigenia, holding the image, led the way to the shore, Orestes and Pylades following with a guard of Taurians.

But when they reached the sea, the fifty Argives were waiting for them, and easily overcame the Tauric guard. Swiftly, then, they all entered the ship and sailed triumphantly away.

They came after an easy voyage to Greece, and there by command of Athena, the image of Artemis was set up in a temple near Athens, and Iphigenia continued to be its chief priestess. But never again was human sacrifice offered to it.

Orestes and Pylades reached Mycenae in safety, and there Orestes married Hermione: when Menelaus died they became King and Queen of Sparta as well, and both lived happily into old age.

Electra married Pylades, and they reigned happily in Phocis, when King Strophius died, and had three sons who were firm allies of King Tisamenes, the son of Orestes and Hermione.

CHAPTER 32

The Adventures of Menelaus

Helen, thy beauty is to me
   Like those Nicaean barks of yore,
That gently, o'er a perfumed sea,
   The weary, wayworn wanderer bore
   To his own native shore.

EDGAR ALLAN POE : *To Helen*

32. The Adventures of Menelaus

WHEN the Greeks sailed away from Troy they did not all sail at the same time or in the same direction, so that various fortunes attended each of them. Menelaus and the majority of the Greek kings sailed later than Agamemnon, Diomedes, and Nestor, and were scattered by a great storm.

Many of the ships were wrecked on the coast of Greece: for King Nauplius, in revenge for the death of his son Palamedes, lit false beacon lights on the rocky coast of Euboea, and the pilots believed them to mark the entrance to a harbour and steered their ships on to the rocks.

Neoptolemus with his followers landed safely in the north of Greece, and instead of returning home marched inland and conquered Molossia. Here he reigned for seven years, with Andromache as his queen; and they had a son called Molossus to succeed them. But at the end of this time Neoptolemus grew tired of Andromache and set out for Sparta to claim Hermione as his wife. On the way he visited Delphi, and not receiving the answer he wanted from the Oracle, plundered the temple and burnt the shrine. When he reached Sparta Neoptolemus carried off Hermione, for at this time Orestes was still being pursued by the Furies during his year of exile. But returning by Delphi, Neoptolemus met Orestes, who had come to consult the oracle: Neoptolemus was killed then and there by the angry people of Delphi and buried under the temple which he had destroyed, while Hermione returned in safety to Sparta.

When the storm scattered the ships, Menelaus actually reached Greece and anchored at Sunium near Athens. But when he tried to sail across the Gulf of Aegina to reach Argos or some port near Sparta, the storm sprang up again and drove him south to the island of Crete.

After wandering about for some time he came to Cyprus, where he met one of the Greek heroes who had failed to reach home after the fall of Troy: Demophon the son of Theseus.

This prince does not seem to have tried very hard to reach Athens, for when he landed in Thrace on his way home, he fell in love with the Princess Phyllis. So he stayed there, married her, and became king. But after a while he grew tired of Thrace and told Phyllis that he must leave her for a few months while he sailed down to Athens to set his affairs in order before renouncing his homeland for ever.

'It is not lawful for the King of Thrace to leave his country,' objected Phyllis. But Demophon pointed out that he was only king by right of his marriage to her, and that *she* must remain where she was.

'But I will not be away longer than three months,' said Demophon, and he swore the most solemn oaths by every one of the Immortals that he would be back in well under a year.

Phyllis bade farewell to him as he entered his ship, and gave him a little golden casket.

'This contains a charm,' she said. 'Open it a year from now if you have not returned by then.'

Demophon promised to do this, and set sail from Thrace. But he made no attempt to visit Athens; instead he steered straight for the island of Cyprus, and settled there.

He did not keep one of his oaths, but on the appointed day he opened the casket. At that very moment in far-away Thrace poor, deserted Phyllis died of a broken heart, and the Immortals turned her into an almond tree. But Demophon saw something in the casket which drove him mad on the spot. Leaping on a horse, he galloped screaming towards the sea-shore, his drawn sword in his hand; suddenly his horse stumbled, the sword flew from his hand, and Demophon fell upon it and was killed instantly.

As he did so, the bare almond tree in Thrace blossomed into green leaves: and ever after that the Greeks called the new green leaves '*phylla*' after the faithful Princess Phyllis of Thrace.

Menelaus buried the body of Demophon, and set sail from Cyprus. But once again ill fortune befell him, and his ships were scattered in a storm. This time it was much worse than before, since Menelaus was washed overboard; and although he was safely picked up by another of his ships, when the storm ended there was no sign of the royal ship in which Helen was sailing.

Menelaus was in despair: to have sacked Troy for Helen's sake and then to lose her on the way home!

He searched for her up and down the Mediterranean, visiting various places in Africa, Asia Minor and Phoenicia in vain. At last after several years, during which, though he had not found Helen he had collected much treasure, Menelaus came to the island of Pharos, one day's voyage from Egypt. There he landed with the four ships that remained to him, to rest before attempting the voyage home to Greece; for by now he had given up all hope of finding Helen.

But having landed on Pharos, he could not get away. The wind blew steadily from the north – and Menelaus knew that any strangers visiting Egypt were liable to find themselves made into slaves or even sacrificed by King Theoclymenus. Day after day the Greeks remained on Pharos; soon their food ran short, and they were driven to spending all their time catching fish to keep themselves from starving.

At length one day as Menelaus walked by himself on a lonely stretch of the shore, praying to the Immortals for aid, there came up out of the sea the nymph Idothea.

'You are very foolish and feeble-witted, Greek stranger!' she exclaimed. 'Or is it that you and your companions like sitting about on this desert island catching fish?'

Then Menelaus answered:

'Fair nymph, goddess or Immortal, whoever you may be: I do not stay here of my own will, but because we cannot get away. Therefore I beg you to tell me what I must do to escape from this place: for surely the Immortals hold me here because I have neglected some honour which is their due.'

'That I do not know,' said Idothea, 'but my father Proteus, the Old Man of the Sea, can read both the past and the future. If you can catch and hold him, he will tell you. But he is hard to catch and harder still to hold. Yet I will help you, if you will choose your three best men to accompany you, and meet me here at daybreak tomorrow.'

Menelaus promised readily, and Idothea slipped back into the sea. But she was waiting for them next morning, carrying with her four newly-flayed sealskins.

'You must dig yourselves holes here in the sand,' she said, 'and I will cover you with the skins. For at noon the Old Man of the Sea comes out of the waves to sleep here on the shore, and with him comes a great flock of seals to sleep also, and to guard him. He will first number them as a shepherd does with his sheep, and then slumber in their midst. When he is asleep, you four must spring out of hiding and catch hold of him. By his magic he will turn himself into all manner of creeping creatures, and maybe into fire and water as well; but if you can hold him tight, in the end he will return to his own shape, and you may ask him what you will and he will return a true answer.'

So saying Idothea covered them with the sealskins and left them there; nor did they pass a very pleasant morning, for the skins above them stank in the hot sun.

But at last the seals began to arrive and stretch themselves out to sleep on the sunny sands; and when they were all assembled Proteus came himself, the Old Man of the Sea, and counted his

Menelaus and Proteus

fishy flocks just as Idothea had said. When he was satisfied that
all was well, he laid himself down to rest in their midst, not far
from where Menelaus and his three companions were concealed.

As soon as he was asleep they sprang out and seized hold of him.
At once Proteus woke and in a moment turned himself into a fierce
lion, and after that into a snake, a leopard, and a great wild boar.
Still the four Greeks clung to him, and he turned himself
into running water, and then into a tall tree. But, seeing that he
could not shake them off, he returned to his own strange blue shape,
and said:

'Hmm! Menelaus of Sparta! Doubtless some Immortal has
told you how to catch me!'

'Old Man of the Sea,' replied Menelaus, 'you know everything:
so why ask me these vain questions?'

'Hmm! Exactly!' grunted Proteus, a merry twinkle in his bright
blue eyes. 'You want to know why you are kept on this desert
island? Yes, of course. Well, all you've to do is to fit out one ship
and sail in her to Egypt. You've a sacrifice to offer there – and what
is fated to happen, will happen! Hmm! Yes. And you'll get safely
back to Greece as soon as you've done that, with four ships. You'll
find that Agamemnon has been murdered by Aegisthus and Cly-

temnestra; and unless you hurry, Orestes will have avenged him by the time you land at Nauplia. . . . You want to know about anyone else? Old Nestor got home first: you'll see him. Calchas met a prophet cleverer than himself, and died of fury. . . . You said "How sad?" No, I thought not! . . . Odysseus? He's a prisoner on Calypso's enchanted isle. But he'll get back to Ithaca after ten years, it's all arranged in Olympus. . . . You and Helen? Oh yes, you'll live happily ever afterwards in Sparta, and you won't die, either. The Immortals will carry you both to the Elysian Fields which are at the world's end. . . . That's all I can tell you. . . . Now off you go to Egypt. . . . Hurry!'

With that Proteus winked knowingly, and jumped backwards into the sea before they could prevent him.

However Menelaus knew enough now, and deciding to trust Proteus implicitly, he launched one of his ships and set sail for Egypt. The north wind blew steadily, so that the voyage was easy: but when they drew near to the mouth of the Nile, the wind increased suddenly to a gale, and dashed the ship to pieces on a reef of hidden rocks.

Menelaus and most of his men swam to the shore, and took shelter in a cave, drenched and miserable.

In the morning Menelaus set out alone, still encrusted with sea salt and grime, and perfectly disguised by the miserable raggedness to which the rocks had reduced all his fine clothes.

When he reached the city he was directed to the Temple of the Strange Hathor, where wanderers might find shelter, and reaching it he knelt down at the altar in the courtyard.

There the greatest surprise of all his adventures befell him: for presently the Priestess of Hathor came forward to the altar, and it was none other than Helen herself, attended by four handmaidens.

Very quickly Menelaus made himself known to her, and Helen was filled with joy. But fear came quickly on the heels of joy.

'If you are discovered, they will kill you!' she cried. 'And my death is near me also. For Theoclymenus, Egypt's King, comes this day to make me his wife by force. When the ship brought me here, his father the king who has recently died called me the Strange Hathor and made me Priestess of Hathor, which is their name for Aphrodite, here in this temple.

'But Theoclymenus is of another spirit and cares little for what we think right and wrong. Priestess though I am, he will make me his wife: all that troubles him is the thought that you, my husband, may still be alive.'

Then, their wits sharpened by the danger, they thought of a scheme to outwit Theoclymenus and win safely away, though the ship in which Menelaus came to Egypt had been dashed to pieces.

When Theoclymenus came to the Temple later that morning, Menelaus, still in his rags, knelt at the king's feet and cried:

'My lord, I bring news! Menelaus, King of Sparta, is dead! His ship was wrecked on your coast and I alone escaped from the angry sea and the sharp rocks. But Menelaus was killed: I saw with my own eyes how the rocks crushed his bones before the waves carried his body out to sea!'

Theoclymenus was delighted with this news, and turned to Helen exclaiming:

'Now there is nothing to keep us apart!'

'Nothing indeed,' sobbed Helen, 'and I will marry you of my own wish and with full consent. But first grant me a request. Menelaus was a great king, and I loved him once: let me celebrate his funeral rites after the true Greek style.'

'Certainly you may,' said Theoclymenus, 'all that I have is yours. Do as you please, for I know not the funeral customs of the Greeks.'

'Then we must have a ship,' said Helen, 'for the rites of those lost at sea must be performed on the sea itself, at a spot where the land is only just in sight. I must have a bull to sacrifice: this shipwrecked sailor can come and attend to that, since he is a Greek and knows well what to do. Then my Menelaus was a warrior, so I must have a fine suit of armour to cast into the sea in his honour. And there must be garments and ornaments too: and an offering of wine and bread. . . .'

'All shall be as you desire,' said Theoclymenus. 'A ship of mine, manned by enough of my sailors to row or sail it shall be ready in an hour, and this Greek, since he is to perform the ceremony, shall be in command of it.'

So all things were prepared: Helen led the way, followed by her handmaidens who carried rich robes, jewels, and other offerings, and Menelaus followed. On the quayside his own sailors who had survived the shipwreck joined them, since the bull proved difficult and could not be placed on board without their aid.

The ship set sail, and the wind blew suddenly from the south until soon the land grew dim behind them.

'Now for the sacrifice!' cried Menelaus, and slew the bull in fine style. 'And now,' he added, 'let us cast these Egyptian barbarians into the sea, to swim back to King Theoclymenus if they can, while we sail for Hellas!'

The Egyptians were soon overpowered, and, being good swimmers, most of them reached the shore to tell Theoclymenus how Menelaus had tricked him. But Menelaus himself sailed triumphantly away, was joined by his three ships as he passed the island of Pharos, and came safely to Greece without any further adventures.

They landed at Nauplia, to find that Orestes had just killed Aegisthus and Clytemnestra and was about to be stoned by the people. But Apollo appeared at the right moment to save Hermione, whom Orestes and Electra had captured as a hostage, and when Orestes set out on his wanderings, Helen and Menelaus took their daughter back to Sparta to await his return.

When Neoptolemus came and carried her off, Menelaus prepared to set out in pursuit of them. But news came that the wicked son of Achilles had perished miserably at Delphi, and Hermione was on her way back to them, safe and unhurt.

A year later Orestes returned, his madness cured and his deeds forgiven and purified, and his wedding with Hermione was celebrated with all joy and honour.

Not long after they had gone to claim their kingdom at Mycenae, and ten years since the fall of Troy, a stranger prince arrived at Sparta. He was welcomed by kindly Menelaus, and that evening as he sat feasting in the great hall of the palace, Helen came forth from her fragrant chamber as bright as golden Artemis and still the loveliest woman in all the world, and greeted the young prince.

'Noble sir, none have I ever seen so like another, man or woman, as you are like one of the noblest of the Greeks, who suffered many things and did deeds unforgettable at Troy for my poor sake. Surely you must be Telemachus, the son whom Odysseus left as a new-born child in his palace when first he sailed for Troy?'

Then the stranger answered: 'Queen of Sparta, I am indeed Telemachus, the son of Odysseus. It is ten years since Troy fell, and he alone of all the heroes who fought there has not returned home: yet no news has come to us of his death.'

Then Helen and Menelaus welcomed Telemachus as warmly as if he had been their own son, and he told them how the palace at Ithaca was filled with evil men who were the suitors of Queen Penelope, urging her to marry one of them and declaring that Odysseus was surely dead.

'He is not dead, and he will return this very year!' cried Menelaus. 'For so Proteus, the Old Man of the Sea, told me. Odysseus, he said, was held prisoner by the nymph Calypso in her magic isle, but would return to Ithaca ten years after the fall of Troy!'

CHAPTER 33

The Wanderings of Odysseus

Yet endure! We shall not be shaken
  By things worse than these;
We have 'scaped when our friends were taken,
  On the unsailed seas;
Worse deaths have we faced and fled from,
  In the Cyclops' den,
When the floor of his cave ran red from
  The blood of men.

ANDREW LANG : *The World's Desire*

33. The Wanderings of Odysseus

WHEN the great storm scattered the Greek fleet as it sailed away from Troy, Odysseus and his twelve ships were driven northwards to Ismarus, a town in Thrace. They landed there and took the town by storm: for the Thracians were allies of the Trojans, and they knew that Odysseus had killed their king, Rhesus.

Odysseus, however, took care that no harm was done to Maron the priest of Apollo, and in gratitude Maron gave him twelve jars of wine so strong that each needed to be mixed with twenty times the quantity of water for a man to drink of it without intoxication.

Soon the Thracians from further inland came to attack Odysseus, and he put to sea as the lesser of two evils. The storm wind had veered round by now, and it drove him south for ten days and nights until he came to the land of the Lotus-eaters. Now whoever eats of the lotus fruit forgets his home and all worthy things, desiring only to lie in the warm, sunny meadows and eat the lotus for the rest of his life.

Odysseus sent some of his men to see who dwelt in that land; and these, when they had tasted the lotus, forgot even to come back and tell him. So he set out with another party, found them and forced them back to the ships in spite of their prayers and lamentations. Then they sailed on, and came to a big, fertile island on which grazed many sheep. Cautious Odysseus left his fleet behind a rocky islet nearby and landed on the main island with twelve men, leaving one ship with the rest of its crew ready to sail at a moment's notice.

Up the beach went Odysseus and his twelve companions, and presently they came to a big cave in which were jars of milk, big cheeses, and huge piles of firewood, besides many kids and lambs playing in their wattle pens.

'Some shepherd must live here,' said Odysseus, 'and shepherds are usually friendly people. Let us wait until he returns, and see if we can buy cheeses and other stores from him.'

Evening seemed slow in coming, and while they waited the men lit a fire and helped themselves to some of the cheeses for their supper.

Then suddenly the owner of the cave arrived, driving his flocks before him and carrying a dead tree over one shoulder. Odysseus and his companions fled to the very back of the cave and hid there, quaking in terror: for he was a terrible Cyclops, a giant with only one eye which was in the middle of his forehead.

When the Cyclops, whose name was Polyphemus, had milked his goats and ewes, he heaped wood on to the fire, and the light revealed the men hiding in the darkest corners.

'Ho–ho!' cried Polyphemus in a great voice. 'Who are you? Pirates, sea-robbers come to bring ill upon other men and other men's goods?'

'Not so, mighty sir,' answered Odysseus, overcoming his fear with difficulty. 'We are poor Greeks returning from the sack of Troy, seeking our homes after many years of war. I beg you to deal kindly with us: for Zeus brings evil upon those who harm a stranger.'

Polyphemus laughed cruelly. 'Mad or foolish you must be, stranger,' he cried. 'For no Cyclops pays any heed to Zeus, nor indeed to any of the Immortals, save only Poseidon, ruler of the sea, for he is my father. But tell me, where did you leave your ship? In some safe bay of the island, I hope.'

Then Odysseus, fearing the worst, spoke words of guile. 'Alas,' he said, 'Poseidon who shakes the earth broke our tall ship to pieces on the rocks, and we poor few escaped only with our lives.'

Hearing this, the Cyclops growled angrily, and reaching out his great hand he seized two of the sailors in it, dashed out their brains on the rocky floor, cut them up and devoured them for his supper, even crunching up the bones with his strong teeth. Then he drank several vats of milk, and grunting happily, settled down on the floor and fell fast asleep.

Now Odysseus was minded to see if with a careful sword-stroke straight to the heart he could kill the monster as he slept. But he realized in time that to do so would mean their certain death since Polyphemus had placed across the doorway of the cave a mass of rock so huge that twenty men could not have stirred it.

In the morning Polyphemus awoke, milked his flocks, ate two more men, and went out for the day, blocking the cave-mouth carefully behind him.

Then Odysseus set to work with the help of his terrified companions. He cut a great stake like the top of a mast, sharpened one end and hardened the point in the fire. Scarcely was this done and the weapon concealed under a pile of dung, when back came Polyphemus, driving his sheep and goats before him. As on the previous evening he began by replacing the great stone over the cave-mouth; then he attended to his flocks; and after that made his supper on two more of the companions of Odysseus.

When his meal was complete and he was just settling down

for a good drink of milk before going to sleep, Odysseus stepped forward and bowing low held up a great wooden goblet filled with red wine: for by great good fortune he had brought with him one of the jars of strong wine which grateful Maron had given to him in Thrace.

'Cyclops, take and drink wine after your feast of man's flesh, so that you may know what sort of cargo our good ship held,' he said politely.

Polyphemus grabbed the cup and drained it at a gulp; then, smacking his lips, he handed it back to Odysseus demanding more: for he had never tasted wine.

'Fill again,' he hiccoughed, 'and then maybe I will give you a gift. For never have I drunk anything so good.'

Odysseus filled the cup yet again, and the Cyclops began to grow very intoxicated.

'Tell me your name, stranger,' he said. 'Then I can drink to your health.'

'Noble sir,' answered Odysseus, 'my name is Nobody. That's what my father and mother and my dear wife, and all my friends call me.'

'All right, Nobody,' grunted the Cyclops, 'this is my gift to you in exchange for the delicious drink – I'll eat you last of all your companions!'

And with that he sank down on the cave floor and fell fast asleep, snoring like a whole herd of swine.

Then Odysseus and his companions took the sharpened stake, and having made the end hot in the fire, they plunged it into the single eye of Polyphemus and twirled it round until he was blinded.

Polyphemus let out the most fearful yells and tried in vain to catch Odysseus and the rest of the men. Presently, hearing his cries, one Cyclops after another came running from their caves nearby to see what had happened.

'Polyphemus!' they called. 'Whatever makes you yell like that in the middle of the night? Surely no one is driving off your flocks; and even more surely you are not being slain by force or craft?'

Then Polyphemus shouted back from within the cave: 'Nobody is slaying me by guile! Nobody is slaying me by force!'

'Oh, if nobody is hurting you,' they answered crossly, 'you must be suffering from some pain sent by an Immortal. So pray to your father Poseidon, and let us get some sleep!'

Then they returned to their own caves, and Odysseus laughed to himself at the ease with which he had beguiled each foolish Cyclops.

Odysseus and the Cyclops

Morning came, and Polyphemus opened the cave, since the sheep and goats had all to go out and graze. But he seated himself at the cave-mouth and felt each sheep as it passed him to make sure that the Greeks did not escape. But Odysseus tied the sheep together in sets of three, and under the middle sheep of each three he bound one of his men. Then he himself seized hold of the greatest ram in the flock and hung on to the thick wool under its belly.

'Alas my poor ram!' said Polyphemus as he stroked its back. 'Usually you run frisking to the pasture before any of the ewes. But today you linger behind: maybe you are sorry for your poor master whom this accursed Nobody has blinded!'

When they were clear of the cave, Odysseus released his companions and they hastened down to the ship, driving with them many of the sheep and goats.

As the ship sailed out from the land Odysseus stood in the stern and shouted aloud:

'Cyclops! You have not been cheated and blinded by a mere Nobody! If anybody asks who robbed you of your eye, you may tell him that it was Odysseus the sacker of cities, the son of Laertes, King of Ithaca!'

Polyphemus flung a mighty rock which almost hit the ship; but his second throw raised a great wave which washed it well out of his reach. Then he prayed to his Immortal father:

'Poseidon, girdler of the earth, grant that Odysseus the son of Laertes may never win home to Ithaca! But if it is ordained that he must return, then may he come late and in an evil plight; may he come in the ship of strangers, having lost all his companions, and may he find sorrows waiting for him in his home!'

Over the dancing waves sailed Odysseus, and he might have won home in spite of the Cyclop's curse had it not been for the greed and stupidity of his own men. For he came next to the Isle of the Winds, and there King Aeolus who held the winds in charge to loose or bind at the will of Zeus gave them all to Odysseus in a great oxhide bag. So they sailed peacefully home until they could see the very smoke rising from the chimneys in Ithaca. But then Odysseus, feeling that they were safe at last, fell asleep and his men opened the bag because they thought that it contained gold which he was keeping for himself. Out rushed the winds, and drove them back into unknown seas, and King Aeolus would not bind them again for Odysseus, who had missed his chance.

Now the curse of Polyphemus began to work upon them, for they were driven far across the sea and landed in the country of the Laestrygonians who were fierce cannibals. These people dropped huge rocks from the cliffs that sank all but one of the ships, and then caught the wretched sailors as they swam ashore.

Odysseus escaped in his own ship by cutting the cable, and they came sadly to the island of Aeaea where dwelt Circe the enchantress, the sister of Aeetes the king of Colchis whom Jason and Medea had visited many years before.

Not knowing what sort of entertainment to expect, Odysseus divided his company into half and cast lots as to which should go first to the buildings which they saw among the trees in the distance.

The lot fell on Eurylochus, who set out with his two and twenty companions, and came to a fair palace where Circe welcomed them kindly. All entered except Eurylochus who hid in the wood to see what would happen. Circe led the men to a table in the long hall and set before each of them a great bowl filled with cheese and honey and barley meal and wine: but with each there was mixed also a magic drug. When the men had drunk, she touched them with her wand, and at once they were all changed into swine which she drove out of the palace and shut up in a sty at the back.

315

Eurylochus returned with his terrible news, and Odysseus set out to punish Circe and try to restore his companions. As he walked through the wood Hermes the Immortal Messenger met him:

'Odysseus, you may not overcome Circe by your own strength and cunning,' said Hermes. 'But take this herb which is called "moly" and cast it, unseen, into the cup which she will mix for you. Then drink it without fear, and when she strikes you with her wand, draw your sword and threaten to slay her unless she restores your companions and vows to do no further harm to any of you. Then you must live here with her for a year, and she will make you her lord and the master of this island. But at the end of that time I will come again and see to it that she sends you on your way with all things needful for your voyage.'

All fell out as Hermes had said: the magic swine were restored to their human shapes, and Odysseus and his men passed a pleasant year in the enchanted palace of Circe.

At the end of that time the enchantress sent Odysseus on his way with his ship well-stored, but advised him first to seek guidance from the blind prophet Tiresias.

'He is numbered with the dead,' Circe told him, 'but you may come to the verge of the Realm of Hades by way of the Ocean Stream, the magic flood that girdles all the earth. Beach your ship where Acheron flows into Cocytus, a branch of the River Styx, and both run by a great white rock into Ocean. There, hard by the Poplars of Persephone, dig a trench, and pour forth the offerings, and the spirits of the dead will draw near to you. But keep them from the trench until Tiresias comes and you have learnt from him all that you need to know.'

Away sailed Odysseus from the fair Aeaean isle and came to the white rock and the Poplars of Persephone. There he did as Circe had instructed him, and learnt many things from the ghost of Tiresias. There also he saw the spirits of many a famous hero and heroine: his own mother, whom he did not know had died, was the first to greet him, and after her came Alcmena and Leda with many others who had been the brides of Immortals. He saw also the ghost of Agamemnon and learnt of his miserable end; and he saw Achilles and the other heroes who had fallen at Troy: but when Ajax came he would not greet Odysseus, being still angered over their quarrel concerning the armour of Achilles. Heracles came also, and many more: yet these were but shadows, for Heracles himself dwelt among the Immortals, and Achilles walked the Elysian Fields with the dead heroes.

Then Odysseus sailed away, back to the world of light, and

presently drew near to the island where the two Sirens still dwelt, though the rest of their number had perished when Jason passed by them unscathed, thanks to the song of Orpheus.

Now when the ship drew near, Odysseus instructed his men to bind him to the mast and not to release him until the danger was passed. But to the men themselves he gave lumps of wax which they put into their ears so that they might not hear the fatal singing.

On they sailed, and the Sirens sang their wonderful song, so that Odysseus forgot even his wisdom at the sound, and shouted to his men to unbind him. But they only bound him the tighter, and rowed on with great strokes of their oars.

Then the Sirens sang again in their irresistible voices:

'Come hither, hither over the wave,
Glory of Greece – Odysseus brave,
    And hark to our magic song.
For none has passed us over the main
Till he harkened the honey-sweet voice of us twain,
    And tested what joys belong
    To the Siren maids: for all things we know,
Past, to come, and the end of woe
    In the bliss of our magic song!'

Odysseus shouted and struggled until he was exhausted, and when the Sirens' isle was left far behind his men released him and drew the wax from their ears.

Thus Odysseus was the only man who ever heard the Sirens singing and lived to tell of their song: for the music of Orpheus had drowned their singing when the Argonauts passed by. But the two Sirens fell from their rocks and died: for this doom was decreed if once a mortal escaped them after he had heard their song.

The next danger came to Odysseus as his ship sped between Italy and Sicily: for on one side of the straits was the great whirlpool of Charybdis, and on the other the sea-dragon Scylla lurked in her cave. Remembering Circe's advice, Odysseus steered well away from Charybdis: but just as they swept by, Scylla appeared at her cave-mouth and grabbed six men with her octopus-like tentacles. While she was feasting on these, the ship passed into safety, and they anchored at Trinacria, an island of the Sun.

Here grazed the golden cattle of the Sun Titan Helios, which Tiresias had warned Odysseus not to touch. Odysseus passed the warning on to his men. But after they had been becalmed there for many days, and were growing hungry, they disobeyed his orders and killed several of the cattle on which they feasted for six days.

The wind rose on the seventh and they sailed away: but Helios had reported the theft to Zeus who hurled a thunderbolt which split the ship and drowned all save Odysseus, who clung to the mast and floated away. He could not steer, and saw with terror that he was drifting towards the whirlpool of Charybdis. Into the whirlpool went the mast and was sucked down: but Odysseus leapt from it just in time and caught hold of a wild fig-tree which grew from the cliff above. To this he clung until he saw the mast shot up from the depths by the whirlpool: then he cast himself on to it, and was washed away. When he was nearly dead from exhaustion, the mast came to land on the island of Ogygia.

In this magic isle dwelt the nymph Calypso, daughter of the Titan Atlas. She welcomed Odysseus, tended and fed him, and begged him to remain with her for ever.

'I will make you immortal,' she said, 'for indeed on this magic isle old age does not come. Here we may live for ever, the King and Queen of fair Ogygia, and you will have no more troubles, for suffering and sorrow shall be far from you.'

But Odysseus, faithful to his home and longing for his wife Penelope, refused to wed Calypso or to vow to remain with her for ever. But he could not escape since his ship was lost and she would allow him no tools with which to build a new one. And she kept him there for seven long years while he sat day after day on the sea-shore, gazing across the blue waves towards distant Ithaca and wearying his heart with longing.

At length Athena, who took special care of Odysseus, went to Olympus and begged Zeus to grant him a safe homecoming.

'My heart is torn for wise Odysseus, that hapless one,' she said. 'It is ten years since Troy was taken and still he alone of heroes has not won to his home. But now the guileful daughter of Atlas keeps him for the seventh year in her sea-girt isle striving to make him forget Ithaca: but Odysseus, yearning to see if it were but the smoke rise upwards from his own land, desires else to die.'

Then Zeus made answer to wise-eyed Athena:

'My daughter, I have not forgotten the much enduring Odysseus whom Poseidon, girdler of the earth, keeps from home in his anger at the blinding of his Cyclops son Polyphemus, whose mother was Thoosa, child of the Sea Titan, giant Phorcus. And now I will send Hermes the Messenger to Ogygia: for the time approaches when Odysseus shall come home.'

So Hermes came to Calypso and told her the commands of

Zeus: and she, weeping sorely, gave Odysseus all the tools that he needed to construct a big raft, and stores of wine, grain, and dried flesh to take when it was made.

Then she bade him farewell and he sailed over the smooth sea with a glad heart. But Poseidon, returning to Olympus from the land of the Ethiopians, and not knowing the will of Zeus, saw Odysseus nearing the land of Phaeacia on his raft. Then in a fury Poseidon called up the stormwinds, and whirling Odysseus into the deep, went on his way well pleased, deeming that this was the end.

But Odysseus came safely to shore, and was found by the Princess Nausicaa who brought him to her father the King of Phaeacia, who entertained him kindly, listened to all his story, and at length sent him home to Ithaca in one of his own ships.

As it sped over the sea Odysseus fell into a deep sleep, and the kindly Phaeacians landed him still sleeping and left him under a tree, surrounded with rich and generous gifts. Thus after ten years of wandering, Odysseus came home.

CHAPTER 34

Odysseus in Ithaca

Penelope for her Ulysses' sake
  Devised a Web her wooers to deceive
In which the work that she all day did make
  The same at night she did again unreave.

SPENSER: *Sonnet xxiii*

34. Odysseus in Ithaca

WHEN Odysseus awoke from sleep a mist lay over all the place and he did not know where he was. At first he lamented, thinking that the Phaeacians had landed him on some desert island and left him to his fate. But presently Athena came to him and drew back the mist. Then Odysseus knew his home, and kneeling down kissed the soil of Ithaca in his joy and thankfulness.

'There is still much trouble before you,' Athena warned him. 'For a hundred and eight suitors have gathered in your hall to woo your wife Penelope. They dwell in the town, but come each day and feast riotously on your possessions; your flocks and herds grow few, your wine is well-nigh exhausted. But still your faithful Penelope holds them at bay, though she nears the end of her strength.'

Then Athena told Odysseus how Penelope had baulked the suitors for three years with a cunning almost equal to his own.

'I cannot choose a husband,' Penelope had said, 'until I have woven a fine robe to be the winding shroud against the day the hero Laertes shall die, Laertes, father of my lord whom you say is dead. It must be a worthy robe, fit for a hero: alas that I could not weave one for my lord Odysseus!'

So Penelope wove at her loom day by day, working hard to make the shroud for Laertes; but every night she stole secretly to her loom and unravelled all that she had woven during the day. But at the end of three years some of her maids, who had fallen in love with several of the suitors, betrayed her, and the suitors lay in wait and caught her unpicking the web.

Then they came in a body and told her that she must make her choice without any more delay. Penelope begged for a few weeks in which to decide, and this they allowed.

'But today is her last day of grace,' ended Athena, 'and to-morrow they will demand her answer. It was when she knew that the end was near that she sent Telemachus to seek news of you. He is at Sparta, but I have been to him there, and he will return today. Go now to the cottage of Eumaeus the faithful swineherd, whose father was a Prince of Phoenicia from whom he was stolen in childhood and sold as a slave to your father Laertes: him you may trust, and Philoetius the herdsman. But you must go in disguise. . . .'

Athena spoke more words of advice to Odysseus, and helped him to make himself like an old beggar. After this she departed

323

to guide Telemachus across the sea from Pylos to Ithaca in such a way as to avoid a band of suitors who had laid an ambush for him between two islands: Athena came to Telemachus in the guise of his wise tutor Mentor, and brought him safely home that day.

Meanwhile Odysseus hid all the Phaeacian gifts in a cave, and trudged up the beach in his rags and came after a short walk to the cottage of Eumaeus. Out rushed the dogs to drive off the beggar, and Odysseus sat down hastily, to show that he was a friend – a sign which Greek dogs still understand!

Eumaeus came forth, welcomed the beggar kindly into his cottage and fed him well, though he had no idea whom he was really entertaining. Odysseus did not reveal himself until Telemachus came; but then they rejoiced together and made their plans against the suitors.

That evening Telemachus returned to the palace, and when the suitors had gone home to bed, he removed all the weapons and armour which usually hung on the walls and pillars in the great hall where the feasts were held. He did not tell Penelope that Odysseus was in Ithaca, nor anything of the plan, but he suggested that, next day when the suitors came to demand her hand in marriage for one of them, she should consent to marry whoever could bend the bow of Odysseus and shoot an arrow through the rings in the heads of twelve axes set up in a row – a feat which Odysseus himself had often performed in the days before he sailed to Troy.

Next morning Odysseus the beggar came up to the palace, and on the way he met Melanthius the goatherd who jeered at him and kicked him in the side, calling him vile names.

'If ever the great Odysseus returns,' said Eumaeus sternly, 'you will suffer for treating a stranger like this.'

'Oh, he'll never return,' cried Melanthius. 'Depend upon it, he lies dead in some foreign field – and I only wish Telemachus was as dead as he is!'

Odysseus passed on to the palace, and at the gate he saw his ancient hound Argus, blind and mangy, lying in the dirt where the suitors had kicked him out to die. But as he drew near the old dog knew him, even after all those years: he struggled to his feet, sniffed at Odysseus, then licked his hand, whining with joy, and wagging his tail feebly – then sank down dead.

There were tears in his eyes as Odysseus stopped to stroke his old friend and lay him out gently by the palace wall.

Inside the courtyard Odysseus begged food from the suitors, and was not kindly received. And there a real beggar called Irus tried to drive him out; for Irus was ravenously greedy, and spent all his time eating and drinking, and feared that the new beggar might take some of the food which would otherwise come to him.

Odysseus argued with him gently, but Irus would not be reasonable and challenged him to fight with fists. The suitors gathered round laughing to watch the duel between the two beggars, and promised to see fair play and reward the winner.

When Odysseus bared his strong arms, Irus was afraid and would have slunk away; but the suitors jeered at him and made him fight, calling him a bully and a cowardly braggart – as indeed he was.

So Irus rushed in with a yell and struck Odysseus on the shoulder; but Odysseus struck back, though not as strongly as he could have done, and stretched Irus bleeding on the ground. Then he dragged him out of the palace, propped him up against the wall, and left him, saying:

'Sit there now, and scare off the swine and dogs; and do not bully beggars again, or a worse thing may befall you!'

Odysseus then returned to the palace, and Penelope sent for him since she had heard that he could give her news of the fall of Troy, and perhaps even of her lost husband.

Odysseus told her as much as seemed good for her to know at that moment, and when his tale was ended, Penelope bade the old nurse Euryclea wash his feet for him and find him some decent clothes to wear – for she knew that he spoke the truth and had really met her husband on his wanderings as he brought her a sure token.

As Euryclea washed his feet with warm water, she came to the scar from the wound which a boar had made on Mount Parnassus when Odysseus was a boy, and she recognized it and knew then who he was.

She would have cried out with joy, but Odysseus put his hand over her mouth quickly.

'Do you want to cause my death?' he whispered. 'If the suitors know, they will murder me at once. Keep my return a secret, even from the Queen: the time will soon come when justice shall be done.'

After this he slipped back into the hall and waited quietly. Presently Penelope came in, fair and stately, carrying the great black bow and a quiverful of arrows. At her command twelve axes were set up in a line, and then she said:

'Princes and nobles, I can stand out against you no longer. Therefore whoever among you can string the bow of Odysseus and shoot an arrow through the rings in the axe-heads as he used

'Penelope came in, carrying the black bow'

to do, the same shall be my husband and the lord of rugged Ithaca, and Zacynthos and wooded Same.'

So the suitors began in turn to handle the great bow; but not one of them could so much as string it. Then they grew angry, and declared that it was some trick of Penelope's, and that the bow could not be strung by any mortal man.

'Let me try,' said Odysseus, but the suitors cried out at the impudence of the beggar, and one of them flung a stool at him.

'He shall try if he likes,' cried Telemachus, and it seemed as if a

326

quarrel were about to begin. So he turned to Penelope and bade her go to her room with all her maidens; and when she had gone he sent Euryclea to lock them in. While this was happening Philoetius slipped into the courtyard and locked the gates also, that none might come out or in.

Then, at a word from Telemachus, Eumaeus picked up the bow and carried it to Odysseus. He took it in his hands, turning it this way and that lovingly, testing it to see that all was well with it; then suddenly he bent it and slipped the string into place as easily as a minstrel strings his lyre. And beneath his fingers the bowstring sang like a swallow, yet with a deeper, fiercer note telling of war and of the death of men.

While the suitors sat back in anger and amazement Odysseus set an arrow to the string, drew, and loosed so surely that it sped through all twelve of the rings without touching one with its brazen barb.

'Telemachus, your guest does you no shame!' cried Odysseus, and with a bound he was on the high threshold with the arrows ready to his hand and the beggar's rags cast from him. 'Lo, now is the terrible trial ended at last,' he continued, 'and I aim at another mark!'

Even as he spoke an arrow hummed from the bow, and one of the suitors fell back dead in his seat, pierced through the throat.

'Mind where you're shooting!' shouted some of the suitors, still not recognizing him and thinking that the last shot had been a mistake.

'That will I indeed,' was the answer, 'for you have much to answer, you who thought that I would never come back from the land of the Trojans, and therefore wasted my goods and insulted my wife. Now death waits for you, one and all, at the hand of Odysseus, the sacker of cities!'

Then, while the great bow sang and the swift shafts hummed, the suitors strove vainly to get at him and pull him down. First they sought for weapons, but these were not in the usual places on the walls. Then such as carried swords attacked him, using tables as shields; but Telemachus brought helmets, spears, and shields for himself and faithful Eumaeus and Philoetius, and armour for Odysseus also, and the battle raged furiously.

Once it was almost lost, for false Melanthius the goatherd slipped into the store-room and brought out several weapons for the suitors: but Telemachus caught him in time and tied him up, to be punished afterwards.

On and on shot Odysseus, and Athena spread panic among the

suitors so that they did not rush the four all in a single body as they might have done. When his arrows were exhausted, Odysseus took up the spears which had been flung at him and returned them to the suitors with deadly aim; and drawing his sword he leapt amongst them, crying his terrible war-cry. At his side fought brave young Telemachus, and Eumaeus the faithful swineherd, and Philoetius the cowherd; and all of them were wounded in that terrible fray.

At length the suitors lay dead, every man of them: but Odysseus spared Phemius the minstrel who had done no harm, and a slave who chanced to be in the hall and hid under an ox-hide.

Then Odysseus called for Euryclea, and she brought the hand-maidens, and together they carried the bodies out of the palace, and cleansed the hall, and set all in order.

When this was done, Euryclea went to fetch Penelope who all the while had been sleeping peacefully in her inner chamber.

'Awake, dear child!' cried the old nurse. 'Awake and see the day for which you have prayed so long! For Odysseus has come – he is here in his own house, and has slain the proud suitors who troubled you so and devoured all his substance!'

But Penelope would not believe the good news, not even when she came into the hall and found Odysseus waiting for her.

'I have heard it said,' she replied when Telemachus reproached her, 'that traitor Paris put on the form of Menelaus and so beguiled fair Helen my cousin. And well I know that the Immortals can wear what shape they will!'

Then Odysseus said to Telemachus:

'Son, your mother speaks wisely: for we have tokens that we twain know, secret from all others.'

Then Odysseus was bathed and clad in fair garments, and Penelope felt almost sure that he was indeed her husband. But still she doubted, and as a test she said:

'Noble sir, let us wait until tomorrow before we test one another further. But now I will command my maidens to bring forth the bed of Odysseus, whom you swear that you are – even his bridal bed and mine, which stands in the innermost chamber.'

Then Odysseus turned upon her, saying:

'This is a bitter word that you speak! Who has been interfering with my bed? For there is no man living, however strong, who could lift it and bring it here. And I will tell you why: when I married you, and built on our chamber to the palace, there stood an olive tree as thick as a pillar; round this I built the room, and roofed it over, but the lower branches of the tree I lopped off, and used the tree, still growing, as one of the corner posts of the

328

bed. Lady, here is a token for you! I say that the bed cannot be brought out to me, unless some man has cut away the stem of the olive tree.'

When she heard this, Penelope's last doubt was gone. She broke into weeping, and ran up to him, cast her arms about his neck and kissed him, saying:

'Odysseus, my husband! None but you and I knew of the olive tree that is part of the bed in our secret bridal chamber. Now I know you indeed, and now I am truly happy once more!'

Then Odysseus held her in his arms; and in the happiness of that moment it seemed that all his toils and all his wanderings were but little things compared with so great and true a joy.

CHAPTER 35

The Last of the Heroes

... My purpose holds
To sail beyond the sunset, and the baths
Of all the western stars, until I die.
It may be that the gulfs will wash us down;
It may be we shall touch the Happy Isles.

TENNYSON: *Ulysses*

35. The Last of the Heroes

AND that is where the old tales come to an end, for Odysseus was really the last of the heroes. There were no stories about Telemachus or his children: the old books say that he had a son called Perseptolis – but that is only because doubtless some Greek family claimed descent from him. In his lifetime the great grandsons of Heracles came back to Greece from exile in the north and conquered most of it – but that is where history begins and legend ends.

For the Heroic Age ended when Odysseus died: its brief, golden gleam lasted only a little while – scarcely longer than the triple lifetime of Tiresias – and then the Immortals ceased to mingle visibly with mankind, and neither Zeus nor any of them married mortals or had mortal children. Helen was the youngest child of Zeus.

When Homer wrote his two wonderful epic poems, *The Iliad* and *The Odyssey*, nearly three thousand years ago, he looked back less than two centuries to events which had already become legends, and wove them into immortal works which were the centre of all later poems and plays about the Immortals and the heroes. All other tales of Troy fit into what Homer had already written.

The tales end with Odysseus, but how did Odysseus end? The Greeks asked this question very early, and a poet made a short poem which is now lost. But what we know of it is very slight, and it was simply made to fit what Homer tells us.

For when Odysseus called up the ghost of Tiresias he received instructions as to his future course, and a veiled prophecy that, in his old age, death would come to him 'from the sea'.

When the suitors were dead, their friends and relations wanted to kill Odysseus, and he was only saved by Athena who came from Zeus to make peace and send Odysseus on his last voyage to seek for the place of sacrifice of which Tiresias had told him. So Odysseus set sail for the mainland, and when he reached the shore he went into the interior on foot, carrying an oar over his shoulder.

For weeks and weeks he went on, until at last he came to the land of the Thresprotians. And one day he passed two men working in a field, and one said to the other:

'Whatever is that stranger carrying on his shoulder?' And the other replied:

'It must be a winnowing fan for separating chaff from corn. I'm sure I can't think of any other use for it!'

Then Odysseus knew that he had reached a country where

Ithaca

men had never heard of the salt sea, and thankfully he set the oar
in the earth and offered the necessary sacrifice to Poseidon whom
he had offended long ago when he blinded Polyphemus the Cyclops.

On his way home Odysseus tarried for a while with Queen
Callidice and helped her to overcome the Brygians who were
invading her country. Then he returned home and lived happily
with Penelope and a son who was born to them after his return
from Troy called Poliporthes, while Telemachus he made King of
Ithaca.

But Odysseus had another son of whom he knew nothing. His
name was Telegonus, and his mother was Circe the enchantress.

When he was grown up, Telegonus set out to seek for his father,
and he sailed in vain to many lands. At last a storm drove him to
Ithaca, and he landed without knowing where he was, and his men
killed some of the cattle and began to drive off the rest.

Then old Odysseus set out to chase away these thieves. But
as Telegonus entered his ship he turned and flung a spear tipped
with the poisonous spine of the sting-ray. And, as was decreed,
this wounded Odysseus, who never recovered but fell quietly
asleep.

Then the Immortals carried him away to the Elysian Fields
at the World's End, there to live happily for ever with the other
heroes:

'No snow is there, nor yet great storm, nor any rain; but always
ocean sendeth forth the breeze of the shrill West to blow cool –
where life is easiest for men.'

ENVOI

Pass with a ringing laugh, a friendly word,
    Thinking of Rhintho resting here alone:
The Muses' smallest, least-remembered bird
    Plucked from their hill this garland of his own.

From the Greek of Nossis

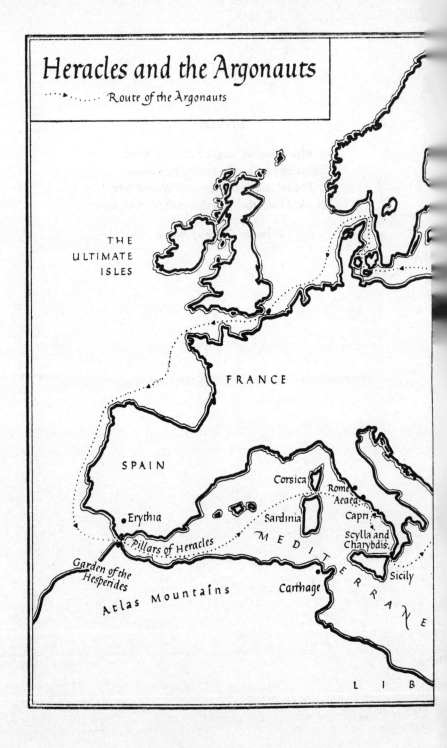

Heracles and the Argonauts

······▸······ Route of the Argonauts

THE
ULTIMATE
ISLES

FRANCE

SPAIN

Corsica

Rome
Aeaea

Sardinia

Capri

Erythia

Scylla and
Charybdis.

Pillars of Heracles

M E D I T E R R A N

Sicily

Garden of the
Hesperides

Atlas Mountains

Carthage

L I B

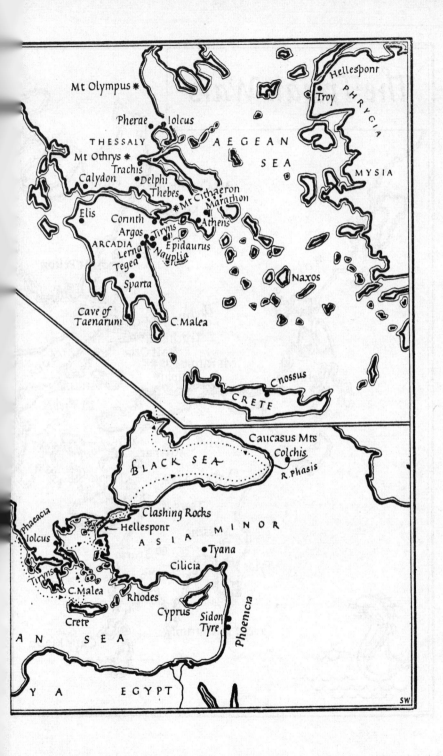

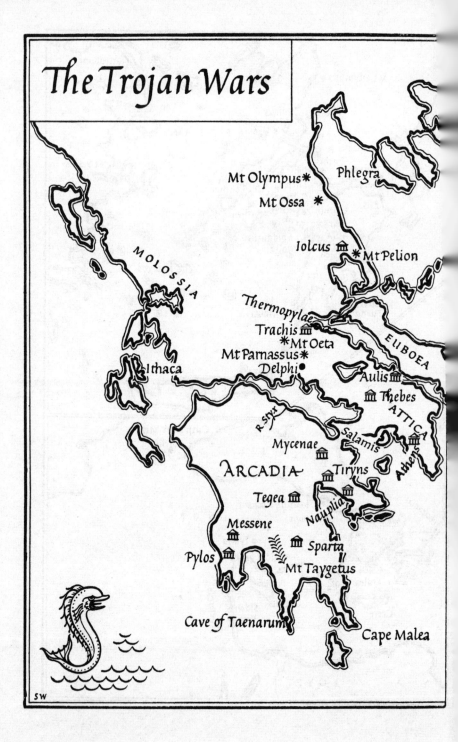

The Trojan Wars

Mt Olympus ✳
Phlegra

Mt Ossa ✳

MOLOSSIA

Iolcus 🏛 ✳ Mt Pelion

Thermopylae
EUBOEA

Trachis 🏛
✳ Mt Oeta

Mt Parnassus ✳
Delphi ●
Aulis 🏛

Ithaca
Thebes 🏛

ATTICA

R. Styx

Mycenae 🏛
Salamis

ARCADIA
Tiryns 🏛
Athens 🏛

Tegea 🏛
Nauplia

Messene 🏛
Sparta 🏛

Pylos 🏛
Mt Taygetus

Cave of Taenarum
Cape Malea

SW

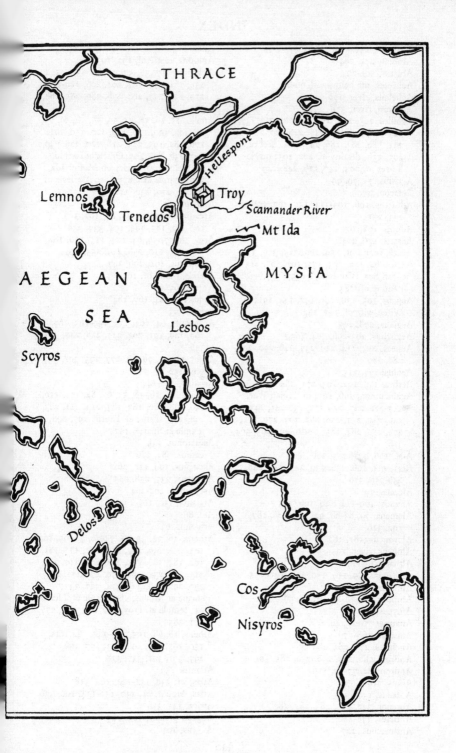

INDEX

Absyrtus, 154, 155, 160, 164
Acamas, 271, 284
Acastus, 202-204
Achaetes, the helmsman, 66-68
Achelous, river, 170
Acheron, river, 316
Achilles, 205, 206, 219-222, 227-232, 237,
  227-232, 237-240, 246, 248-260, 265,
  271, 280, 283, 286, 287, 316; heel of,
  205, 256; destiny of, 202, 203; magic
  horses of, 204, 240, 246, 248, 249
Acrisius, 73, 79, 99
Actaeon, 63
Admetus, 106, 109-114, 150, 167, 196,
  233, 271
Adonis, 102, 103
Aeacus, 176, 204
Aeaea, island of, 159, 160, 315, 316, 336
Aeetes, 64, 152, 153, 155, 162, 163, 315
Aegean Sea, islands of, 43, 57, 337, 339;
  naming of, 144
Aegeus, 105, 139, 141, 142, 144, 191;
  Witch-wife of, 141, 142
Aegialia, 278, 293
Aegisthus, 293-296, 304, 307
Aeneas, 213, 214, 229, 237, 246, 270, 284,
  288, 289
Aeolus, 177, 315
Aethra, 139, 192, 193, 271, 284
Agamemnon, 196, 197; in Trojan War,
  217-222, 227, 229-232, 238-241, 245,
  246, 249, 257, 258, 260, 267, 270, 271,
  278, 280, 284, 285; death, 293-295, 304,
  316
Aias, 196, 271, 285, 286
Ajax, 175, 196, 238, 239, 245, 246, 248,
  256-258, 316
Alcaeus, 79
Alcestis, 109-114, 149, 196, 233
Alcmena, 79, 83-88, 94, 177, 186, 187,
  192, 316
Alcyoneus, 181, 182
Alpheus, river, 104
Althaea, 167-170
Amazons, 115, 119, 150, 175, 191, 255
Amphion, 63
Amphitryon, 79-88, 91, 94, 99
Amycus, 151
Anaurus, river, 149
Ancaeus, 168-170
Anchises, 213, 284, 288
Andromache, 237, 238, 250, 285, 301
Andromeda, 77-79, 119
Anius, 218
Antaeus, 130-132
Antenor, 227, 269, 283, 284, 287
Anticlus, 278-280
Antimachus, 227

Aphareus, 194
Aphidna, castle of, 192, 193, 284
Aphrodite, 17, 38, 57, 59, 64, 85, 102, 103,
  134, 161, 171, 182, 204, 206, 210-214,
  229, 233, 237, 268, 278, 280, 285, 288,
  305
Apollo, 15, 16, 18, 21, 30, 55, 56, 59, 65,
  66, 102, 109, 110, 119, 120, 150, 161,
  176, 182, 213, 218, 227, 229, 230,
  247, 256, 296, 307; Oracle at Delphi,
  see Delphi; sanctuary on Mount Ida,
  229; temple at Cumae, 103; priests of
  Apollo, 219, 230, 311
Arachne, 35
Arcadia, 25-30, 35, 43, 44, 102, 167,
  170-172, 183, 184, 194, 337, 338
Ares, 16, 57, 59, 64, 104, 115, 130, 182,
  183, 195, 210, 238, 249, 255, 259
Areopagus, 191, 296, 297
Aretias, island of, 104
Argave, 65, 68
Argo, 150-164, 167, 184
Argolis, 73
Argonauts, 64, 104, 133, 150-163, 167,
  168, 186, 191, 202, 217, 228, 288, 317,
  336
Argos, 69, 73, 79, 86, 277, 293, 301, 337
Argus, 150
Ariadne, 142-144
Artemis, 15, 16, 18, 53, 63, 84, 102, 110,
  150, 168, 169, 182, 183, 213, 221, 223,
  298, 307; shrine at Tauris, 297, 298;
  temple at Sparta, 192
Ascalaphus, 135
Ascanius, 284, 289
Asclepius, 109, 110, 261
Astyanax, 237, 238, 285
Astydamia, 202-204
Atalanta, 150, 167-172
Ate, 86
Athamus, 63
Athena, 16, 34, 35, 38, 74-76, 79, 95, 100,
  104, 134, 136, 141, 150, 171, 178, 181,
  182, 184, 186, 195, 204, 206, 210, 211,
  213, 230, 231, 258, 270, 275-277, 285,
  296, 297, 318, 323, 324, 327, 333;
  shrine at Athens, 18; temple at Thebes,
  94; temple at Troy, 267, 269, 275, 277,
  278, 285
Athens, 18, 68, 105, 139-142, 144, 145,
  150, 191, 193, 196, 271, 277, 296,
  297, 301, 302, 337, 338
Atlantis, 159
Atlas, 21, 130, 132-134, 160, 318
Atlas, Mount, 21, 130, 132-134, 160, 336
Attica, 141, 338
Augean Stables, 104, 125
Augeas, 104

340

Aulis, 217-223, 276, 286, 293, 298, 338
Autonoe, 63
Aventine, Mount, 122, 123

Bathos, 183, 184
Battus, 27, 28
Baucis, 45, 46
Briseis, 230, 231, 239, 251
Bronze Age, 43
Brutus, 289
Brygians, 334
Busiris, 130
Butes, 161

Cacus, 122, 123
Cadmus, 54-64, 68, 94
Calais, 150, 151, 288
Calchas, 219-222, 228, 229, 230, 258, 267, 276, 286, 305
Callidice, 334
Calydon, 164-170, 172, 337
Calydonian Boar, 163-170, 175, 184, 191, 196, 202
Calypso, 305, 307, 318, 319
Capri, island of, 160, 336
Carthage, 288, 336
Cassandra, 213, 214, 275, 277, 285, 293, 294
Cassiopea, 77, 78
Castor, 150, 184, 193-196, 284
Catreus, 214
Caucasus, Mount, 36, 37, 129, 152, 337
Celeus, 69
centaurs, 103, 191, 203. *See also* Chiron, Nessus, Pholus
Cepheus, 77, 78
Cerberus, 134-136, 150, 193
Cercyon, 140
Cerynites, river, 102
Cerynitian Hind, 102
Ceuta, 121
Ceyx, 172
Charon, 134, 135, 150
Charybdis, 161, 317, 318, 336
Chiron, 103, 109, 149, 203, 204, 206, 228
Chryseis, 230, 231
Chrysothemis, 293, 294
Cilicia, 53, 337
Cinyras, 218
Circe, 152, 159, 160, 315-317, 334
Cithaeron, Mount, 15, 63, 88-92, 100, 337
Clashing Rocks, 151, 152, 337
Clytemnestra, 192, 197, 217, 221, 222, 278, 293-296, 304, 305, 307
Cocalus, river, 144, 145
Cocytus, river, 316
Colchis, 64, 150-155, 162, 191, 217, 315, 337
Corinth, 105, 125, 140, 164, 337
Coronis, 109

Corsica, 160, 336
Corythus, 209, 265
Cos, island of, 177, 178, 183, 339
Creon, 83, 84, 94, 95
Crete, 20, 54, 55, 105, 141-145, 162, 163, 214, 301, 337
Cretan Bull, 105, 141, 142
Creusa, 284
Cronos, 19, 20, 25, 34, 36, 53, 74, 201
Cumae, 103, 184, 289
Cyclopes, 20, 73, 99, 110, 311-315
Cycnus, son of Ares, 130
Cycnus, son of Poseidon, 228, 233
Cyllene, Mount, 25-30
Cyllene, nymph, 26, 27
Cyprus, 214, 218, 301, 302, 337
Cyzicus, 151

Daedalus, 105, 144, 145, 162
Danae, 73-75, 78, 79, 84, 99
Danaus, daughters of, 135
Dardanus, 57
Death, the messenger, 110-114, 177, 247
Deianira, 170, 172, 175, 184, 185
Deidamia, 206, 219-221, 255, 259
Deimachus, 175
Deiphobus, 213, 267-269, 275, 278, 280, 284
Delos, island of, 15, 218, 219, 339
Delphi, 18, 20, 30, 47, 56-58, 301, 307, 337, 338; oracle at, 30, 47, 57, 63, 73, 94, 95, 99, 295, 301
Demeter, 16, 19, 20, 53, 69, 70, 135, 160, 192, 340
Demophon, 271, 284, 301, 302
Deucalion, king of Thessaly, 38, 39, 46-49
Deucalion, king of Crete, 162, 163
Dictys, 74, 75, 78, 79
Dido, 288, 289
Diomedes, king of Thrace, 105, 114; horses of, 105, 106, 114, 115
Diomedes, son of Tydeus, 196, 219, 220, 229, 237-241, 245, 255, 258-260, 269, 278, 293, 301
Dionysus, 17, 53, 64-70, 79, 84, 103, 136, 144, 182, 184, 193, 218, 219
Dodona, branch of, 150, 159
Dolon, 240, 241
Dryope, 30

Earth, Mother, 19, 20, 47, 49, 53, 130, 132, 181
Echion, 168, 280
Echo, 9
Egypt, 10, 53, 66, 130, 214, 302-307, 337
Eilithyia, 86
Electra, nymph of Samothrace, 57
Electra, daughter of Agamemnon, 293-295, 298, 307
Electryon, 79, 83
Eleusis, 69, 140

Elis, 104, 337
Elissa, 288
Elysian Fields, 59, 155, 187, 250, 287, 305, 316, 334
Enceladus, 183, 184
Enna, 69, 160
Eos, 85, 255, 256
Epeius, 270, 271, 280
Ephialtes, 182, 183
Epidaurus, 139, 140, 337
Epimetheus, 21, 33, 34, 38, 39, 46
Eriginus, 93, 94
Erigone, daughter of Icarius, 68
Erigone, daughter of Aegisthus and Clytemnestra, 296
Eris, 204
Eros, 17, 182
Erymanthia, 103
Erymanthian Boar, 102, 103
Erymanthus, 102
Erythia, 121, 122, 336
Ethiopia, 43, 130, 255, 256, 319
Etna, Mount, 56, 184
Euboea, 301, 338
Eumaeus, 323, 324, 327, 328
Eumelus, 196, 271
Eumenides, 297
Europa, 54-56
Euryclea, 325, 327, 328
Eurydice, 150, 161
Eurylochus, 315, 316
Eurypylus, 177, 178
Eurystheus, 79, 86, 94-106, 115, 121, 125, 132-134, 136, 139, 141, 175, 192, 196
Eurytion, 169, 202
Evenus, river, 172

Fates, Three, 110, 167
Floating Islands, 161
Furies, 193, 209, 295, 296, 297

Ganymede, 120, 175, 204
Geryon, 121, 122; cattle of, 121, 122-125
Giants, 19; war with gods, 36, 48, 49, 63, 79, 84, 85, 129, 130, 177-184, 201
Gibraltar, 121
Glauce, 164
Golden Age, 25, 26, 30
golden apple of Discord, 204, 206, 210, 211, 278
golden apples of the Hesperides, 125, 129-134, 160, 171, 172
Golden Fleece, 63, 64, 145, 149-154, 167, 175
Gorgons, 75-77. See also Medusa
Gorgon's head, 69, 134, 184
Graces, 211
Grey Sisters, 75

Hades, 18-20, 25, 55, 69, 70, 75, 76, 86, 110, 112, 113, 134, 135, 150, 155, 160, 161, 183, 184, 192, 193, 195, 209, 248, 250, 284, 295, 316
Harmonia, 57-64
Harpies, 151, 217, 288
Hebe, 120, 186, 195, 204
Hecate, 154, 182, 287
Hector, 177, 209, 213, 228, 231, 237-239, 245, 246, 248-255, 265, 283, 286
Hecuba, 18, 176, 177, 209, 250, 275, 283, 287
Helen, 85, 333; in Sparta, 192, 193, 196, 197, 211; in Troy, 214, 217, 219, 222, 227, 229, 232, 233, 234, 237, 251, 265-269, 271, 278-286; return to Sparta, 10, 295, 302, 305-307
Helenus, 267, 287
Helicon, Mount, 21, 29
Helios, 21, 25, 33, 35, 85, 122, 152, 161, 181, 317, 318
Helle, 63, 64, 145
Hellen, 47
Hellespont, 64, 115, 151, 286, 287, 337, 339
Hephaestus, 17, 36, 38, 57, 64, 104, 162, 177, 181, 182, 201, 204, 249
Hera, 17-20, 59, 64, 65, 69, 70, 86-88, 94, 95, 115, 119, 123, 125, 130, 132, 134, 149, 177, 181, 182, 184, 186, 201, 204, 206, 210, 211, 214, 217, 231, 288
Heracles, birth of, 79, 85-88; choice of, 91-94; labours of, 94-136; slavery, 139, 145; the Quest of the Golden Fleece, 150-153, 159, 160, 162, 163, 336; the Calydonian Boar Hunt, 167, 170-172; at first fall of Troy, 175-178, 202, 209, 267; in battle against the Giants, 181-184; death, 184-191, 193, 227; as an Immortal, 186, 260, 261, 316; poisoned arrows of, 101, 186, 196, 227, 258-261, 266; pillars of, 121, 122, 160, 336
Hercules, *see* Heracles
Hermes, 17, 18, 25, 27-30, 35-38, 43-46, 54-57, 59, 65, 69, 74, 75, 78, 79, 85, 134-136, 183, 187, 206, 210, 214, 316, 318
Hermione, 197, 214, 233, 259, 265, 278, 295, 296, 298, 301, 307
Heroic Age, 9, 48, 202, 333
Hesione, 119-121, 175, 176, 196, 202, 214, 217
Hesperides, 130, 133; the Garden of the, 125, 130-134, 153, 160, 171, 336
Hesperus, 130
Hestia, 17, 19, 20, 213
Hippolyta, 115, 119; belt of, 115, 119, 121
Hippolytus, 191
Homer, 286, 333
Hope, 39

Hyacinthus, 9
Hydra, 100, 101, 125, 185, 227, 259, 266
Hylas, 150, 151
Hyllus, 185, 186
Hypnos, 177, 247

Iapetus, 21
Iasus, 167, 170, 171
Icarian Sea, 144
Icarius, king of Athens, 68
Icarius, father of Penelope, 197
Icarus, 144
Ida, Mount, 206-213, 229, 233, 248, 266, 267, 270, 280, 284, 288, 339
Idas, 150, 194
Idothea, 303, 304
Iliad, 286, 333
Illyria, 129
Ilus, 213, 267
Immortals, the coming of, 15-19; war against the Titans, 19-20; home of, 20; battle with Typhon, 53-56; at wedding of Cadmus and Harmonia, 59; war against the Giants, 36, 48, 49, 84, 129, 130, 178-187; at wedding of Peleus and Thetis, 203, 204
Inachus, river, 73
India, 66
Ino, 63-65
Iolaus, 96, 100, 101, 125, 175
Iolcus, 109, 110, 145, 149, 150, 163, 164, 202-206, 277, 337, 338
Iole, 185, 186
Iphicles, 86, 87, 92, 95
Iphiclus, 228
Iphigenia, 221-223, 276, 293, 297, 298
Iphitus, 139
Iris, 217
Iron Age, 202
Irus, 324, 325
Isle of Winds, 315
Isles of the Blest, 250, 257
Ismarus, 311
Ithaca, 15, 196, 217, 218, 305, 307, 315, 318-329, 334, 338
Ixion, 135, 191, 193

Jason, childhood, 149, 203; the Quest for the Golden Fleece, 145, 149-164, 191, 196, 217, 315, 317; at the Calydonian Boar Hunt, 167, 168
Justice, see Themis

Knossus, 105, 142, 337; labyrinth of, see Labyrinth

Labyrinth, 105, 142-144, 162
Lacedaemon, 197, 277
Ladon, dragon, 130-133, 160
Laertes, 150, 196, 217, 323

Laestrygonia, 159, 315
Lamos, river, 65
Laocoon, 275-277
Laodamia, 280
Laomedon, 119-121, 175, 176, 202, 209, 213, 217
Lapiths, 191
Larissa, 79
Latinus, 289
Lavinia, 289
Leda, 192, 316
Lemnos, island of, 17, 177, 201, 227, 259-261, 339
Lerna, Lake, 69, 337
Lernean Hydra, see Hydra
Lesbos, island of, 255, 256, 339
Lethe, river, 193
Leto, 18, 110
Leucippus, 194
Lichas, 184, 185
Lindos, 134; ox of, 134
Linus, 88
Lotus-eaters, 311
Lycaon, 44, 46
Lycia, 248
Lycian army, 246, 247
Lycomedes, 206, 219, 258
Lycurgus, 66
Lycus, 95
Lynceus, 150, 194

Machaon, 261
Maenads, 66, 68
Maia, 18, 25, 27, 28, 30
Malea, Cape, 57, 162, 295, 337, 338
Man, creation of, 25
Marathon, 105, 141, 142, 337
Maron, 311, 313
Medea, 10, 152-164, 217, 315
Medusa, 74-79, 135
Megapenthes, 69
Megara, 94, 96
Melanion, 171, 172
Melanippe, 119
Melanthius, 324, 327
Meleager, 150, 163, 167-170, 196
Memnon, 255, 256
Memory, see Mnemosyne
Menelaus, marriage to Helen, 196, 197; in Trojan War, 214, 217, 218, 222, 227, 232-237, 240, 245, 257-259, 265, 267, 269, 271, 278, 280, 283-286; return to Sparta, 10, 295, 298, 301-307, 328
Menestheus, 191, 193, 196, 271
Mentor, 324
Messene, 194, 338
Metis, 20, 21, 34
Midas, 65
Might, demon, 36
Minos, the first, 162

Minos, the last, 105, 142, 144, 145, 162, 191
Minotaur, 105, 142, 143, 162, 191
Mnemosyne, 21
Molossia, 301, 338
Molossus, 301
Moon, *see* Selene
Muses, Nine, 21, 29, 59, 204
Mycenae, 73, 196, 197, 217, 221, 293-298, 307, 338
Myrmidons, 219, 220, 222, 230, 231, 246
Mysia, 151, 220, 221, 337, 339

Narcissus, 9
Nauplia, 73, 105, 119, 218, 304, 307, 337, 338
Nauplius, 229, 301
Nausicaa, 319
Naxos, island of, 144, 337
Nemea, 99
Nemean Lion, 99, 100
Neoptolemus, 220, 259-261, 278, 283, 285-287, 301, 307
Nephele, 63
Nessus, 103, 172, 185, 186
Nestor, 150, 167, 168, 184, 220, 231, 238-240, 257, 271, 293, 301, 305
Nicostratus, 197, 214
Nile, river, 305
Nisyros, Rock of, 183, 339
North Wind, 150, 151
North Wind, land at the back of, 75, 102, 159
Northern Sea, 159
Nyctimus, 44
Nymphs, 15, 16; mountain nymphs, 20; sea nymphs, 47, 57, 65, 66, 77; water nymphs, 67, 151; northern nymphs, 75-77; Illyrian nymphs, 129; nymphs of Artemis, 163
Nysa, Mount, 65

Ocean, 21, 34, 201
Ocean Stream, 316
Odysseus, 10, 15, 48, 150; in Trojan War, 196, 197, 217-221, 227, 229, 237, 238-245, 249, 257-261, 267-271, 276, 278-284; wanderings of, 161, 305, 307, 311-319; return to Ithaca, 323-334
Odyssey, 286, 333
Oeax, 229
Oedipus, 9, 83, 84, 161
Oeneus, 170, 172
Oenone, 209, 211, 213, 233, 265-267
Oeta, Mount, 185, 227, 338
Ogygia, 318
Oicles, 175, 176
Oileus, 150, 196, 271, 285

Olympus, Mount, 20, 21, 25, 29, 30, 34-36, 43, 53, 54, 69, 70, 85, 86, 88, 120, 177, 181, 182, 186, 194, 195, 201, 204, 249, 260, 261, 318, 319, 337, 338
Omphale, 139, 145
Orestes, 221, 293-301, 305, 307
Orpheus, 150, 151, 153-159, 161, 162, 193, 317
Ossa, Mount, 182, 338
Othrys, Mount, 109, 337
Otus, 182, 183

Palamedes, 217, 218, 220, 229, 276, 301
Palladium, 267, 269, 270, 277, 284, 298
Pallas, the Titan, 35
Pallas Athena, *see* Athena
Pallas, uncle of Theseus, 139, 141, 142
Pan, 15, 30, 54-56, 59, 63; Pan-pipes, 30
Pandarus, 229, 237
Pandora, 38, 39, 43, 46
Panopeus, 25, 33, 46
Paris, 177; judgement of, 206-214; in Trojan war, 217, 222, 227, 229, 232, 233, 237, 238, 245, 246, 250-256, 258, 261-269, 278, 283, 284, 328
Parnassus, Mount, 15, 29, 30, 47, 57, 325, 338
Patroclus, 220, 231, 246-250, 257
Peleus, 119, 121, 150, 167-169, 175, 176, 201-209, 219, 220, 240, 246, 248, 250, 267
Pelias, 109, 149, 150, 164, 202
Pelion, Mount, 154, 182, 203, 204, 206, 338
Penelope, 197, 218, 278, 307, 318, 323, 325-329, 334
Peneus, river, 104
Penthesilia, 255
Pentheus, 68
Periphetes, the Clubman, 139, 140
Persephone, 16, 69, 70, 76, 113, 135, 160, 192, 193, 316
Perseptolis, 333
Perseus, birth, 73, 74; slaying of Gorgon, 74-78, 135; death, 69, 79; descendants, 83-85, 81, 91
Phaeacia, 161, 162, 319-324, 337
Phaedra, 145
Pharos, 302, 303, 307
Phasis, river, 152, 154, 337
Phemius, 328
Pherae, 106-114, 337
Phexippus, 168, 169
Philemon, 45, 46
Philoetius, 323, 327, 328
Philoctetes, 186, 196, 227, 255, 259-261, 266
Phineus, 78, 151, 288
Phlegathon, river, 135
Phlegra, 178-182, 338

344

Phocis, 298
Phoenicia, 54, 55, 214, 288, 302, 323, 337
Pholus, 103
Phorcus, 75, 318
Phrixus, 63, 64, 145, 154
Phrygia, 44-46, 86, 337
Phyllis, 301, 302
Pirithoüs, 191-193
Pittheus, 136-139
Podarces (Priam), 176
Poeas, 163, 186, 260
Poliporthes, 334
Polites, 275, 283
Polydectes, 74, 75, 78
Polydeuces, 150, 151, 184, 193-196, 284
Polyxena, 251, 275, 286-288, 293
Porphyrion, 182
Poseidon, 16, 17, 19, 20, 46, 66, 105, 119,
    120, 130, 176, 183, 204, 228, 240, 246,
    275, 277, 285, 312, 313, 315, 318, 319,
    334
Priam, 18, 19, 176, 177, 209, 211-217,
    227-229, 232, 240, 250-255, 265,
    275-277, 283, 286, 287, 293
Procrustes, 10, 140, 141
Procyon, 68
Prometheus, 21, 25, 30, 33-43, 46-48, 63,
    88, 129, 130, 152, 181, 201, 202
Protesilaus, 228, 237, 246
Proteus, 69, 73
Proteus, Old Man of the Sea, 201,
    303-305, 307
Pylades, 294-298
Pylos, 184, 220, 324, 338
Pyrrha, 38, 46-49
Pyrrha (Achilles), 206, 219, 220
Python, 30

Rhea, 20, 340
Rhesus, 240, 241, 245, 311
Rhodes, 134, 337
Rhoio, 218
Rome, 122, 289, 336

Salamis, 175, 214, 338
Same, 326
Samothrace, 57
Sardinia, 160, 336
Sarpedon, 246, 247
Satyrs, 26, 27, 28, 35, 65, 66, 144
Scaean Gate, 249, 250, 256
Scamander, river, 249, 286, 339
Scamandrius, 237
Sciron, 140
Scylla, 161, 317, 336
Scyros, island of, 206, 219, 220, 258, 259,
    339
Scythia, 123-125
Scythian snake-maiden, 123-125
Selene, 21, 27, 85, 181, 340

Semele, 64, 65, 70, 136
Seriphos, 74, 78, 79
Sibyl, 289
Sicily, 56, 69, 144, 145, 161, 184, 288, 317,
    336
Sidon, 66, 214, 337
Silenus, 26-28, 35, 65, 184
Silver Age, 25, 43
Sinis the Pinebender, 140
Sinon, 270, 271, 276, 277, 280
Sirens, 160, 161, 317
Sisyphus, 135
Sky, see Uranus
Sleep, see Hypnos
Sparta, 150, 184, 192-194, 196, 197,
    211-214, 217, 233, 265, 266, 277, 295,
    298, 301, 304-307, 323, 337, 338
Sphinx, 83, 84, 161
Sterope, 184
Sthenelus, 79, 83, 86
Strange Hathor, Temple of, 305
Strophius, 293-295
Stymphalian Birds, 104, 105
Stymphalus, Pool of, 104
Styx, river, 135, 136, 150, 205, 206, 256,
    338; oath of, 28
Sun, see Helios
Sunium, 301
Syrinx, 9

Taenarum, cave of, 134, 192, 337, 338
Talos, 162, 163, 186
Tantalus, 135
Tartarus, 20, 21, 25, 28, 36, 110, 135, 181,
    183, 191, 297, 337
Tauris, 297, 298
Taygehis, 15, 338
Tegea, 167, 170-172, 184, 338
Telamon, 119, 121, 150, 167, 168, 175,
    176, 196, 202, 209, 214, 267
Telegonus, 334
Telemachus, 218, 307, 323-328, 333
Telephus, 220, 221
Tenedos, island of, 227, 271, 339
Tenes, 227
Teucer, 196, 271
Teumessian Fox, 84
Theano, 269, 284
Thebes, 58, 63-65, 68-88, 92-96, 109, 110,
    187, 337, 338
Themis, 21, 132, 167, 204, 284
Theoclymenus, 303, 305-307
Thermopylae, 185, 338
Thersites, 255
Theseus, 10, 18; early adventures,
    136-142; slaying of Minotaur, 105,
    142-145, 162; with Argonauts, 145, 150,
    163, 167; in Hades, 191-193;
    descendants, 271, 284
Thessaly, 46, 106, 337

Thestius, 92, 95
Thetis, 66, 177, 201-206, 220, 227, 228, 231, 240, 248-250, 256-259
Thoas, 297, 298
Thoosa, 318
Thought, see Metis
Thrace, 54, 55, 65, 105, 114, 151, 240-242, 245, 301, 302, 311, 339
Thrasymedes, 239, 242, 271
Thresprotians, 333
Tiber, river, 289
Time, see Cronos
Tiphys, 151, 152
Tiresias, 87, 88, 316, 317, 333
Tiryns, 73, 79, 86, 96-106, 115, 121, 125, 132, 134, 136, 175, 196, 337, 338
Tisamenes, 298
Titans, 19-21, 25, 34, 36, 43, 49, 53, 135, 181
Tithonus, 255, 256
Toxeus, 168, 169
Trachis, 172, 175, 184, 185, 337, 338
Trinacria, island of, 317, 318
Troezen, 136, 139
Troilus, 10, 229
Tros, 120, 175
Troy, 43, 57, 86, 115-121, 150, 151, 168, 337, 339; first fall of, 175, 177, 186; siege of, 202, 203, 206, 209, 211, 213, 214, 217-280, 338; final fall of, 283-293, 301, 307, 311, 312, 316, 318, 325; Wooden Horse of, 269-280; luck of, see Palladium
Tyana, 44, 337
Tydeus, 170, 196
Tyndareus, 184, 192, 193, 196, 197, 295

Typhon, 49, 53-57, 63, 74, 184
Tyre, 66, 337

Ultimate Islands, 159, 336
Underworld, see Hades
Uranus, 19, 20, 53, 74

Venice, 287
Vesuvias, Mount, 184
Vice, 91, 92
Virtue, 91, 92

Western Ocean, 132, 159
Wine-growers, 218, 219
Wooden Horse, see Troy

Zacynthos, 326
Zetes, 150, 151, 288
Zethus, 63
Zeus, king of Immortals, 17-19, 109, 110, 120, 194-196, 204-206, 213; at war with the Titans, 20, 21; father of Hermes, 25, 27-30; conflict with Prometheus, 25, 33-39, 129, 201; visiting mankind, 43-46, 333; the flood, 46-49; battle with Typhon, 46-63, 74; father of Dionysus, 63-70; father of Persephone, 69, 192; father and protector of Heracles, 84-96, 121, 122, 129, 134, 177, 186, 187; judge of the Argonauts, 159, 160; battle with the Giants, 79, 181-184, 201; father of Helen, 192, 193; participation in Trojan War, 202-206, 210, 213, 217, 220, 231, 233, 237, 239, 250, 261, 267, 286, 318, 319